INTRODUCTION TO EDUCATIONAL INTERPRETING AND TRANSLATION

Judy Cortés, PhD, CA-CCI, CSI

Copyright © 2024 Judy Cortés

Published by Culture & Language Press, a division of Cross-Cultural Communications, LLC.

All rights reserved.

This work and any parts thereof may not be reproduced in any form or by any electronic or mechanical means without written permission from the publisher. For further information, contact the publisher.

Culture & Language Press
10015 Old Columbia Road, Suite B-215
Columbia, Maryland, 21046
USA
+ 1 410-312-5599
www.cultureandlanguage.net
clp@cultureandlanguage.net

Graphic design
Goran Skakic

ISBN: 978-1-7332491-9-5

"A different language is a different vision of life."
—Federico Fellini

"To learn a language is to have one more window from which to look at the world."
—Chinese proverb

"To have another language is to possess a second soul."
—Charlemagne

I dedicate this book to all the interpreters and translators who provide invaluable translation and interpreting services in public schools.

Contents

Advisory vi

Acknowledgments vii

About the Author viii

Preface ix

Introduction xii

Chapter 1: Overview of the U.S. School System 1

Chapter 2: Who Is Interpreting? Whom Will You Interpret For? ... 17

Chapter 3: Introduction to Interpreting in Special Education ... 41

Chapter 4: Interpreter Ethics in Educational Interpreting 57

Chapter 5: Modes of Interpreting: Consecutive 73

Chapter 6: Modes of Interpreting: Simultaneous 95

Chapter 7: Modes of Interpreting: Sight Translation 107

Chapter 8: Written Translation in School Settings 121

Chapter 9: Language Proficiency and Certification 133

Chapter 10: Legal Requirements in Educational Settings 157

Chapter 11: Interpreting for Assessments 171

Chapter 12: Practice for Interpreting and Translating in School Settings ... 187

Resources for Educational Interpreters and Translators 234

Bibliography 243

Bilingual Glossary for Educational Interpreters 245

Advisory

The information in this book is deemed to be correct at the time of printing. Many of the role plays are based on the author's personal experiences.

Acknowledgments

I would like to acknowledge the following teachers and interpreters for their valuable suggestions regarding the role plays: Vanessa Chapman, a special education teacher from the Delhi Unified School District in Delhi, California; Mark Feisthamel, a middle school math teacher from the Gilroy Unified School District in Gilroy, California; Barry Murphy, a retired history teacher from the North Monterey County Unified School District in Moss Landing, California; Dr. Carolina Serna, associate professor at Biola University, Ann E. Susmar, MA, CCC-SLP, retired speech and language pathologist, and Karin Wigren, 4th and 5th grade teacher from the Pájaro Valley Unified School District, California. I would also like to thank Dr. Linda Bynoe, and Dr. Christine Sleeter, emeriti professors, for their continued support and encouragement.

These incredible Spanish/English interpreters shared information about their assignments, which guided the creation of some role plays: Elizabeth Camacho León, from the Simi Valley Unified School District in Simi Valley, California, a district interpreter and translator; and Sergio Terán, a community liaison and translator/interpreter for the Special Education Local Plan Area (SELPA) at the Monterey County Office of Education, Monterey, California, who also contributed to the listing of the most common special education assessments in Chapter 11.

Translations into Arabic were provided by Mustafa Abid, senior faculty development specialist; into Russian by Svetlana David, senior faculty development specialist; into Korean by Namju Cha, assistant professor of Korean; all from the Defense Language Institute in Monterey, California.

I also appreciate Yu-Wen Wei's contribution for her Mandarin Chinese translation.

About the author

I grew up in Uruguay and arrived in California as a high school student. In college at the University of California (UCLA), I planned to become a United Nations (UN) interpreter. I applied to study abroad to perfect my French because I would be needing a third working language if I were to work for the UN. That was not meant to be. I studied abroad at the University of Madrid, in Spain, and this event changed the course of my career. The Spanish language and its literature took the place of French and became my focus. Upon returning to Los Angeles, I completed my undergraduate studies and graduated with a bachelor of arts (BA) in Spanish. A year later, I received my master's degree. I then taught Spanish for a brief period at the Defense Language Institute (DLI) in Monterey, California, before continuing my studies at UCLA in the area of Hispanic languages and literatures.

I completed my doctor of philosophy (PhD) while teaching as assistant professor in the Modern Languages Department at the University of Hawaii. Back in California, married, I first taught translation courses for the then Monterey (now Middlebury) Institute of International Studies. I also spent two years at the DLI as a content developer for the Spanish Basic Course, a project that led to the creation of several volumes of teaching materials for the intense Spanish language course offered at the DLI for military students.

After obtaining my state interpreting certification, I worked on a part-time basis as a court interpreter. I also passed the American Translators Association (ATA) exam. Subsequently I embarked on a career in bilingual education. For 15 years I taught various grade levels in public school settings and became active interpreting and translating for my school district. I became a frequent presenter at conferences: California Association for Bilingual Education (CABE), American Association of Teachers of Spanish and Portuguese (AATSP) and National Foreign Language Resource Center (NFLRC), always focusing on educational interpreting. My dedication and interest in interpreting led to my long-term involvement with the administrative office of the U.S. courts as a rater of candidates taking the oral portion of the federal court interpreter's exam.

The year California State University, Monterey Bay (CSUMB), opened its doors to incoming students, I was hired as the field placement coordinator in the Teacher Education Department, overseeing the placement and supervision of future teachers, multiple subject credential candidates in the tri-county area: Monterey, San Benito, Santa Cruz. I taught courses, such as "Pedagogy for Linguistically and Culturally Diverse Students," and various levels of Spanish, including a graduate course highlighting the works of Latin American literature.

In 2007, I became a Fulbright Scholar at the Universidad Católica de Temuco in Chile where I taught an interpreting course.

I have authored stories and written workbooks, primarily for third and fourth graders, in Spanish for Macmillan and Santillana publishers.

As of now, I teach for CSUMB, and I continue to interpret in legal, medical and educational settings.

—Judy Cortés

Preface

☞ Why I wrote this book

The topic of interpreting and translating in school settings is one I am both familiar with and passionate about. I have spent most of my career as a public school bilingual teacher and a trainer of bilingual teacher candidates. Most of the parents I worked with spoke Spanish at home. These Spanish-speaking parents needed assistance when communicating with school personnel, with monolingual English-speaking teachers, principals, psychologists, speech pathologists, office assistants and other school personnel.

Existing laws require that schools inform parents or guardians about school programs and activities and the children's progress *using a language the families and guardians understand*.

Furthermore, educators such as teachers and administrators have often found themselves in positions where they could clearly determine there was a need for an interpreter or translator, yet didn't know how to find one.

All families and guardians who cannot fluently speak the language of a particular school district can benefit from the services of a translator or interpreter. Language assistance enables a meaningful exchange of information and ideas. In such cases, it is critically important to transmit messages accurately and professionally. Everyone present needs to understand the information being shared so they can make important decisions.

An important term in the field of community interpreting is communicative autonomy, which refers to the capacity of all participants in an encounter to be responsible for, and in control of, their own communication (García-Beyaert, 2015, p. 363). Without interpreters and translators in schools, achieving communicative autonomy and meaningful communication will be impossible for many.

I have often witnessed situations where English-speaking school personnel with limited knowledge of Spanish attempt to communicate with a monolingual Spanish-speaking parent. Sometimes older or younger siblings, or other relatives or friends, come to act as interpreters. Most often, however, that communication is not precise or accurate.

Interpreters and translators are the critical link that make clear communication possible in a variety of educational settings.

After working in elementary and middle schools, my involvement in bilingual education continued when I became coordinator of field placements at California State University, Monterey Bay. During my tenure as coordinator, I continued my quest to ensure that student teachers seeking a multiple subject or secondary credential in our program understood the need to have ongoing meaningful communication between school staff and parents who do not speak English through interpreters to reduce or eliminate language barriers.

In the courses I taught for the Teacher Education Program, such as the "Pedagogy for Linguistically and Culturally Diverse Students" course, I stressed the importance of keeping parents and guardians informed in a language they understood and preferred, typically their primary or native language.

The services of a qualified interpreter make clear, direct communication possible. Such communication is required to be offered in many different school meetings and events. Ongoing communication also promotes parent participation.

It is important for these parents to receive notices in their primary language indicating that interpreting services will be provided at the meetings they are invited to attend. Notices to alert families about important school activities and events, including parent-teacher conferences and meetings about special education or disciplinary procedures, are only a few examples of documents that should be translated.

I had the good fortune of working with many bilingual English-Spanish credential candidates and bilingual paraprofessionals. My goal for all was to make them aware of what could be done to decrease the communication gap that existed between school personnel and parents who could not communicate in English.

Bringing in a qualified competent interpreter will address and resolve communication problems across a range of school scenarios. The language disparity is hugely reduced when a qualified interpreter or translator provides their services.

The meaning of messages conveyed in one language should not be lost through mediocre translation or interpretation attempts by unqualified individuals. Thankfully, there are now many well-qualified bilingual staff in schools with linguistically diverse student bodies. Some are employed by school districts, while others work as freelance interpreters for language services or independently. Many provide spoken language interpreting as well as translation; others provide sign language interpreting, either for parents and families or to Deaf and Hard of Hearing students throughout their school day.

Ongoing training for all these interpreters and translators should be prioritized by school districts. A growing number of them do provide it or require it. The overall number in the U.S., however, remains small.

I have interpreted in school settings for about 15 years. I have had the opportunity to participate in many formal and informal situations where interpreting and translation played a critical role. As a native speaker of Spanish, and as a certified translator and court-certified interpreter in California, I continue to interpret in legal, medical and community scenarios. This involvement allows me to refine my skills, particularly as we incorporate telephonic over-the-phone interpretation (OPI) and video remote interpreting (VRI) into our skill set.

How can schools best serve the growing number of families who need to understand how schools work? How will they understand the progress their child is making at school? Questions and answers must be provided in a language that parents speak and understand.

This book will provide school interpreters with useful tips and training exercises based on situations commonly found in schools. It describes levels of language competency for interpreters and translators. It explains the three interpreting modes and how they correspond to specific situations in schools, followed by role plays and exercises for practice in all three modes. There is also an introduction to written translation that includes short exercises based on documents that are common in U.S. school settings.

Some of the role plays and exercises are in both Spanish and English, the most frequently used language combination in U.S. schools. However, most role plays and exercises allow practice for interpreters in any language pair that includes English. A sample simultaneous practice appears in Arabic, a consecutive in Korean, one sight practice is in Mandarin and a sample written translation appears in Russian.

Most of the situations and scenarios in this book are based on actual school interactions that have taken place in Monterey County, California. A glossary of English educational terminology with Spanish translations is included at the end of the book. Interpreters of other languages can translate the English terms into their own language. It is important for U.S. interpreters both to understand and be able to interpret these terms.

The information and practice in this book are intended to be easy to read and understand. The level of language and difficulty in role plays and exercises ranges from simple to complex. I hope that the book helps to support the training and education of interpreters and translators in schools. I also hope it helps to professionalize this critically important field.

—Judy Cortés Feisthamel

Chapter — Introduction to Educational Interpreting and Translation

Introduction

☛ Purpose of this training manual

The book is intended to help train, educate or guide interpreters to perform educational interpreting in elementary, intermediate (middle or junior high) and high schools, commonly referred to as K–12. It also briefly addresses how to translate basic documents that interpreters in U.S. schools are often asked or expected to translate.

This manual is based on standard best practices for community interpreting. It seeks to help interpreters in schools perform their work at a professional level.

☛ A worldwide audience for a U.S. book

This book primarily addresses a U.S. audience. Every country's school system is somewhat different. U.S. interpreters in schools need to understand the context in which they interpret. Interpreters in other countries will need to study their own school districts and systems.

That said, there are surprisingly few resources available to help educate and train educational interpreters in any country. As a result, despite the specificities of U.S. educational systems discussed in this book, there are enough educational commonalities across national borders today to make this book useful in other countries besides the U.S.

☛ Spoken language vs. sign language interpreters

Although the content in this book is oriented primarily toward spoken language interpreters, much of it will also be useful for sign language interpreters, especially American Sign Language (ASL) interpreters, who interpret for parents and guardians in schools.

In the U.S., interpreters of signed languages who interpret for parents are often referred to as community interpreters. In contrast, educational interpreters for Deaf and Hard of Hearing children are ASL educational interpreters who often accompany and interpret for one child throughout the school day; they work in a particular specialization of interpreting that is not discussed in this book.

☛ Who will find the book useful

This book addresses interpreters in school districts, both public and private. However, it focuses primarily on public schools. The audience for this book includes:

- Trainers and educators of interpreters.
- Interpreters in schools who seek a resource for self-study.
- Remote interpreters (over-the-phone, video remote, video relay service or remote simultaneous interpreters) who interpret in schools.

- Staff in K–12 schools or school districts, including:
  - Language service coordinators.
  - Language access staff.
  - Parent liaisons (who interpret and translate).
  - Bilingual staff (who interpret and translate).
  - Outreach workers (who interpret and translate).
  - Other school staff or administrators who need to understand the work of interpreters and translators.
- Language bank interpreters in school districts.[1]
- Language service providers (language companies and nonprofit interpreter services), including language companies that specialize in remote interpreting.
- Universities and colleges with interpreting programs.
- Trainers licensed by the publisher (CCC-licensed trainers).

The urgent need for this book

Interpreting in school settings is a topic of urgent interest to many who work with or in schools, from educators and school administrative or support staff to language services and nonprofit organizations that provide services to schoolchildren and their families.

The topic of how to interpret in schools is also of special interest—of course—to interpreters.

So little has been written about this topic. Yet in the U.S. and around the world, the need for interpreting and translation in schools has soared dramatically.

Much of that need stems from migration. There were an estimated 281 million global migrants in 2020—3.6 percent of humanity.[2] At no time in the history of the world have so many families been on the move. Many of them have children who need to attend school. The parents also need to support their children's education.

Without interpreters and other forms of formal language assistance, such families struggle to support the education of their children.

---

[1] Community language banks, including those found in many U.S. school districts, are groups of bilingual individuals in the community who are called on by school districts to interpret in K–12 schools. They may or may not be qualified, trained, tested and skilled interpreters (some may simply be informal language assistants). They are typically paid less than interpreters in other specializations or interpreters sent by language companies to work in schools.

[2] Retrieved from: https://www.un.org/en/desa/international-migration-2020-highlights

In addition, there is a growing awareness, in the U.S. and around the world, that for Deaf and Hard of Hearing students to have meaningful access to a quality education, they too will need interpreters. The same is true for children of the Deaf, whose parents need interpreters if the parents are to provide meaningful support to their school-age children.

But both migrants and families with Deaf children or parents will need *trained, qualified* interpreters. Without the resources to train interpreters, it will be incredibly difficult to build a global corps of competent interpreters.

As a result, this book fills a huge void. It is a resource. School interpreters and translators have few such resources available. Educators who work with families who do not speak the language of school realize they need more guidance for the interpreters and translators in their schools. However, most often they do not know where to find materials to guide or train them.

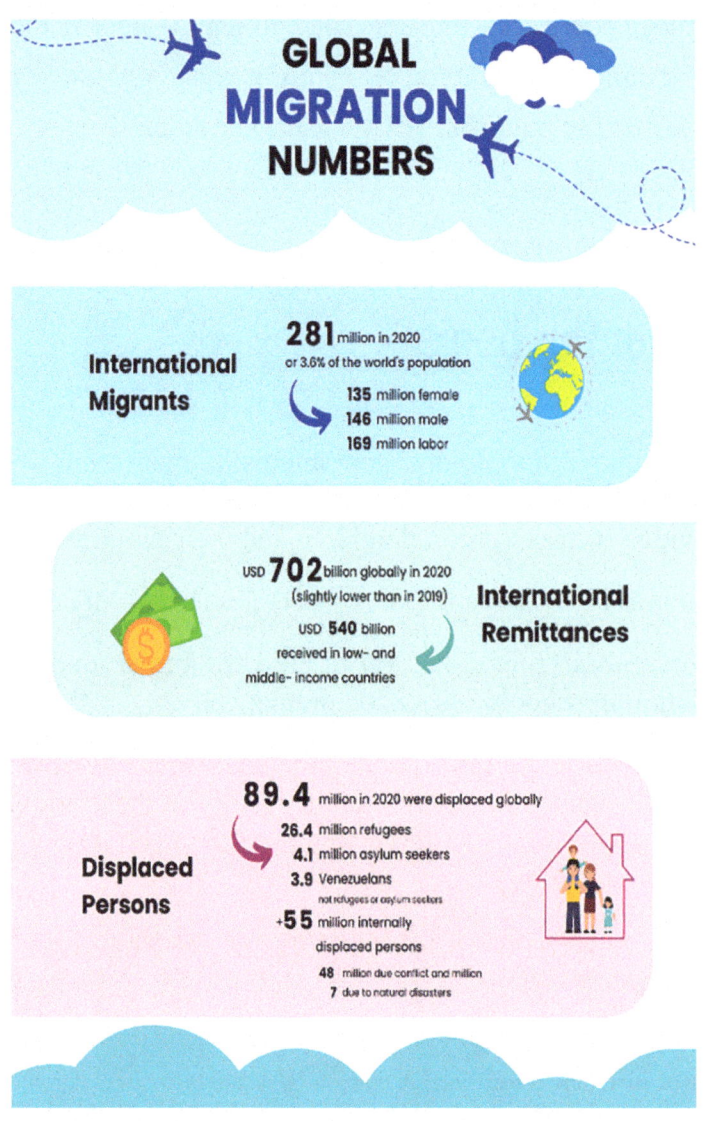

Figure i: UN World Migration Report 2022: Selected Infographics

Retrieved from: https://worldmigrationreport.iom.int/world-migration-report-2022-selected-infographics

How to use this book

👉 Guidance for school districts

If you interpret in schools
See the guidance for individual interpreters on the next page.

If you work in a school language service
If you work with or coordinate school interpreters and translators, consider using this book to set up a training program that values inclusiveness.

- Engage a professional trainer or educator of interpreters to present a program based on this book.
- Spend time through question-and-answer, presentations and interactive discussions to help interpreters gain a sound understanding of the school system overall, including special education programs, parent-teacher meetings and disciplinary procedures.
- Allot ample time for practice, both for role plays and translation exercises.

  Consider bringing in language coaches who are professional interpreters and translators to help provide each group of three interpreters with feedback on roles and translations, including language-specific feedback.
- Provide a copy of this book to anyone who interprets or translates in your schools.

If you are a school administrator
Make sure that anyone in your school or district who either interprets or helps to coordinate language access or language services gets a copy of this book. If possible, read it yourself. Then consider:

- Setting up a program to train the school or district's staff interpreters, bilingual staff, parent liaisons and any other school staff who interpret using this book.
- If possible, engage a professional interpreter trainer or educator to deliver the program.
- Also consider using material in this book to set up a program to train other staff members how to work effectively with school interpreters.
  - In particular, for those staff members who work as teachers, guidance or school-based counselors (licensed therapists) or in special education or assessment or with disciplinary procedures, help make them aware of how to work with interpreters in schools.

☞ Guidance for trainers and educators

There is ample material in this book to make the foundation for a one-semester program, with many role plays and translation exercises. The content can easily be adapted to mirror the types of programs used to educate medical, social services or legal interpreters. See the guidance provided above on how to do so.

☞ Guidance for individual interpreters

Whether you work as a contract interpreter, staff interpreter, bilingual school employee who sometimes interprets, a parent liaison, anyone employed by the school or as a member of a school language bank, assuming no one is using this book to train you, use it for self-study.

If possible, try to do the following:

- Find one or more interpreters to study with (ideally, they will share your languages).
- Read each chapter and discuss it with your partners.
- Perform role plays together for practice, following the guidance in this book.
- Complete the other exercises in the book and discuss your answers or translations.
- The basis to create a training program for your interpreters who perform educational interpreting in schools.
- As a gift or resource to provide to your interpreters.

☞ Guidance for language services

Whether you are a large, medium or small language company, a nonprofit interpreter service or an organization that provides remote interpreting in schools, this book can be used as:

- The basis to create a training program for your interpreters who perform educational interpreting in schools.
- As a gift or resource to provide to your interpreters.
- A resource for your staff in quality assurance, language access and inclusiveness.
- A tool to help guide the promotion and delivery of your services to school districts and schools.
- Concrete information to help guide conversations with school staff about educational interpreting and how it should be performed (for example, if school staff have questions or have had unfortunate experiences with unqualified interpreters from other organizations or language services).

Overview of the U.S. School System 1

Chapter 1

- Introduction
- Key aspects of the U.S. school system
- Grade levels of U.S. schools
- Legal mandates to provide language assistance in schools
- Chapter 1 review
- Chapter 1 activities
- Answer key for Chapter 1 activities

Introduction

This chapter provides interpreters with a broad view of the U.S. school system, including school districts and school structures, how they work and why interpreters need to understand them.

Chapter 1 also examines types of schools and how they operate at a district and local level. It also notes why language assistance, including interpreters and written translations, are required by a number of federal, state and local laws, a topic explored in more detail in Chapter 10.

Key aspects of the U.S. school system

Interpreters need to understand the school system where they will interpret. Otherwise, it will be difficult for them to interpret accurately, clearly and professionally.

However, school systems are complex institutions. In many cases, they can be quite confusing—and not only for interpreters.

Understanding how a school system works can help interpreters by providing:

- Clarity and context.
- Ways to understand and process terminology.
- Insight into how to find equivalent terms in the target language.
- Knowledge and understanding of administrative, legal, medical, assessment-based and pedagogical processes to reduce confusion and misunderstandings by the interpreter.
- Guidance on how the interpreter can take action if misunderstandings arise during the session.
- Awareness of when to request clarifications, both for accuracy and clear communication.
- A clear sense of the role of the interpreter and relevant professional boundaries.
- Rationale for why interpreters should not explain the system or its working to parents or explain parental culture to educators and school staff.

A better understanding of the U.S. school system can also help interpreters cope with emotional situations that may arise. For example, when parents are faced with an unexpected or unpleasant event, confrontations may erupt.

👉 Basis and impact of confusion about school systems

School systems are often confusing to both families and interpreters for many reasons. Perhaps the most important reason, at least for interpreters, is that they will usually interpret for families from countries in which school systems are structured differently than in the U.S.

Even sign language interpreters may interpret for parents or students for whom English is not usually a native language.

Other factors why school systems are often confusing for both families and interpreters include:

- School systems are large, complex and bureaucratic.
- Each school district may have distinct professional cultures, norms, practices and terminology.
- School systems differ greatly from state to state and among local jurisdictions.
- School districts, at least in the U.S., deal constantly with legal issues and concerns, legal documents and legal processes, all of which have helped shape their complex cultures.
- Educational requirements in the U.S. have resulted in a great deal of complex paperwork and expectations; interpreters often perform written translation (whether or not they are trained and qualified to do so).
- Common major interpreting topics in U.S. schools include special education programs for students with disabilities; programs for gifted and talented students; cognitive, speech-language, audiology and other assessments; and standardized testing. These practices and programs may not exist in a family's (or interpreter's) previous country.

Almost anyone involved and confused about school systems can be impacted. Confusion can arise not only for families and interpreters but also school staff—including administrators and teachers, special education teams, support staff, school counselors (guidance counselors or licensed therapists, often known in the U.S. as school-based counselors).

Such confusion also affects bilingual-bicultural workers in schools. They are often called family liaisons, among many other names, and they will be discussed later in this chapter.

Confusion arises from cultural misunderstandings, conflicts of belief, differing expectations and so on. For example:

- A parent might have no idea what a progress report is, what its notations mean or how it relates to their child's academic work.
- A teacher might be unaware that the child's religious practice means the child is fasting from dawn to dusk for weeks at a time and might not be taking prescribed medications or water.
- A school administrator might unknowingly face a cultural expectation by some parents and their children that cheating is not bad: it is simply a way that some children help other children.

👉 Authority and control

The United States has a federal organization, which means that higher level guidance is provided at the federal level and many practical decisions are taken at state and local levels. The U.S. Department of Education (ED) is the governing body over policies related to education. It also provides guidance to schools, administers grants to states and collects information and statistics about the nation's schools.

At the core of the ED mission is a commitment to assure equal access to educational opportunities for all students. It keeps close ties with state departments of education. These are found in all states, including commonwealths and territories of the U.S. These state departments are responsible for the maintenance and operations of public schools within their borders. They also regulate curriculums, teaching methods and instructional materials.

Authority and control of individual schools most often rests with school districts. A school district functions as a unit usually operating several schools in a geographic area. Its board members determine policy and curriculum selection.

School districts are led by a superintendent, the person who oversees the whole school district. Below the superintendent of schools is the assistant superintendent who leads various departments. However, not all school districts have an assistant superintendent.

Several individual schools operate within a district. The principal is the person who manages and oversees the daily operation of a school. Larger schools employ one or more assistant principals. The state education agency determines school boundaries, and these boundaries can include between one and one hundred schools and cover all grade configurations.

For a number of years, the U.S. district with the highest enrollment has been the New York City Department of Education, followed by the Los Angeles Unified School District.

School board meetings

School boards are important entities. Its members are usually locally elected officials. Many interpreters provide interpreting services for their meetings. Boards typically consist of five to nine members. They represent the community's values, views and expectations. Meetings are typically held monthly.

Public comments at board meetings can deal with specific items on the agenda or with general items. The public, usually parents and guardians, can address the board directly.

Prior to the COVID-19 pandemic, board meetings were held in person. During the pandemic, they were held virtually (meaning that interpreters worked remotely). Over time, new practices evolved that included returning to in-person meetings but in many cases holding hybrid sessions.

Hybrid sessions mean that meetings today can be held face to face (for those choosing to attend in person) and at the same time over a videoconference platform, such as Zoom or Google Meet (for those who attend remotely).

Grade levels of U.S. schools

How are schools in the United States organized? Generally, it's a three-level structure within the U.S. school system:

1. Elementary school (kindergarten (K) and grades 1 through 5 or 6)
   May include or be connected to an intermediate school (grades 3 through 6)
2. Middle school and junior high school (grades 6, 7, 8, and sometimes 5 or 9)
3. High school (grades 9, 10, 11, 12)

The following chart shows the two most common school configurations:

1. Elementary (K–5 or 6), intermediate or middle (6–8) or junior high school (7–8, sometimes higher) and high school (typically 9–12)
2. Elementary (K–8) and high school (9–12)

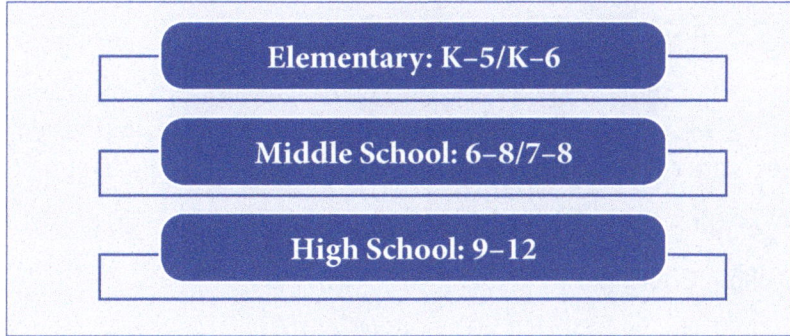

Figure 1.1: Common U.S. school structure, configuration 1.

Or

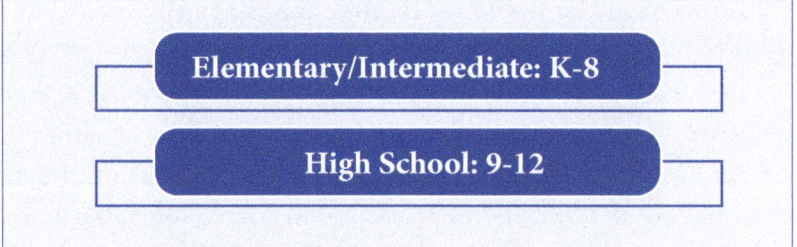

Figure 1.2: Common U.S. school structure, configuration 2.

☛ How grade levels in schools are organized

Elementary grades usually follow the configuration of K–5 or K–6 grade levels, while middle or intermediate schools usually span grades 6 through 8 or grades 7 and 8. Many school districts around the country have restructured elementary and middle school into K–8 schools.

High schools generally cover grades 9 through 12, although some districts have clusters of 9th graders in junior high or middle school.

There are certainly a number of other possible configurations. Rural schools, for example, may have one K–12 school or only a K–8 school and a high school. Such differences vary from state to state, but also in some cases from one municipality to another. Some of the most common variations are:

1. Elementary school districts that operate either grades K–6 or K–8 schools only.
2. Secondary school districts for 7–12 or 9–12 schools.
3. Joint school districts, including districts that belong to more than one county.

4. Intermediate school districts as part of a government agency that is organized at the county or multicounty level to provide services and programs to local school districts or directly to students.
5. Unified school districts that operate elementary and secondary schools.
6. Independent school districts, which vary by state. In Texas, this term denotes that the district is separate from any county or municipal-level entity.

Educators in the United States should be aware that the school systems of other countries can be organized in different ways.

☞ Higher education

The United States is a popular destination for international students. Many of them come from non-English speaking countries, primarily China, South Korea or Taiwan, seeking higher education degrees. These students enroll in the following types of institutions as they seek their chosen degree or coursework:

- Private universities
- Public universities or colleges
- Community or junior colleges
- Graduate schools
- Institutes
- Trade schools

Most institutions assist these foreign students by enrolling them, if necessary, in English as a second language (ESL) classes. Many students, as they adapt to their new settings and culture may, nevertheless, need the services of interpreters and translators. Services may also be desired for their non-English speaking family members who are joining them in the U.S.

Additionally, some of these students may need to get their coursework, references, course descriptions, transcripts and legal documents translated and oftentimes validated at these institutions. Interpreters and translators may be called on to communicate effectively with non-English speaking families or parents needing interpreting services.

☞ By comparison: Mexico

The Mexican education system provides an example of a different school system. It includes three levels of basic education followed by higher education:

- Elementary school (*primaria*), for grades K–6
- Junior high (*secundaria*), for grades 7–9
- High school (*preparatoria*), corresponding to grades 10–12
- Higher education (*educación terciaria*), taking place after high school

Once students complete the 12th grade, they can receive a vocational certificate or a diploma called *bachillerato*.

Basic education, also known as primary and secondary education, typically lasts for nine years and is mandatory for children ages 6 to 15. During these nine years, students are introduced to a range of subjects, including mathematics, science, social studies, languages and arts.

Upper secondary education, also known as high school, typically lasts for three years and is not mandatory, although it is highly encouraged. At this stage, students can choose to specialize in a particular subject, such as science or arts, depending on their interests and future career plans.

Higher education in Mexico includes vocational and university education. Vocational education provides students with practical skills and training in a specific trade or profession, while university education leads to a bachelor's degree and prepares students for more advanced careers.

In addition to public schools, there are also private schools in Mexico that offer a similar education. Some private schools are affiliated with international boards of education, such as the International Baccalaureate (IB).

Overall, the school system in Mexico provides students with a comprehensive education that prepares them for both their academic and professional lives. The government of Mexico has made significant investments in education in recent years and is working to improve the quality of education and increase access to it for all students.

☞ By comparison: India

The school system in India follows the 10+2+3 pattern of education, which means ten years of elementary education, followed by two years of secondary education and then three years of higher secondary education.

Elementary education is mandatory and is provided free of charge to children ages 6 to 14 under the Right to Education Act of 2009. During these 10 years, students are introduced to a range of subjects, including mathematics, science, social studies, languages and arts.

Secondary education, also known as high school, typically begins at the age of 14 and lasts for two years. At this stage, students can choose to specialize in a particular subject, such as science or commerce, depending on their interests and future career plans.

Higher secondary education, also known as pre-university education, lasts for three years and prepares students for university education. This stage is also known as the Plus Two stage and is considered to be an important benchmark for students who want to pursue higher education in India.

In addition to government-run schools, there are also many private schools in India that follow the same syllabus and offer a similar education. Some private schools are affiliated with national or international boards of education, such as the Central Board of Secondary Education (CBSE), the Indian School Certificate (ISC) or the International Baccalaureate (IB).

Overall, the school system in India is diverse and dynamic, and it provides students with a range of educational opportunities to choose from, depending on their interests and future goals.

☛ Public vs. private schools

The major difference between public and private schools in the U.S. is funding. Public schools receive funds from public sources, primarily federal, state and local taxes. Private schools are funded through nonpublic sources, such as endowments, foundation grants, nonprofit organizations that support education and tuition fees, the latter being the most common significant funding source. Public schools do not charge tuition fees.

Admission to public schools is guaranteed even for undocumented children; admission is based on legal criteria, most often the home address of the child's parents or guardians. However, being admitted to a private school is not guaranteed. Most private school students are assessed prior to admission. Many private schools have a particular religious affiliation, although students of other faiths can attend some of them. Public schools are not allowed to align themselves with any religion.

More racial and ethnic diversity is found in public schools. Public schools hire teachers who are credentialed by the state, while private schools do not need to meet this requirement. Public schools are obligated to educate all students, regardless of any type of disability, while private schools can reject students. Private schools tend to have fewer students in their classrooms.

☞ Charter schools vs. magnet schools

Charter schools and magnet schools are distinct types of schools that share certain features.

Both are free of tuition. Both can enroll students K–12 but may house only certain grades.

Magnet schools are public schools. They are held accountable by the state and the local school board but have specialized courses or curricula. For example:

- A tech magnet might be a school that focuses on programs for science, technology, engineering and mathematics (STEM), including practicums, internships, special laboratories and more.
- An International Baccalaureate program may provide a curriculum for the last two years of high school based on a program used in 140 countries that prepares students for successful higher education.
- A world languages school might have immersion programs or special foreign language or American Sign Language programs.

Charter schools are accountable to their own charter. They are publicly funded. There is a great deal of debate about whether they are actually "public" schools. Some U.S. states, such as Florida, call them public schools, but legal experts differ on their status.

Charter schools may or may not be a formal part of a public school district. Either way, they are not required to follow the state-dictated curriculum and standards for public schools. Instead, charter schools operate autonomously through individual agreements, or charters, with state or local governments that specify the school's rules and performance standards.

However, charter schools are subject to all the mandates of the Individuals with Disabilities Education Act (IDEA), discussed in Chapter 3.

Legal mandates to provide language assistance in schools

School administrators often wonder why interpreting services must be provided to facilitate communication between school staff and families who speak languages besides English—or who are Deaf or Hard of Hearing—when the children of these families (including Deaf children) attend U.S. schools.

Providing interpreting and translation services to families and school staff is not a choice. It is required by law. Language assistance is mandated by laws set forth by the federal government and, in many cases, also by state and local governments.

Chapter 10 discusses many of these laws. Here are just a few examples of the U.S. laws explored in that chapter.

Federal laws:

- Title VI of the Civil Rights Act of 1964
    - Requires recipients of federal financial assistance to take reasonable steps to ensure equal access to public (federally funded) services.
        - Those steps typically include language assistance, translation and interpreting, especially for large school districts.
    - Provisions bolstered by Executive Order 13166 of 2000.
- Equal Educational Opportunities Act (EEOA) of 1974
    - Requires public schools to provide support and services that allow students and their parents and guardians to participate "meaningfully and equally" in educational activities.
- Americans with Disabilities Act of 1990
    - As with Title VI, it requires recipients of federal financial assistance to take reasonable steps to ensure equal access to public (federally funded) services, including language assistance for the Deaf and Hard of Hearing.
    - May include the services of full-time, one-on-one educational interpreters for Deaf and Hard of Hearing students who interface with school staff outside of classes.
- Elementary and Secondary Education Act (ESEA) of 2001
    - Addresses parental involvement in Sec 1118.
    - Also known as The No Child Left Behind Act
- Public Law 94-142 (1975) later renamed Individuals with Disabilities Education Act (IDEA) of 1990—previously named Education for All Handicapped Children Act (EHA)
    - Makes available a free appropriate public education to eligible children with disabilities.
- Executive Order 13166 of 2000
    - Brings another layer of enforcement to Title VI; seeks to expand and ensure meaningful access by parents needing interpreting services at schools through federally funded programs and services.
    - Requires federal agencies to examine the services they provide, identify any need for services to parents needing language assistance and develop and implement a system to provide those services so that these parents can have meaningful access to them.

—U.S. Department of Education website

Executive Order 13985 of 2021 and Executive Order 14091 of 2023

- Both further advance racial equity and support for underserved communities, and specifically address language access in Section 8 of 14091 as follows:

(e) improve accessibility for people with disabilities and improve language access services to ensure that all communities can engage with agencies' respective civil rights offices, including by fully implementing Executive Order 13166 of August 11, 2000 (Improving Access to Services for Persons with Limited English Proficiency)

☛ State and local language access laws

Virtually every U.S. state has some form of language access law that typically applies to entities that receive state funding. California alone has 57 such laws (Youdelman, 2019, p. 4).

However, some of these laws apply only to a special area of services, such as healthcare. Others apply more broadly to publicly funded services, including education. Examples of states with language access laws that affect education directly are California, Hawaii, Maryland, Minnesota and New York, as well as the District of Columbia.

A few examples of municipalities with their own language access laws that apply to entities that receive local government funding include Anchorage, Austin, Boston, Chicago, Detroit, Minneapolis, New York City, Oakland, Philadelphia, San Francisco, San Jose, Seattle, Tucson and many more.

See Chapter 11 for details about language access requirements in education.

Parental participation

Language access laws are critically important for allowing families to understand parent-teacher conferences, meetings with speech therapists and board meetings. Provisions for language access are a critical way to support the large body of research demonstrating that parental involvement and engagement leads to students' success.

Therefore, it is of vital importance for school districts to take necessary measures to address the need for proper communication between parents and school staff. Welcome signs, announcements and postings informing parents about available interpreting services are strongly encouraged. Accessibility to programs, events and meetings is a right afforded to all parents.

📖 Chapter 1 review

In this chapter, you have learned about the U.S. school system, including federal and state responsibilities, school districts, types of schools and their operations at the district and local level. The U.S. Department of Education (ED) and state departments of education oversee policies related to education, while operational control of schools lies with local entities, including school districts and independent schools.

School systems can be confusing for families and interpreters because of their intrinsic complexity, the variations in policy implementation across the country and the differences with school systems in other countries. The impact of such confusion can lead to a range of issues, from cultural misunderstandings to legal processes. As an interpreter, understanding the school system will help you interpret accurately and professionally. The chapter also notes that interpreters should not explain the school system or its workings to parents or educators.

In the U.S., the school system is divided into elementary schools (K–5 or K–6), middle or intermediate schools (6–8 or 7–8) and high schools (9–12). Some districts have K–12 schools or K–8 schools. In other countries, school levels may be organized differently, even when the everyday words used to describe them appear to be similar. For example, primary education in other countries may refer to a range of grades different from those associated with elementary schools in the U.S.

In terms of funding and mandates, public schools are funded through taxes and are required to educate all students regardless of disability, while private schools are funded through nonpublic sources and are not mandated to serve students with disabilities. A subset of public schools includes charter schools and magnet schools. Magnet schools are public and accountable to the state; charter schools are publicly funded but operate autonomously.

Interpreting and translation services in schools are mandated by federal and local laws to ensure equal access for speakers of less common languages or Deaf and Hard of Hearing persons.

Chapter 1 activities

1. Multiple choice

Circle the letter that corresponds to the best response.

1. The United States school system:
    a. Does not include special education.
    b. Is the same for every state.
    c. Is easy to understand.
    d. Can differ from state to state.

2. Schools in the United States are typically organized:
    a. Into three different levels.
    b. Into four or five different levels.
    c. Into one K–12 school.
    d. By independent joint school districts.

3. Public schools:
    a. Receive most funding through grants and endowments.
    b. Charge tuition fees.
    c. Are free of tuition costs to students.
    d. Employ few credentialed teachers.

4. School boards:
    a. Are headed by a school principal.
    b. Determine policies for schools.
    c. Usually hold two yearly meetings.
    d. Don't accept public comments.

5. The school district with the highest enrollment in the United States is the:
    a. Hawaiian State Department of Education.
    b. Miami-Dade County Public Schools.
    c. New York City Department of Education.
    d. Los Angeles Unified School District.

2. Open-ended responses. Describe the following.

1. The role of the school board.
2. The role of the U.S. Department of Education.
3. The role of the school principal.

Overview of the U.S. School System — Chapter 1

3. Define the following federal laws.
    1. Title VI of the Civil Rights Act of 1964.
    2. Equal Education Opportunities Act (EEOA) of 1974.
    3. Individuals with Disabilities Education Act (IDEA) of 1990.
    4. Executive Order 13166 of 2000.

4. Indicate if these statements are true (T) or false (F).   T   F
    1. Magnet schools are free of tuition.   ___ ___
    2. Private schools tend to have more students in their classrooms.   ___ ___
    3. All states have language access laws that affect education.   ___ ___

5. Match the school characteristics with the descriptors by placing the correct letter (or letters) in the corresponding category.
    A. These schools are public funded.
    B. Oftentimes this type of school is specialized in its program.
    C. These schools operate through an agreement with the state, county or local government.
    D. These are not subject to IDEA.

Types of schools

Public	Private	Magnet	Charter

☑ Answer key for Chapter 1 activities

1. Multiple choice
1. D
2. A
3. C
4. B
5. C

2. Open-ended responses. Describe the following.
1. The members of the board determine school policies and curriculum selection.
2. This is the government body that maintains educational policies, provides advice to schools, administers grants to states and collects information about the nation's schools.
3. Principals take care of the daily activities within a school. They also manage school budgets and monitor teacher performance.

3. Define the following federal laws.
1. The Civil Rights Act ensures equal access to public services, including those of interpreters and translators, thus prohibiting exclusion of individuals from federally funded activities.
2. EEOA requires public schools to provide support and services that allow students and their parents to participate meaningfully and equally in educational activities.
3. IDEA makes available free appropriate public education services to eligible students with disabilities.
4. Executive Order 13166 expands the enforcement of Title VI of the Civil Rights Act and ensures meaningful access by families needing interpretation services to federally funded programs.

4. Indicate if these statements are true (T) or false (F).
1. T. 2. F. 3. F.

5. Match the school characteristics with the descriptors by placing a number or numbers in the corresponding category.

Public	Private	Magnet	Charter
A	D	A, B	A, C

Who Is Interpreting? Whom Will You Interpret For? 2

Chapter 2

- Introduction
- Types of educational interpreters
- Budgeting for language assistance
- Whom will you interpret for?
- Chapter 2 review
- Chapter 2 activities
- Answer key for Chapter 2 activities

Introduction

If you want to interpret in public schools today, it is important to know two essential categories of people: those who already interpret in schools and those who need your services.

You need to know who is interpreting in schools today because so many different types of people perform this role—from family members and children to bilingual school employees or freelance, agency and remote interpreters. This will help you see where you fit in and how confusion arises from the fact that not all these individuals provide *professional* interpreting services.

For example, if you interpret everything someone says (or signs), doing so might surprise them. They might burst out, "Oh, I didn't want you to interpret *that*. I was just talking to *you*."

In another example, if someone asks you for advice, and you simply interpret that request to the other person, the first person might wonder why you don't give advice because other people who interpret for them often do.

Similarly, you need to understand the people you will interpret *for*. Many people in schools need your services. On the school staff side, you might interpret for a teacher, a learning specialist or a school office assistant. That is quite a different experience from interpreting for a school board meeting, a disciplinary hearing or a schoolwide multicultural event.

Interpreting for assessments creates another different set of interpreting demands. You might interpret for a speech-language pathologist, an audiologist or a school psychologist. Your job is to listen carefully to the messages and to convey the information from one language to another in the best and most accurate way possible, without deletions or additions.

This chapter will introduce you to the people who interpret in schools and the people you may interpret for. That way, you can better prepare for the daily realities of interpreting in public schools.

Types of educational interpreters

Many people interpret today in schools around the world, including the U.S., who are not interpreters. They are simply bilingual individuals who happen to be available to assist school staff and families.

This section will examine who is interpreting in U.S. public schools as well as some of the limitations of those who interpret without professional assessment, training or qualifications.

☞ Language assistants

Often parents go to school to speak to a teacher, an administrator, special personnel, a coordinator, or paraeducators. When parents and school staff find themselves in need of an interpreter. The parents may want to communicate a concern, understand a matter related to a student or a school or district, get an explanation or participate in a meeting. School staff need to respond.

Many individuals have taken on the role of interpreter in schools, such as bilingual family members and friends, including children. These individuals are rarely trained to interpret. People "pulled in" to interpret simply because they are bilingual are often called ad hoc interpreters or language assistants.

Many specialists do not want to call them ad hoc interpreters because interpreters is a term reserved for those who perform the work professionally.

Here are some concerns when language assistants try to act as professional interpreters.

Concerns about language assistants

Allowing language assistants, such as friends and family, to interpret in school settings is not ideal, for many reasons. Untrained interpreters:

- Typically do not follow standard protocols for interpreting (such as professional introductions, transparency, use of direct speech and intervention protocols).
- Are usually unaware of the existence of codes of ethics for interpreters and would have no idea which code or behavior to follow.
- Tend to summarize.
- May offer advice and guidance to family members they interpret for.
- Often add to, omit, or change parts of the message.
- Frequently get into side conversations that exclude one or more participants from understanding.

As a result of these challenges, school staff and families who then work with professional interpreters (those who have professional training and qualifications) can become confused when working with unqualified language assistants.

In addition, language assistants may omit or change the information they interpret. Sometimes these omissions are due to embarrassment or unwillingness to interpret certain messages. Countless anecdotes exist describing children who interpret for their parents and fail to interpret negative information about their grades or behaviors.

In other cases, family members may soften or change a message out of sensitivity or cultural concerns.

Who provides language assistance in schools?

The following groups of individuals commonly take on the role of ad hoc interpreter, usually when the school does not have interpreters on staff or on call. Note the specific concerns about these types of untrained language assistants.

Family members and friends

Family members and friends usually lack adequate vocabulary for interpreting educational terminology and school-specific terms, particularly those belonging to special education. These individuals may care deeply about a student and have the child's best interests at heart, yet they have probably never had interpreter training.

In addition, they may not know that it is important to interpret the whole message and not add to it. Sometimes family members and friends may want to avoid conveying bad news. They might be tempted to add their opinions or ask their own questions. They could choose to omit certain information and then give advice without interpreting it.

Family members and friends are unlikely to be aware of the legal risks and consequences of interpreting in schools. For example, many special education and disciplinary meetings, and the sight translation of the documents that a parent or guardian must sign, involve *legal processes*.

Children

In addition to the issues raised in the previous subsection, asking a child to assume the responsibility of interpreter can embarrass, confuse and even traumatize that child. Doing so also inverts family roles (children acting as parents).

Having children interpret in nonemergency situations for siblings, cousins or friends might also constitute a potential violation of federal and state laws governing language access in U.S. schools. (See Chapter 10.)

A fact sheet issued by the U.S. Department of Health and Human Services (HHS) based on federal laws specifically cautions against having friend or family members, "especially children," interpret unless the family has been advised of their right to have a competent interpreter and still wants that family member to interpret.[3]

Not all information needs to be shared with a young child or even a teen. In addition, some of the educational terminology, including its acronyms, can be confusing. A child may be put on the spot when certain information is not conveyed accurately by either side. The child might be tempted to omit or ignore some of the negative comments and may prefer to summarize the information being shared. This does not mean though that children will cease to interpret when there is no professional interpreter available.

Consequences for children who interpret

There may be negative consequences to having a child interpret, particularly for a younger child. A child should not be placed into such an uncomfortable situation. Requesting an interpreter ahead of time would be the optimal approach in most situations.

Research about the psychological and socioemotional outcomes of language brokering has been mixed. For some children it can be stressful, shameful or burdensome, while for others it might lead to greater academic performance. See Weisskirch (2010) for a discussion of some of the risks and challenges for child language brokers in immigrant families experiences.

A generally accepted best practice that allows older children to interpret while protecting them is to train interested high school students to interpret. A growing number of pipeline interpreting programs now exist. These are high school courses that introduce students to potential career paths in interpreting. Students can then practice interpreting at school wide events in an emotionally safe and supervised environment.

Custodial staff

Custodial staff help to maintain and clean school buildings. A teacher may call on them when there is no one available to interpret for a parent. These requests put the custodian in an awkward situation. Interpreting is not the role or job of custodial staff.

Certainly, having a maintenance worker give or transmit brief instructions when a person is lost or asks for directions can be helpful. Schools should not ask custodial staff to interpret for a parent-teacher conference or a special education meeting.

Bilingual school staff

The assumption that anyone who speaks two languages can interpret is easily disproven by a basic interpreter skills test. In addition, not every bilingual individual trained to interpret can do so: interpreting is a complex, demanding skill.

---

[3] See Guidance to Federal Financial Assistance Recipients Regarding Title VI Prohibition Against National Origin Discrimination Affecting Limited English Proficient Persons. Retrieved from: https://www.hhs.gov/civil-rights/for-individuals/special-topics/limited-english-proficiency/guidance-federal-financial-assistance-recipients-title-vi/index.html

Bilingual school employees who are asked or expected to interpret may be either language assistants or interpreters. If they are screened, tested and professionally trained to interpret, they can become qualified interpreters.

Sometimes school office staff and other school staff who are bilingual also translate or interpret. However, this work should be undertaken only after they have taken some type of interpreter training with substantial practice.

In addition, not all bilingual individuals or school staff members want to take on the role of an interpreter. Some may be reluctant to do so because of time, workload or a potential liability issue.

The following are examples of U.S. school staff who often are asked to interpret, whether or not they are qualified to do so.

Paraprofessionals or instructional aides

Paraprofessionals assist teachers with classroom instruction under teacher supervision. Many paraprofessionals are bilingual and some expect to interpret at the school site. Others prefer not to do so.

Onsite administrators

At times an administrator may want to speak to a parent in the parent's native language even though their understanding and communication skills in that language may be rather rudimentary. It is commendable for individuals to try to communicate in a new language they are learning. However, professional interpreting may be needed to ensure that accurate information is conveyed and to help assure understanding for all participants.

Naturally, if the administrator is fluently bilingual, they may speak to a family member who speaks that language without calling in an interpreter. They may also feel comfortable speaking at assemblies or meetings in front of parents or students. Nevertheless, when addressing sensitive or legal issues, the services of a qualified interpreter will be needed if they are going to be explaining complex school issues, such as expulsions, disciplinary actions, retentions or any matter related to special education. (See Chapter 10 for details.)

Teachers

Some bilingual teachers might be willing to act as interpreters. They might be excellent at the task, but most are not qualified to do so and have never been trained to interpret. This interpreter role is also above and beyond what they have been hired to do and can be a burden. Bilingual teachers working in Dual–Immersion sites possess, however, the ability and training to work with students and parents in two languages.

Alternatively, if a school wants to assess a teacher's language skills, train them to interpret, test them for interpreting skills and compensate them for this service outside their regular working hours, their services might be welcome.

Special personnel

Special personnel are professional school staff. They include, for example:

- School psychologists
- Guidance counselors
- School-based counselors (licensed therapists)
- Speech-language pathologists
- Special education teachers

Some special personnel are hired not only for their specialty but also their bilingual skills. Many can perform their jobs in two languages. They should however first be tested for language proficiency.[4] Otherwise, there is no reliable way to be sure they are sufficiently bilingual.

If they are truly bilingual, they may already possess vocabulary specific to their field in both languages. They can communicate well with everyone present at a meeting. They may also be able to administer exams in the child's primary language without the assistance of an interpreter or translator.

However, many people, including special personnel themselves, confuse providing services in another language with interpreting. Most are not trained or qualified to interpret. Those special personnel who need an interpreter or translator should have at their disposal a list of available bilingual school employees who are qualified to interpret and also agencies that employ certified or qualified interpreters.

The work that special personnel in schools perform is incredibly important. They cannot do it adequately, in many cases, without interpreters.

Parent or community liaisons

Parent or community liaisons provide communication and outreach services between schools and families. Many school districts, K–12 schools and alternative schools employ them year-round. These districts and schools prefer to employ their own inhouse staff to interpret and translate, even though these employees have additional duties.

These employees receive various titles: community liaison, bilingual office assistant or administrative assistant, bilingual paraeducator, family coordinator, parent support liaison or administrative assistant/bilingual.

There is a lack of consistency among the job titles. What is clear is that these bilingual employees perform multiple tasks that include support for families, family-school communication, interpreting and translation.

When openings for these positions take place, potential supervisors take into account a person's linguistic background and training. In most cases, language skills are screened or assessed prior to an interview.

---

[4] Ideally, all U.S. professional school staff who want to provide their services in another language would score ILR-3 or ACTFL Superior or higher on an accredited language proficiency test. For information about language testing and scores, see Chapter 10.

It is important to note that these individuals bring with them a wealth of cross-cultural knowledge and understanding. They continuously navigate cultures and can advocate for English learners or Deaf parents or guardians who may not have a clear understanding of the education systems and cultures of the United States.

Staff interpreters

A growing number of U.S. schools today, especially in states such as California, Texas and Washington, have engaged full-time staff interpreters (or, in many cases, staff interpreters/translators).

Staff interpreters are not bilingual employees doing additional jobs at a school while also interpreting or translating part-time. The staff interpreter's job title is that of an interpreter or interpreter/translator. This job is to provide professional language assistance to school staff and families needing interpreting services.

These employees are hired to interpret and/or translate. They either come qualified to do so, or the school district tests and trains them.

Particularly in states such as California, Texas and Washington, procedures are in place to establish a district-wide, professional corps of interpreters and translators. Some districts even provide their staff interpreters with continuing education and opportunities to attend conferences.

Many districts, schools and educational institutions now require at least a two-year community college degree before employing interpreters or translators. This is particularly true for American Sign Language (ASL) interpreters. A few districts even prefer a bachelor's degree in translation and interpreting or in a related field, but that requirement is rare (though, again, less rare for sign language interpreters).

Training and testing bilingual staff who interpret

School districts continue seeking bilingual employees to interpret and translate. It follows that some of these talented bilinguals should receive the necessary testing, training and credentialing.

Many U.S. school districts have implemented their own bilingual certificate programs for paraprofessionals and other bilingual school staff who interpret. This type of endeavor is commendable and should be encouraged, especially with differential pay for those who obtain the certificate.

Ideally, such training will be offered to staff who already perform this type of work as well as to other bilingual employees in the school district who are interested in becoming interpreters and translators. The best practices approach is as follows:

1. Screen bilingual employees to determine if they are interested and might be qualified to become interpreters.
2. Test the candidates for language proficiency.

3. Train the employees 40 hours or more in community interpreting with a focus on educational interpreting. That program will ideally include interpreting ethics, standards, protocols, skills training in all three modes of interpreting (consecutive, simultaneous and sight translation), educational terminology and information about educational services, assessments and programs, among other topics.
4. Test the employees for basic interpreting skills.
5. Provide yearly professional development workshops about interpreting for staff interpreters.

If the school district does not have the personnel qualified to offer testing and training programs, it could locate and contract with an agency or organization that offers such tests and programs. This approach would enable bilingual school personnel who are qualified and interested to practice and improve their interpreting skills.

Interested paraprofessionals and other bilingual staff members could also enroll in translation and interpreting classes offered at a community college or online.

Should any bilingual staff at schools be trained to interpret?

Not all school employees who are bilingual may want to take part in formal interpreter training or act as interpreters in schools. However, they can continue to perform an invaluable service in classrooms while assisting students and classroom teachers in another language.

Teachers depend on bilingual paraprofessional staff, in particular when the student's primary language has to be used for instructional purposes. Such work by paraprofessionals is generally well established in many classrooms across the U.S. for the Deaf and Hard of Hearing but far less often for children who are English language learners.

However, such work is not the same as the interpreting needed for parent-teacher conferences, special education meetings, disciplinary procedures and hearings, schoolwide events, meetings with counselors and so on.

School districts should continue to seek and hire paraprofessionals with bilingual skills and other qualified bilingual staff to interpret. They should all, however, be tested and trained before interpreting. Compensating them for their extra skill and talent would be appropriate.

Special education departments appear to have the greatest need for the services of interpreters and translators. (See Chapter 3 for details.)

☞ Contract interpreting services

When qualified bilingual employees who are tested and trained as interpreters are not available, districts or special education departments can contract with interpreting agencies or professional freelance interpreters.

The availability of professional interpreters and translators is gradually becoming more common and widespread in districts with a large number of non-English speaking families and families with Deaf or Hard of Hearing children or parents.

☞ Professional interpreters

Many specialists dislike the term *professional* interpreter. In their view, any interpreter who is not professional is not an interpreter!

That said, interpreters and translators who work at a professional level are fluent speakers of two or more working languages. They have acquired the necessary skills to become experts in both the oral and written system of both or all these languages.

Interpreters are also ambassadors of cultural understanding. They navigate the nuances that characterize many cultures, including customs, fears, attitudes, beliefs and behavior.

Furthermore, most interpreters have gone through professional training and testing. Training is available in person and online for those interested in this type of career.

Although most U.S. training is for legal or medical interpreting, it addresses all modes of interpreting: simultaneous, consecutive and sight translation.

Specialized training for educational interpreters and translators is slowly increasing, especially in Texas, Arizona, Washington State and California.[5]

Interpreting is mostly an oral (or oral and signed) activity, so bilingual oral skills are critical. However, at other times written information, instructions and documents need to be read and translated. Therefore, interpreters and translators should be able to read and write in both or all their working languages.

☞ Freelance interpreters

School districts typically request interpreting and translation services on an as-needed basis. Some districts and regional or school offices will sign contracts with language services that provide contract interpreters. However, many schools directly work with individual, qualified interpreters who have proven to be competent at the interpreting task.

Some of these freelance interpreters sign up with two or three school districts if the number of English learner (EL) or Deaf families is low, particularly for less common languages.

☞ School language banks

In a number of cases, U.S. school districts have engaged a whole group of freelance interpreters for various languages. They sometimes test and train these interpreters.

This model is sometimes referred to as a language bank. It is less costly than paying a language company or a nonprofit interpreter service. However, it puts the burden on schools to screen, assess and often train and test interpreters. It may also require the district to provide the necessary equipment when simultaneous interpreting services are provided.

---

[5] Cross-Cultural Communications (CCC), the publisher of this book, provides community interpreting and training-of-trainer programs tailored specifically to educational interpreting. CCC programs are taught nationwide. See www.cultureandlanguage.net or contact info@cultureandlanguage.net for details.

Most schools do not have the resources to run their own language service in a professional way. This language bank model has limitations. Over the years, however, some school districts have developed more sophisticated models than traditional language banks by contracting with language services agencies, particularly in states with high numbers of immigrant families, such as California.

☛ Language services

A number of language services all over the U.S. provide professional translation and interpreting, both face to face and remotely (over phone and video).

These agencies can be for-profit language services (language companies) or nonprofit services run by community organizations, such as refugee resettlement agencies or other nonprofit agencies that serve immigrants and refugees.

Professional language services can be called on to assist school staff and linguistically diverse families—both English learner (EL) and Deaf or Hard of Hearing families. In principle, language services should employ, or contract with, only qualified interpreters. In reality, many U.S. language services have provided interpreters (and translators) who lacked adequate training, qualifications and experience.

Today, however, a growing number of language services provide qualified interpreters. Most provide needed equipment, such as headsets, receivers and a transmitter with a microphone for the interpreter. Many of the interpreters are certified in legal and medical interpreting. Prior to the COVID-19 pandemic, most of them provided their services primarily in person.

Schools and districts establish contracts with such services, and, as long as funding is available, often engage two or three different language services to assure adequate language coverage.

☛ Remote interpreting

Many U.S. languages today provide over-the-phone interpreting (OPI) and video interpreting. Video remote interpreting (VRI) is used for both spoken and sign language interpreting. Video relay service (VRS) is used only for sign language interpreting. Remote simultaneous interpreting (RSI) is almost always via video and used primarily for public meetings.

Thanks to remote interpreting, whether OPI, VRI, VRS or RSI, those who need an interpreter can log in and access one without the interpreter (or even the school staff or family members) being physically present at a school. Remote interpreting is becoming more convenient and popular for all people as participants become more familiar with this platform. A hybrid model has gained favor too. This occurs when some participants are physically present while others access the meeting or the event remotely. Many school board meetings offer this option.

Figure 2.1: An interpreter working remotely.

Since the COVID-19 pandemic began, remote interpreting in general and VRI in particular have become far more common in schools. VRI is often provided over Zoom, Google Meet, Webex, or other video conference platforms. RSI can also be used on such platforms, or it may be provided over a conference interpreting platform.

For OPI services, the use of a telephone might be adequate, especially a dual-handset phone (a phone with two receivers) if a teacher or a parent is in the same room and only the interpreter is remote. However, a computer and headset will provide higher quality audio that makes the exchange much easier to understand.

Conference calls can also be used whereby three or more people connect via a phone. One person initiates the calls and dials the others to join. Most iPhones allow up to five participants to join such calls. However, VRI interpreting is preferred because all participants can see one another as long as their cameras are turned on.

For VRI, VRS and VRI, all people need access to a reliable video platform. Headsets and quality microphones are also a necessity—for interpreters, school staff and, when possible, for families.

Budgeting for language assistance

Today, most U.S. school districts have contracts with one or more language services to guarantee that services are provided throughout the year. (Legal requirements for translation and interpreting are discussed in Chapter 10.)

Compensation for these services must be budgeted at the district level. Outsourcing this expense is often addressed on a yearly basis so that all schools with large numbers of EL families or with Deaf students or parents can receive language assistance.

When funding discussions take place, school board members need to keep in mind that laws affect all families with children, regardless of their language dominance, particularly those who need the services of an interpreter or translator.

Meaningful language assistance requires qualified interpreters and translators. Ongoing training for staff interpreters and translators should also be budgeted.

If language assistance is required at meetings, then necessary steps must be taken to provide qualified interpreters. As a result, all parents, guardians or families who require language assistance have equal access to educational services. They can, as a result, make informed decisions.

Interpreters must have strong listening, speaking, reading and writing skills in both languages in order to successfully provide communication between school personnel and parents needing language assistance.

Whom will you interpret for?

As you have seen in this chapter, many different people work in schools, and many families require language assistance. Let's look at the types of people who will need your services.

Parents and guardians

Often, recent arrivals to the United States do not speak fluent English. Moreover, it may take many of these parents years to feel comfortable when hearing and using the English language. Some may not even speak it after having lived in this country for years.

Similarly, for Deaf individuals who grow up in the U.S., English is not usually their native language. American Sign Language (ASL) might be their native language.

From the moment a parent or guardian who needs language assistance goes to a school in person to enroll a child, an interpreter or language facilitator should be present to make the enrollment process smooth and understandable.

While some parents may register their children by going to the school in person, others may choose to do so online with the assistance of English-speaking friends or relatives, especially when the available enrollment forms are in English only.

Today, many schools provide these forms in various languages. Some provide an online translation application (app) such as Google Translate to assist families with online forms (although the accuracy of such apps is often limited).

Bilingual relatives or friends may also ask for family assistance by calling the school or district when the forms do not have appropriate translations available. There are three ways parents can request and interpreter: in person, by phone, or online.

School personnel

Many U.S. school offices employ office assistants, coordinators and community liaisons who speak only English. Monolingual English-speaking staff will be at a disadvantage when parents need the services of interpreters or when school staff needs to get information across to families needing interpreting services.

In addition, every type of school employee discussed earlier in this chapter, with the exception of custodial staff, is someone you might interpret for. They include administrators, teachers, special personnel (professionals), paraprofessionals and community liaisons, among others. In addition to those staff members discussed previously, you might also be asked to interpret for the school nurse or health aide.

That is a broad array of staff, each with their own terminology, forms, protocols and requirements. That is why this book exists: there is a great deal of complexity to interpreting in schools.

In addition, you will need to provide your services in various settings, from parent-teacher conferences in empty classrooms to disciplinary meetings about a student in administrative offices, board meetings, individualized education programs (IEP) meetings and at other functions taking place in both school and district offices and even in students' homes.

Students

You will also, almost certainly, interpret for students. A linguistically diverse student will most likely be placed in a classroom where the teacher either speaks the student's language or has the preparation that addresses the needs of the student.

There will certainly be times when this may not be the case, however, especially with a child who speaks a less common language in the United States, such as Pashto, Kinyarwanda, or Kekchi. For this child, English language exposure, development and acquisition begins right away. Experienced and well-prepared teachers will be able to address this student's needs.

However, even such teachers will sometimes need your services, for example, for disciplinary meetings, concerns about what might be going on at home or to discuss complex topics, such as graduation requirements,

In 2021, there were an estimated 4.9 million children classified as English language learners (ELLs) in U.S. schools, about 10 percent of the public school population. In the fall of 2018, the percentage of ELLs ranged from a low of .08 percent in West Virginia to a high of 19.4 percent in California. How often your services are needed for such students (and their families) will obviously depend greatly on where you live.

These figures are part of the result of the initial identification of a student as a speaker of a language other than English, followed by an assessment that is used to determine if the student is classified as an English learner or fluent English proficient.

Amount of work

Anecdotally, Spanish has been a source of significant ongoing employment or contracts for interpreters in U.S. schools. Yet, depending on the state and the city, a swiftly growing number of jobs are also available for interpreters of other languages.

Apart from Spanish being the most common language used at home, students might speak other European, Asian, African or Indigenous languages. The third most spoken language in the United States is Chinese (Mandarin and Cantonese), followed by Tagalog, Vietnamese and Arabic, according to the 2020 U.S. Census Bureau.

Many schools have clusters of students of a certain national group. This is what happens when a large number of Cubans, Mexicans, Afghans, Somalis, Hmong, Ukrainians or Vietnamese settle in a certain neighborhood.

☞ Relay interpreting

There are also a growing number of children of Indigenous arrivals, primarily from Mexico and Central America. These families might speak a language such as Mixtec, Zapotec, Triqui, Nahuatl or Totonac.

Some of these families speak the Indigenous language at home and yet have a working knowledge of Spanish. Others speak almost no Spanish. Interpreting for these parents might need to be done in a relay style, using the services of two interpreters: one familiar with the Indigenous language and Spanish, and the other with a Spanish and English combination.

Relay interpreting is more time-consuming and somewhat awkward for interpreters who are not trained to perform it. It is done in consecutive mode. For details about how to perform Indigenous language interpreting professionally and specifically how to perform relay interpreting for English, Spanish and Indigenous languages, see the training manual *The Indigenous Interpreter®: A Training Manual for Indigenous Language Interpreting* (Allen et al., 2018).[6]

☞ ASL interpreting

To simplify a complex situation, there are broadly speaking two types of interpreters of American Sign Language (ASL) in U.S. schools:

- Interpreters for one or more Deaf students who typically accompany one student throughout their school day. These are usually full-time staff interpreters who are school employees. They are often called educational interpreters.
- Contract interpreters sent by language services. They typically arrive at schools to interpret for school staff and Deaf or Hard of Hearing families (most often the parents and guardians). They will interpret parent-teacher conferences, special education services, disciplinary hearings, schoolwide events, etc. They are often referred to as community interpreters.

---

[6] This training manual and its workbook are available online, free of charge, at https://www.cultureandlanguage.net/products/tii-manual

This book addresses ASL community interpreters but not ASL educational interpreters (in the ASL-specific meaning of both terms).

☛ Remote interpreting

The COVID-19 pandemic made video remote interpreting (VRI) and over-the-phone interpreting (OPI) popular and necessary across many fields in education, including the district, school, county and regional offices.

In addition, there is an increasing amount of video relay service (VRS) for Deaf students and families.

Finally, remote simultaneous interpreting (RSI) is now popular for school board meetings, hearings, media briefings and other public meetings and events in schools. Even if some families attend in person, others may prefer to connect remotely.

This book does not address remote interpreting in detail. *The Remote Interpreter* textbook, in particular the chapter in the forthcoming volume 2 on educational remote interpreting (Allen et al., 2024), provides a wealth of information on this topic. Here is some general information.

Modality of remote interpreting: OPI vs. VRI

Remote connections between all people, school personnel, parents and the interpreter can happen instantly when all people access a link for VRI or VRS and see and hear one another on a screen.

The same is true when someone picks up the phone and dials a language service that offers OPI.

Which is better for everyday interpreting, such as parent-teacher conferences, IEP meetings or assessments: OPI (phone only) or VRI (with video)?

It is generally better if you, the interpreter, can see the faces, expressions and gestures of the participants. That way you can clearly determine what is being stated. In general, schools are sensitive to this need for families and school staff, so if you work directly for a U.S. school today in a common language, you are likely to perform VRI (or VRS for Deaf students or families) rather than OPI.

However, for less common languages, the school might need to obtain your services remotely through a language service. OPI is still less expensive than VRI, although the difference in price is far smaller than it used to be. With OPI, participants connect through a conference form format, by adding phone numbers or people to the initial call. Generally, for U.S. schools, you are more likely to perform VRI than OPI.

Another option is to use a hybrid approach and combine OPI with VRI. For example, an interpreter can communicate with a teacher through VRI while also interpreting for the parent over the phone.

Figure 2.2: Basic set-up for interpreting remotely.

Modes in remote interpreting

Which mode will you perform in remotely—consecutive or simultaneous?

Unless you interpret for a public meeting, you will probably work consecutively in both OPI and VRI. Most OPI and VRI platforms do not allow you to perform simultaneous interpreting, yet some platforms (like Zoom) do offer an RSI feature and you may prefer to use it.

Sign language interpreters are the exception. Even remotely, they will generally work only (or mostly) in simultaneous mode.

RSI

Zoom was the first standard video conference platform to offer a simultaneous interpreting feature for spoken language interpreting. Other platforms have started to do the same. Unfortunately, this feature may not work on all devices and it has other limitations.

For example, for simultaneous interpreting you will generally need to work with a partner. How will you communicate with your partner to let them know it is time for them to take their turn interpreting? You will need to clearly determine what signals to use, and at what point you will be switching roles from primary speaker to support interpreter. There are other considerations.[7]

Special RSI platforms (such as KUDO, VoiceBoxer, Interprefy) are dedicated to RSI and as a result function much more smoothly for both participants and interpreters. However, they are more expensive. So far, most schools seem to prefer to have interpreters work simultaneously over Zoom.

If you are an educational interpreter and you need to perform RSI, consult *The Remote Interpreter* textbook (Allen et al., 2023) for detailed guidance on remote interpreting for educational settings in general and RSI in particular.

Assisting parents with OPI, VRI and RSI

You are the interpreter. It's not your job to be a tech expert, right?

Well—wrong, perhaps! Sometimes, when parents or school staff require the assistance of another person to resolve any connectivity issues for interpreting—they may turn to you.

When interpreters work with small groups of people and with one parent, and they need to go from one language to another and then vice versa, many sound, video and connection issues can arise. You do not have to be an expert—but you will need to be prepared. Consult *The Remote Interpreter* textbook (Allen et al., 2023) or take online classes in remote interpreting.

In particular, the Zoom simultaneous feature can be problematic. While school staff may now be used to remote interpreting, parents may still have difficulties. Parents may not have up-to-date computers, for example. They might have to connect on a tablet or cell phone.

What has worked well for some interpreters are the applications WhatsApp or FaceTime or by simply dialing a parent or guardian's cell phone number. When all participants see one another on Zoom, but additionally connect with the interpreter and the parent through a cell phone, it is possible to achieve a smooth simultaneous delivery. You can mute the microphone on the remote platform when interpreting for the parent and unmute it when interpreting into English.

Check with all participants before you agree on a procedure for a remote meeting. Participants will appreciate it if you act professionally by explaining the optimal mode and method of interpreting for a specific situation. (Modes of interpreting are discussed in Chapters 5, 6 and 7.)

Often, the remote interpreter takes the lead in deciding which mode to use. Some interpreters prefer consecutive interpreting, because it allows all participants more time to hear and to understand the exchanges. Others opt for simultaneous because it is more efficient, saves time and, for many interpreters, is more accurate. At times, however, interpreters may switch from one mode to another *if the platform permits both*.

Remember: traditional VRI and OPI platforms will not let you perform simultaneously.

---

[7] Fortunately, there are also online resources, such as this video from 2021 offering basic tips, tools and techniques for performing successful RSI over Zoom: https://www.youtube.com/watch?v=PUQBPnpdAvA

👉 Technical challenges in remote interpreting

It is important to keep in mind that challenges will come up when you and the participants connect remotely. These challenges relate to download speeds, internet providers, routers, random access memory (RAM), Ethernet, cables, headsets, cameras, backdrops, internet security protocols and more. (See Allen et al., Chapters 2 and 3, 2023.) Ideally a district or school will employ technology technicians who can make the interpreter's job easier, a person who can be in charge of VRI or RSI setups.

Although the pandemic health threat has diminished for many, schools will continue to use remote interpreting in general and VRI in particular. Especially in special education, some school districts will continue to choose VRI for IEP meetings if all participants have access to an electronic device. Parent-teacher conferences have reverted to in-person meetings now that the pandemic health threat has subsided.

For many parents and teachers, nothing is better than an in-person meeting, especially in parent-teacher conferences and open houses. It is difficult to predict how widespread remote interpreting will become in U.S. schools. However, it is here to stay. Following the COVID-19 pandemic, remote interpreting will continue to be an important part of educational interpreting in U.S. schools.

📖 Chapter 2 review

Chapter 2 provides an overview of the realities of interpreting in public schools in the United States. It discusses the various individuals who have taken on the role of interpreter in schools, such as children, parents, custodial staff, bilingual school employees and full-time staff interpreters.

Problems arise when untrained individuals try to help with interpreting, such as nonadherence to standard protocols and legal risks. Untrained interpreters, including family members and friends, not only often lack adequate domain knowledge and vocabulary for interpreting educational content, but they may also not be aware of the risks and consequences of interpreting in schools or may want to avoid conveying bad news. Even bilingual staff or teachers who might be willing to act as interpreters still lack the qualifications and training to do so.

This is why in many U.S. schools, full-time staff interpreters provide professional language assistance to school staff and families who need their services. These can be employees or external professionals who are either qualified to do so or tested and trained by the school district.

Training and testing in community or educational interpreting, along with yearly professional development workshops, are recommended for school district staff interpreters.

The chapter suggests that qualified interpreters should be provided in all cases. When staff interpreters are not available, districts can contract with interpreting agencies or professional freelance interpreters.

Many languages requiring interpreting can be provided through over-the-phone interpreting (OPI), video remote interpreting (VRI), video relay service (VRS) and remote simultaneous interpreting (RSI). Remote interpreting is becoming more common in schools and is often provided over a video conference platform.

Technical challenges in remote interpreting include slow download speeds, unstable internet connections and security protocols as well as the robustness of the technology used. For example, RSI is not possible unless several audio channels are made available. As a result, the capabilities of remote interpreting often dictate the mode to use (consecutive or simultaneous).

Remote interpreting grew exponentially during the COVID-19 pandemic of the early 2020s. Although the pandemic health threat has receded, many schools will continue to use remote interpreting, especially VRI, for IEP meetings as long as participants have access and know how to use these electronic devices.

Chapter 2 activities

1. Multiple choice

Circle the letter that corresponds to the best response.

1. Language assistants include all of the following, except:
   a. Friends of the family.
   b. Sons or daughters of the family.
   c. Professional interpreters.
   d. Aunts, uncles or cousins.

2. Under what circumstances should high school students interpret?
   a. If they participate in an interpretation class or program.
   b. If they are bilingual.
   c. If they want to interpret for their own teacher.
   d. If they are taking a language class.

3. Most training for interpreters falls within what field?
   a. Immigration
   b. Legal
   c. Community
   d. Educational

4. Relay interpreting generally:
   a. Is only used with Spanish speakers.
   b. Is done using the simultaneous mode.
   c. Is quite common in parent-teacher conferences.
   d. Relies on two interpreters.

5. ASL educational interpreters use:
   a. Relay interpreting.
   b. Spoken language.
   c. Sign language.
   d. Microphones.

2. Respond to the questions with short answers.
   a. Why is using a child to interpret not a good idea?
   b. What is the advantage to using a language bank?
   c. What is the difference between a freelance interpreter and a staff interpreter?
   d. What are contract interpreting services?

3. Indicate if these statements are true (T) or false (F).   T   F
   1. Staff interpreters can also receive the title of community liaison.   ___ ___
   2. All bilinguals can interpret.   ___ ___
   3. Bilingual custodial staff can be asked to interpret.   ___ ___
   4. Language proficiency can be tested.   ___ ___
   5. Language assistants are professional interpreters.   ___ ___
   6. Interpreters do not need to be experts in technology connectivity.   ___ ___
   7. All platforms allow interpreters to interpret simultaneously.   ___ ___
   8. Staff interpreters provide language assistance to staff and EL families. ___ ___
   9. Ideally, staff interpreters should be tested and trained.   ___ ___
   10. All bilingual school staff should be able to work as interpreters.   ___ ___

4. Match the acronyms with their equivalent.
   VRI   American Sign Language
   OPI   Remote Simultaneous Interpreting
   RSI   English learner
   ASL   Video Remote Interpreting
   EL   Over-the-Phone Interpreting

☑ Answer key for Chapter 2 activities

1. Multiple choice

1. C. 2. A. 3. B. 4. D. 5. C.

2. Respond to the questions with short answers.

a. Children are not trained in interpreting; they may delete or omit information; they may not know the terminology being used; they may distort the information. They may not be psychologically ready or prepared for the task and content at hand.

b. Language banks provide districts with available and qualified freelance interpreters who can be called on when needed.

c.

Freelance interpreter	Staff interpreter
Works for themselves or through agencies	Works for the district
Has flexibility	Has a specific schedule
Is on call	Availability is more predictable

d. Contract interpreting services are agencies that can provide tested and trained interpreters to work in schools.

3. Indicate if these statements are true (T) or false (F).

1. T. 2. F. 3. F. 4. T. 5. F. 6. F. 7. F. 8. T. 9. T. 10. F.

4. Match the acronyms with their equivalent.

VRI Video Remote Interpreting

OPI Over-the-Phone Interpreting

RSI Remote Simultaneous Interpretation

ASL American Sign Language

EL English learner

Introduction to Interpreting in Special Education 3

Chapter 3

- Introduction
- Educational interpreters need to understand special education
- The special education process
- Chapter 3 review
- Chapter 3 activities
- Answer key for Chapter 3 activities

Introduction

Special education services must be provided to students in public schools once they meet certain requirements. These are based on specific laws, such as the Education for All Handicapped Children Act (EHA), later renamed the Individuals with Disabilities Education Act (IDEA). Interpreters must be present in order to assist English learner (EL) families in understanding the recommendations made by the professional school staff.

They are there to interpret for parents at individualized education program (IEP) meetings. It is here that specialists explain the process, the types of assessments that have taken place and the types of services that can be offered for a child who qualifies for such services. The interpreter follows careful steps in preparing for such meetings, in delivering the information that is shared by all people and in debriefing following these meetings.

Educational interpreters need to understand special education

Special education is a critical part of U.S. educational services. It is also an area of high demand for interpreters in K–12 schools.

Educational interpreters in the U.S. need to have a sound understanding of special education for many reasons, including the following:

- Interpreters in U.S. public schools will probably have *many* assignments for special education services.
- The interpreting complexity of these assignments is extremely high.
- Much of the vocabulary is high register and challenging to interpret.
- A great deal of the terminology is legal.
- Many parents speak languages that do not have equivalents for these high-register or legal terms.
- Many documents are involved; extensive sight translation of these often long, legal documents can be a huge challenge (often the documents should be translated instead).
- Many or most parents do not have prior experience in their countries or cultures with the concept, far less the delivery of special education services. The idea itself of special education may be confusing.
- Teachers and other school staff might not explain special education services in ways that are easy or helpful to interpret.

In addition to these challenges, providing special education services involves extra layers of bureaucratic processes and procedures that can confuse (and even mystify) interpreters.

Where U.S. special education begins

EHA

Public Law 94-142, Education for All Handicapped Children (EHA), was enacted by Congress in 1975. As a result of this law, all public schools that accept federal funding are required to provide equal access to education for all children, regardless of their mental or physical disabilities.

Education must also take place in the least restrictive environment (LRE). In other words, Deaf and Hard of Hearing students, for example, or those with serious emotional, learning or physical disabilities would ideally, where feasible, receive their education in a mainstream (regular) classroom and not in a school for the Deaf. Similarly, children with autism spectrum disorder would ideally attend their local school and not a school only for children with autism spectrum disorder.

To comply with EHA, schools set up frequent meetings and create ongoing programs with specialists and parental input to determine the best plan to assure a quality education for these children.

In an LRE, a child with disabilities would be able to interact with other children. However, when instructional goals cannot be met in a mainstream instructional environment, a child can be moved into a more restrictive environment. Schools for the Deaf and schools for students with certain specific disabilities still exist.

IDEA

In 1990, EHA was reviewed and renamed the Individuals with Disabilities Education Act (IDEA). Modifications were made. The Office of Special Education Programs (OSEP) provides financial support to assist states and school districts in its role as an administrative body to support IDEA.

IDEA Part A lays the foundation to the act and outlines general provisions, including the purpose of IDEA. For students ages 3 to 21, Part B of the act addresses the following areas:

- Determines the need for special services through appropriate evaluations.
- Creates an individualized education program (IEP).
- Places the child with a disability in the least restrictive environment (LRE).
- Provides a free and appropriate public education (FAPE).
- Mandates that parents, and students when appropriate, participate in decision-making.
- Ensures that procedural safeguards are in place.

Parents become active participants in this educational process, and their input is taken into consideration. If parents think that the IEP is not appropriate for their child, they can challenge the team's recommendation. Linguistically diverse parents can voice their concerns through an interpreter. They can also request specific special services if they think their child needs them.

Early intervention services

Under IDEA Part C, eligible children with disabilities from birth to 36 months receive early intervention services. Families receive an Individualized Family Service Plan (IFSP) that addresses the concerns and priorities of the family.

The plan also describes the goals for the child and the steps that can lead to the eventual transition of the child into formal school education. All parents, including EL and Deaf parents, participate in the creation of intervention services that are made available to their child.

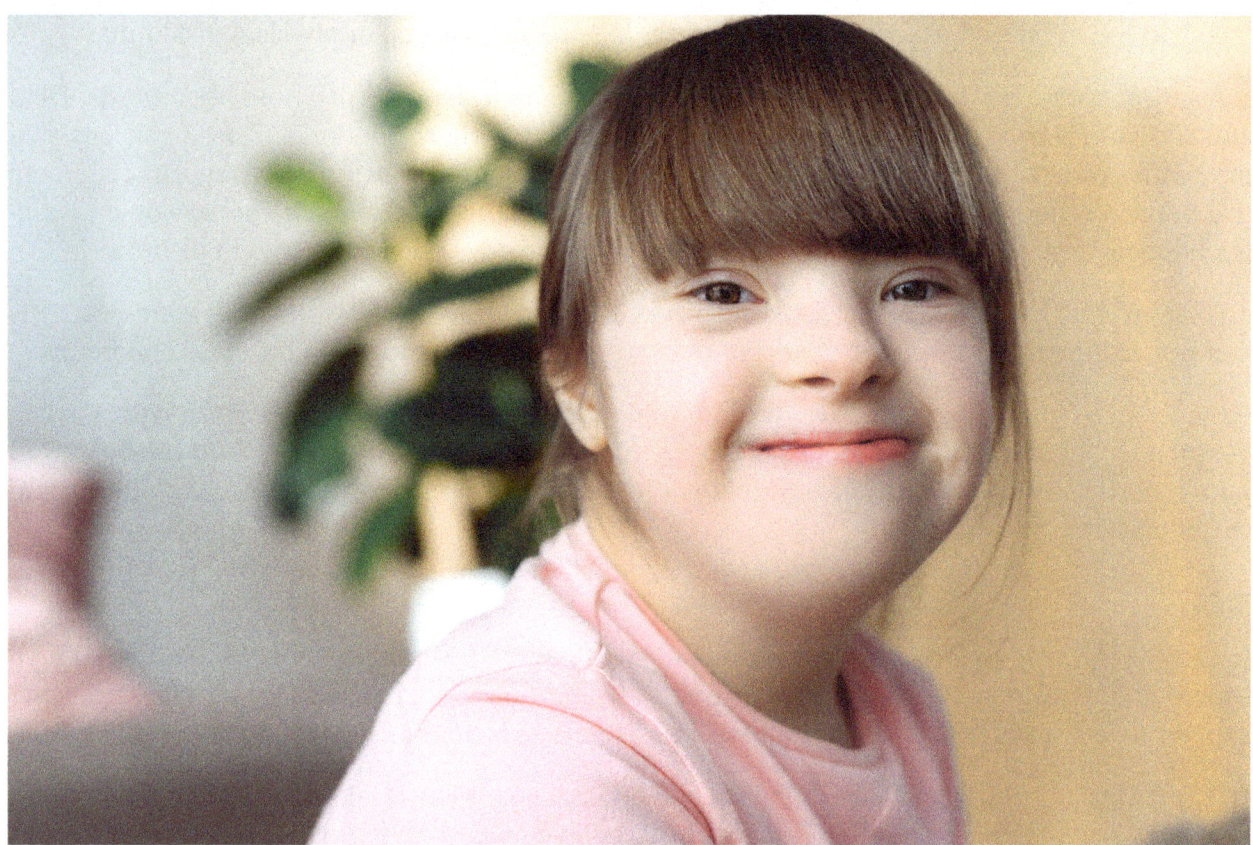

National programs and requirements

IDEA Part D addresses national activities that aim to improve the education of children with disabilities. These provide resources that support programs and projects, including grants for improving the education and transitional services for students with disabilities.

Every U.S. state has a lead person. Some U.S. commonwealths and territories—including the Northern Mariana Islands and the U.S. Virgin Islands—have a lead person. Each lead person oversees either Part B or Part C. The less populous locations work only with Part B. However, all states include a team leader. By law, Congress has to reauthorize IDEA every five years.

A disability vs. a learning disability

Most IEPs address a student's learning disabilities. What is a learning disability?

There are two types of disability addressed in IDEA: a general disability and a learning disability.

Section 1401(3) (A) of IDEA defines a disability in this way:[8]

> The term "child with a disability" means a child—
> - (i) with intellectual disabilities, hearing impairments (including Deafness), speech or language impairments, visual impairments (including Blindness), serious emotional disturbance (referred to in this chapter as "emotional disturbance"), orthopedic impairments, autism, traumatic brain injury, other health impairments, or specific learning disabilities; and
> - (ii) who, by reason thereof, needs special education and related services.

Here is a list of the most common types of disabilities:

- Developmental delays
- Hearing impairment (including Deafness)
- A speech or language impairment
- A serious emotional disturbance
- An orthopedic impairment
- Autism
- Traumatic brain injury
- A specific learning disability
- Multiple disabilities

Section 1401 (30) (A) (B) (C) of IDEA defines a learning disability as follows:

> The term "specific learning disability" means a disorder in one or more of the basic psychological processes involved in understanding or in using language, spoken or written, which disorder may manifest itself in the imperfect ability to listen, think, speak, read, write, spell, or do mathematical calculations.
>
> Such term includes such conditions as perceptual disabilities, brain injury, minimal brain dysfunction, dyslexia, and developmental aphasia.
>
> Such term does not include a learning problem that is primarily the result of visual, hearing, or motor disabilities, of intellectual disabilities, of emotional disturbance, or of environmental, cultural, or economic disadvantage.[9]

All these types of disabilities (both general and learning disabilities) are dealt with through the IEP process. Learning disabilities of lesser concern can be addressed through the Student Study Team, sometimes called Student Success Team (SST). The SST is a group formed within a school to examine a student's academic, behavioral, or socio-emotional progress. Its recommendations are not as enforceable as an IEP.

---

[8] Retrieved from: https://sites.ed.gov/idea/statute-chapter-33/subchapter-i/1401
[9] Retrieved from: https://sites.ed.gov/idea/statute-chapter-33/subchapter-i/1401/30

ESA

Every state has an educational services agency (ESA) in charge of delivering special education services. Different names are used by different states, yet federal mandates related to special education must be met in all states.

For example, New York has the Board of Cooperative Educational Services. Rhode Island works with collaboratives. Connecticut relies on regional education service centers. Indiana has special education cooperatives that provide services.

California's Special Education Local Plan Area (SELPA) provides the required special education services to qualified students and training for parents. SELPA and other ESAs provide EL parents with interpreters and translators at meetings that deal with the educational plans for their child. In California, there are 136 SELPAs that serve 1,515 local educational agencies.[10]

A few states have programs that assist with the administration of special education services. Nebraska's Assistive Technology Partnership works with schools to provide necessary technological devices from a central state pool. Some states, such as Louisiana, Missouri and New Jersey, have created special school districts for students with severe needs that cannot be met by local districts. Louisiana's Special School District, for example, has three specialized schools: one for the Deaf, one the visually impaired and a special education center for orthopedic-impaired students.

Language assistance in special education

Much progress has been made in the special education arena so that parents can understand its steps and requirements. Most ESA websites make information available in Spanish and other languages. At in-person meetings with EL and Deaf parents of special education students, interpreters and translators are brought in to interpret and to translate the plans, steps and recommendations dealing with individualized learning plans in a language that these parents understand.

According to California's Education Code,

> The local educational agency shall take any action necessary to ensure that the parent or guardian understands the proceedings at a meeting, including arranging for an interpreter for parents or guardians with Deafness or whose native language is a language other than English (i).

> The local educational agency shall give the parent or guardian a copy of the individualized education program, at no cost to the parent or guardian (j). [11]

---

[10] Retrieved from: https://selpa.info/

[11] Retrieved from: https://codes.findlaw.com/ca/education-code/edc-sect-56341-5/

The special education process

👉 How the process begins

It is necessary for the interpreters and translators involved at any stage of the special education process to completely understand the process. In particular, both interpreters and translators need to understand the critically important individualized education program (IEP) when they work with children in special education and their parents.

Interpreters play a key role in special education by facilitating conversations between EL or Deaf families and educators. That role often begins before the children are school age with the creation of the IFSP. This early intervention aims to reduce future educational costs. Its goal is to help the family deal with the child's disability and also to facilitate independent living when the child with a disability becomes an adult.

👉 Child Find

Initially, the process of special education for a child and the family begins when someone, usually a teacher or a parent, notices a learning or behavior irregularity in a student. If this concern is noticed before the child reaches school age, a preschool teacher might refer the parent to Child Find, a national program available across the U.S. IDEA includes the Child Find mandate. In addition, IDEA Part C is the program for Infants and Toddlers with Disabilities and is consistent with IDEA Part B.

Child Find specialists make assessments (such as speech, hearing or cognitive assessments) to determine if the child is eligible for special education services under IDEA. If so, Child Find will link the child and family to those services.

👉 504 Plan

This plan is associated with Section 504 of the U.S. Rehabilitation Act of 1973 and ensures that there is no discrimination by organizations and employers against people with disabilities. When this plan is implemented in schools, a team of teachers, specialists and the parent determines what accommodations a student will receive under the plan. The team determines if an IEP or a 504 plan is appropriate.

The 504 plan specifies the accommodations or modifications that are needed so that eligible students can perform at the same level as their classmates. Typically it is used for students who have a medical condition that requires accommodations. The student might require preferential seating, a wheelchair ramp, blood sugar monitoring, extra time on tests, opportunities to turn assignments in late or a keyboard for taking notes. Actual special education services are usually not provided. Interpreters assist EL parents with these and also at SST and IEP team meetings.

☞ SST

If a parent, teacher or other school staff member notes some irregularity in the child's development, a referral is made to the Student Study Team or Student Success Team (SST). The team, usually composed of the teacher, an administrator and support personnel meets with parents or guardians. They discuss the concerns. They create remediation strategies. Interventions are developed, and strategies or interventions are put in place.

After observations and assessments, which may include the participation of the speech-language pathologist, the occupational therapist, the resource teacher and/or the school psychologist, school staff discuss the results of these observations, including classroom interventions, with parents or guardians.

Then the school may recommend one of two pathways. If the concerns can be resolved with or without continued interventions, the student is not referred for additional special education assessments. If the team and the parent do not find a resolution to the concerns through interventions, the student is then referred for special education assessments. The SST team may also refer a child for a Section 504 evaluation. Interpreters are required to assist EL parents during these SST meetings.

☞ The IEP or admission, review and dismissal (ARD) process

When these initial interventions prove to be ineffective, a more formal approach is taken. The student is referred to an IEP meeting by the SST, a teacher, parent, public health nurse, daycare professional or even a doctor. Not all students go through an SST meeting first though. A referral can be made for an IEP meeting without going through the SST process. The referral mostly happens after instructional and behavioral interventions in the classroom have not met with success.

At this point, a team of experts meets to recommend and later administer a number of assessments to identify the child's learning needs. Based on the results of the assessments, the team determines if the student is eligible for special education placement or if the student should remain in the regular classroom with some or no interventions.

Parents participate at these meetings and approve an educational plan. An IEP document based on that plan is then developed and implemented with short-term and long-term goals.

The IEP or ARD team is made up of administrators, parents, teachers and school specialists, such as psychologists and speech therapists. This team creates the IEP that meets the specific needs of the student. The IEP is signed by the participants, including the parent or guardian. The plan is then set in motion and reviewed yearly, or every three years, with the parent or guardian.

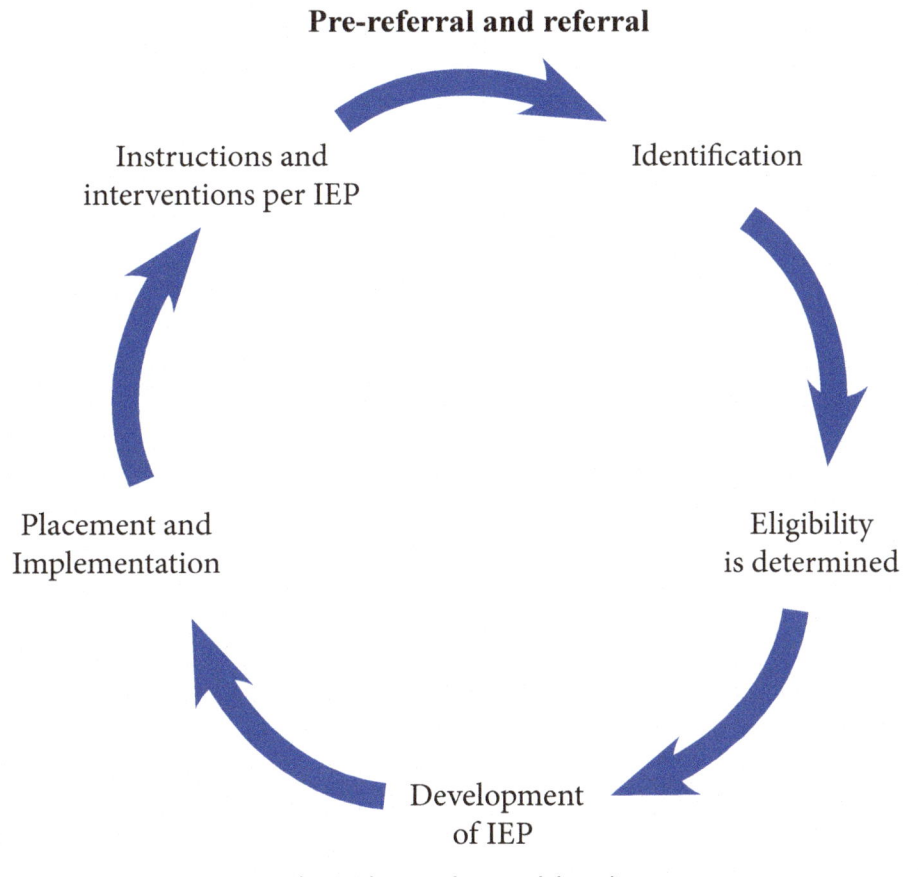

Figure 3.1: **Steps to develop the IEP.**

👉 Common challenges encountered by interpreters working in special education

- There is frequent use of high register terminology. Special school personnel, such as psychologists, speech pathologists and resource teachers, oftentimes explain assessments and goals using formal and pedagogical (intellectual) language, which may confuse the EL parent.
- Much of the explanations include technical vocabulary and acronyms that parents are not familiar with and may be hearing for the first time.
- Some of the vocabulary used by the IEP team may be difficult or impossible to interpret without an extensive explanation, one that the speaker should provide, but does not.
- Lack of understanding by the specialists and school staff regarding the confusion experienced by EL parents, one that the interpreter witnesses frequently and understands well.

- Some expectation by the school staff and by the parent that the interpreter is responsible for making everything understandable. People may think that the interpreter should intervene and explain with greater detail the terminology and the acronyms. They don't understand the role of the interpreter. It is not to counsel. However, the parent can request an explanation of words that are not understood.
- IEP participants might expect that it is up to the interpreter to make everything clear.
- Parents might not understand that most special education (SPED) sessions are legally binding.
- EL parents may lack the understanding of what SPED services mean for the future life, education and career of their child.
- EL parents may lack the understanding about the meaning of learning disabilities and how they can support their children with disabilities.

☛ Most common special education assignments for the interpreter

- The admission, review and dismissal (ARD) process, usually named as such in Texas, is where teams determine if a student is eligible for special education services. If so, the student is assessed, reviewed and can become eligible for an IEP or can be dismissed from services.
- IEP meetings that involve school specialists and parents and determine the direction a student's education will take place after analyzing assessments, observations, data and interviews. As a result, a team creates an individualized program for an eligible student, which is subsequently reviewed yearly.
- Assessments, oftentimes guided by a school psychologist or a speech-language pathologist, focus on auditory, speech, language, cognition and behavior.
- Less common are home visits with school specialists to help observe a student in a home setting.

☛ Participants at IEP meetings

The required participants are:

- A representative of the school system, usually an administrator (a principal or a vice principal)
- One or both parents
- A special education teacher
- A general education teacher

Others who may join the group are:

- A speech-language pathologist
- A school psychologist
- A special needs assistant

- All individuals who conducted assessments
- A person with specific knowledge of the student
- A case manager
- A learning specialist
- The student, when appropriate
- An interpreter, if needed for the parent

☞ Role of parents at IEP meetings

- To be involved in the process
- To ask questions about the assessments and the goals of the IEP
- To clarify any misunderstandings
- To advocate for the child

☞ Recommendations for case managers and IEP team members when working with an interpreter

- Introduce yourselves to the parent and interpreter.
- Know that the meeting may take longer than anticipated.
- Allow the interpreter to share any cultural considerations related to the family.
- Ask the interpreter to select an interpreting style: consecutive or simultaneous.
- Attempt to use simpler language that is not filled with technical terminology.
- Pause when making long statements or when explaining assessment results.
- Speak slowly to allow the interpreter to interpret everything that is said.
- Avoid jargon and abstract words.
- Explain acronyms.
- Avoid side conversations.
- Check for understanding.
- Summarize the key points at the end of the meeting.
- Ask the parent "What questions do you have?" rather than "Do you have any questions?"

☞ Preparation of the interpreter before an IEP meeting

Briefing

- Prior to the meeting you request to meet with the facilitator, case manager or speech pathologist to discuss the purpose of the meeting.

- This facilitator shares relevant information about the student.
- You preview any relevant documents or assessments.
- You familiarize yourself with the assessments that were administered.
- You discuss relevant terminology.
- You ask about the parent's culture that might impact the interaction between the parent and the IEP team.
- You ask about the signal to use for requesting to slow down.
- You discuss the seating arrangements.
- You find out who will be present and the pronunciation of any names.
- You find out how introductions will be handled.

Performance of the interpreter during the IEP meeting

During the IEP

- You interpret everything that is said.
- You seat yourself where you will hear all participants.
- You determine what mode of interpretation to use: consecutive or simultaneous.
- You ask for clarification of terminology when necessary.
- You signal if pauses are needed for you to interpret.
- You use first person language.
- You use notes when interpreting consecutively.
- You let the parent know whom to contact, someone who speaks the home language, if there are follow-up questions.

Interpreter's checklist following the IEP meeting

Debriefing

- Go over outcomes and concerns with the facilitator.
- Review the parent's responses.
- Go over what went well.
- Share any concerns or beliefs about the family culture.
- Confirm when the next session will take place.

It is important for interpreters to know SPED terminology. Check the Department of Education website for glossaries that correspond to your language pair.

📖 Chapter 3 review

Special education is a critical, essential part of the U.S. educational system. There are many laws in the United States that focus on children with disabilities. These laws (EHA and IDEA) must be followed by public schools that accept federal funds. The laws require interpreters for English learner and Deaf parents to understand and participate in their child's education.

School interpreters are present at special education meetings in order to assist EL families in the understanding of the intricate process of special education placement of a child. Interpreters can be present at Child Find before children reach school age. They participate in 504 plans, SST meetings, ARD meetings and IEP meetings.

Interpreters prepare for these meetings with the facilitator or other special personnel, review materials that will be presented, interpret all that is said at these meetings, select the mode that is most appropriate and at the end of the meeting debrief with the participants.

Chapter 3 activities

1. Multiple choice

Circle the letter that corresponds to the best response.

1. The least common assignment for an interpreter is:
   a. An IEP meeting.
   b. A 504 plan meeting.
   c. An SST meeting.
   d. A home visit.

2. An IEP:
   a. Does not need to be signed by the parent.
   b. Includes goals that should be met.
   c. Is reviewed every five years.
   d. Can only be recommended by a teacher.

3. IDEA Part C:
   a. Must be reauthorized every 10 years.
   b. Provides resources and projects that support students with disabilities.
   c. Lays the foundation for the ACT.
   d. Addresses the needs of children with disabilities from birth to three years old.

4. A child's specific learning disability could be:
   a. Related to a brain injury.
   b. Related to an emotional disturbance.
   c. A result of a visual problem.
   d. A result of a hearing loss.

5. An IEP is developed:
   a. By the parent.
   b. At a minimal cost to the parent.
   c. In consultation with a team of school specialists.
   d. Without the need for assessments.

Introduction to Interpreting in Special Education — Chapter 3

2. Indicate if these statements are true (T) or false (F). T F
1. The SST handles less severe learning disabilities. ___ ___
2. ESAs provide special education services. ___ ___
3. Child Find is a national program for school-age children. ___ ___
4. High register words are infrequent in an IEP. ___ ___
5. An administrator must be present at an IEP meeting. ___ ___
6. The IEP participants should avoid explaining acronyms. ___ ___
7. Interpreters must familiarize themselves with the IEP process. ___ ___

3. Define what the following acronyms represent.
a. IDEA
b. FAPE
c. OSEP
d. ESA
e. IEP
f. IFSP
g. SELPA
h. SST
i. ARD
j. EHA
k. LRE

4. Fill in the blank with the appropriate word.
During the IEP meeting
a. You interpret _____ that is said.
b. You seat yourself where you will _____ all participants.
c. You determine what mode of interpretation to use: consecutive or _____.
d. You ask for clarification of _____ when necessary, but not excessively.
e. You use _____ if pauses are needed for you to interpret.
f. You take _____ when interpreting consecutively.
g. You let the parent know whom to _____, someone who speaks the home language, if there will be follow-up questions.

55

☑ Answer key for Chapter 3 activities

1. Multiple choice

1. D. 2. B. 3. D. 4. A. 5. C.

2. Indicate if these statements are true (T) or false (F).

1. T. 2. T. 3. F. 4. F. 5. T. 6. F. 7. T.

3. Define what the following acronyms represent.

a. IDEA: Individuals with Disabilities Education Act
b. FAPE: Free and Appropriate Public Education
c. OSEP: Office of Special Education Programs
d. ESA: Educational Services Agency
e. IEP: Individualized Education Program
f. IFSP: Individualized Family Service Plan
g. SELPA: Special Education Local Plan Area
h. SST: Student Study (Success) Team
i. ARD: Admission Review Dismissal
j. EHA: Education for All Handicapped Children
k. LRE: Least Restrictive Environment

4. Fill in the blank with the appropriate word.

a. Everything or all
b. Hear or see
c. Simultaneous
d. Terminology, words, acronyms
e. Signals
f. Notes
g. Contact or reach

Interpreter Ethics in Educational Interpreting 4

Chapter 4

- Introduction
- What are ethics? And what is a code of ethics?
- Near universal code of ethical tenets and directives
- Educational interpreting codes of ethics and other ethical guidance
- Which ethical guidance should you follow?
- Ethics in remote educational interpreting
- Chapter 4 review
- Chapter 4 activities
- Answer key for Chapter 4 activities

Introduction

The U.S. may have more codes of ethics and ethical guidance documents for educational interpreters (both spoken and sign language interpreters) than any other country in the world, including two national codes. A number of these documents are discussed in this chapter.

A 2023 publication, *The Remote Interpreter,* Vol. 1, examined 240 codes of ethics, standards of practice and other ethical guidance documents for interpreters and translators from 53 countries and territories, in addition to international documents, available in 23 languages (Allen et al., 2023). This analysis suggests that around the world, eight ethical directives or tenets are found in all or most codes of ethics for interpreters.

The first five tenets appear to be universal and the last three tenets are found in the majority of ethical codes and guidelines for interpreters. The eight tenets are:

- Confidentiality (protecting privacy, maintaining secrecy)
- Accuracy (faithfulness and interpreting the whole message)
- Impartiality (taking no sides and avoiding conflict of interest)
- Professionalism (professional conduct)
- Professional development (engaging in continuing education)
- Role boundaries (defining scope of practice and professional boundaries)
- Solidarity (professional relationships that support the profession itself)
- Respect (for all participants)

—Allen et al., 2023, p. 322

In general, codes of ethics for educational interpreters include most or all of these eight tenets, in one form or another.

This chapter provides an overview of what a code of ethics is in the context of educational interpreting and translation. It reviews current codes of ethics and ethical guidance documents for educational interpreters of spoken or signed languages. Finally, it seeks to guide interpreters in public schools, whether they interpret face to face or remotely and whether they work in one or several districts or across the nation.

What are ethics? And what is a code of ethics?

Ethics are often confusing for interpreters—and not only interpreters. Many people in various professions regard ethics and a code of ethics as one and the same. They are not.

Even this nation's two leading law dictionaries add to this confusion.

One, *Black's Law Dictionary,* defines ethics as:

> Directives based on one's ethics and morality. How one lives with others. The foremost concepts and principles of proper human conduct. Socially, it is the collective of universal values, treating each human equally, acknowledging human and natural rights, obeying the law of land, showing health and safety concerns, caring for natural environment. Refer to morality.[12]

The other, *Ballentine's Law Dictionary*, defines ethics more narrowly as:

> A code, system, or body of moral principles or good conduct, particularly a system for a group of people or a profession…In a profession, the sum of professional experience as to standards of professional behavior.
>
> —Ballentine, 1969, p. 422

The fourth edition of *The American Heritage Dictionary of the English Language* includes both definitions for the word ethics:

1. a. A set of principles of right conduct.

    b. A theory or a system of moral values…

2. ethics (*used with a sing. verb*) The study of the general nature of morals and of the specific moral choices to be made by a person; moral philosophy.

3. ethics (*used with a sing. or pl. verb*) The rules or standards governing the conduct of a person or the members of a profession: *medical ethics.*[13]

In short, ethics are what we feel is right and wrong. A code of ethics is guidance about how to conduct oneself professionally.

---

[12] Retrieved from: https://thelawdictionary.org/ethics/

[13] Retrieved from: https://ahdictionary.com/word/search.html?q=ethics

For interpreters, professional conduct is expected and required. That is also true for educational interpreters. Various specializations of interpreting have their own codes. For example, medical and legal interpreting in the U.S. have long-established codes of ethics. The National Association of Judiciary Interpreters and Translators (NAJIT) abides by eight canons (that is, ethical tenets or principles). These eight reflect similar canons in U.S. federal and state court codes of ethics.

The eight NAJIT canons are:

- Accuracy
- Impartiality
- Confidentiality
- Limitations of practice (scope of practice, role boundaries)
- Protocol and demeanor (professionalism)
- Maintenance and improvement of skills (professional development)
- Accurate representation of credentials
- (Removing) impediments to compliance[14]

The U.S. National Council on Interpreting in Health Care (NCIHC) has similar requirements in its national code of ethics, with three significant exceptions:

- The interpreter continuously strives to develop awareness of his/her own and other (including biomedical) cultures encountered in the performance of their professional duties.
- The interpreter treats all parties with respect.
- When the patient's health, well-being, or dignity is at risk, the interpreter may be justified in acting as an advocate. Advocacy is understood as an action taken on behalf of an individual that goes beyond facilitating communication, with the intention of supporting good health outcomes. Advocacy must only be undertaken after careful and thoughtful analysis of the situation and if other less intrusive actions have not resolved the problem.

—NCIHC, 2004, p. 3

Respect is an ethical tenet in a large number of codes of ethics around the world.

The other two tenets above related to cultural awareness and advocacy are found in far fewer codes or standards for interpreters. Both are controversial. For example, NCIHC states:

> The ethical obligation of interpreters is to possess enough understanding of culture and cultural practices and beliefs to be able to facilitate communication across cultural differences, seeking to minimize, and, if possible, avoid, potential misunderstanding and miscommunication based on cultural assumptions and/or stereotyping. Under certain conditions, such as clashing cultural beliefs or practices, a lack of linguistic equivalency, or the inability of parties to articulate the differences in their own words, the interpreter should assist (with the explicit consent of all parties to this intervention) by sharing cultural information or helping develop an explanation that can be understood by all.

—NCIHC, 2004, p. 18

---

[14] Retrieved from: https://najit.org/wp-content/uploads/2016/09/NAJITCodeofEthicsFINAL.pdf

> When the patient's health, well-being, or dignity is at risk, the interpreter may be justified in acting as an advocate…The act of advocacy should derive from clear and/or consistent observations that something is not right and that action needs to be taken to right the wrong. On a deep level, advocacy goes to the heart of ethical behavior for all those involved in health care—to uphold the health and well-being (social, emotional and physical) of patients and ensure that no harm is done.
>
> —NCIHC, 2004, pp. 19-20

In the educational field, a national code of ethics based on the NCIHC code will be discussed later in this chapter. Meanwhile, interpreters can abide by some of the basic near-universal tenets and directives that have proven to be valuable as follows.

Near universal code of ethical tenets and directives

1. Maintain **confidentiality**. The conversations that take place between a parent and educational personnel, such as administrators, teachers, psychologists, speech pathologists and other special educators, are kept confidential.

2. Strive for **accuracy** when conveying messages between the people who need interpretation services. Be faithful to the source language, adhering to the original message and its register, tone and intent when delivering your rendition into the target language.

3. Maintain **impartiality**. Avoid imposing opinions, giving advice, taking sides or projecting biases. Strive to maintain professional distance. Avoid personal disclosures. Declare real and potential conflicts of interest.

4. Conduct yourself with **professionalism**. Dress appropriately, be kind and courteous, observe professional protocols and follow your code of ethics.

5. Engage in **professional development**. Take courses, read journals, attend conferences and webinars, maintain your working languages, etc.

6. Maintain **role boundaries**. Avoid engaging in other work while interpreting or socializing with participants (unless they are colleagues).

7. Treat all participants with **respect**, including families and children, school staff and special personnel. Address participants with appropriate titles and cultural sensitivity.

8. Promote **professional relationships.** Support other interpreters. Join professional associations and participate in interpreter forums and listservs. Avoid criticizing other interpreters or the profession.

Educational interpreting codes of ethics and other ethical guidance

Listed here are examples of ethical guidance available to educational interpreters in the U.S. Three of these documents are national in scope (National Association of Educational Translators and Interpreters of Spoken Languages, NAETISL, 2022, and National Association of Interpreters in Education, NAIE, 2019 and 2021). One of them (NAETISL) is for spoken languages, while two (NAIE) are for signed language.

Spoken language interpreting

- Austin Independent School District. (nd). *Code of Ethics and Standards of Practice for Interpreters and Translators in Educational Settings.*
- National Association of Educational Translators and Interpreters of Spoken Languages. (2022). *Code of Ethics and Standards of Practice for Educational Translators and Interpreters of Spoken Languages.*
- Orange County, California, Department of Education. (2017). *Guidelines for Educational Interpreters.* A document that includes a code of ethics and standards for interpreters.
- University of Minnesota and Minnesota Department of Education. (2015). *Code of Ethics and Standards of Practice for Educational Interpreters of Spoken Languages.*

Signed language interpreting[15]

- Arkansas Department of Education. (2019). *Arkansas Standards for Educational Interpreters and Transliterators.*
- Educational Interpreter Performance Assessment. (2007). *Guidelines of Professional Conduct for Educational Interpreters.*
- Florida Statewide Task Force on Interpreters. (1986). *Florida Code of Ethics for Educational Interpreters.*
- Minnesota Registry of Interpreters for the Deaf. (1996). A comparison of four adaptations of RID code of ethics for educational interpreting (part of a training manual), pp. 34-50.
- National Association of Interpreters in Education. (2019). *Professional Guidelines for Interpreting in Educational Settings.*
- National Association of Interpreters in Education. (2021). *Educational Interpreter Code of Ethics.* A national code of ethics for ASL educational.
- Ohio School for the Deaf Interpreting and Sign Language Resources Advisory Committee. (2011). *Ohio Guidelines for Educational Interpreters.*
- Registry of Interpreters for the Deaf. (2010). *An Overview of K–12 Educational Interpreting,* p. 2.

---

[15] The codes in this list may also apply to cued or tactile languages and typically must address spoken language interpreting as well. Some appear to apply to educational interpreters in the ASL context: that is, interpreters who accompany the Deaf student throughout the school day and who, as school employees, may also tutor and otherwise assist the student, depending on the employment requirements. Some, such as the NAIE codes, apply to any interpreting of sign language, cued language and oral language interpreting and transliterating in educational settings.

Spoken and sign language interpreting

- Denver Public Schools. (nd). *DPS Interpreters Code of Ethics*.

Some departments of education at colleges and universities are developing codes of conduct for interpreters who work in special education.

Which ethical guidance should you follow?

If you are an educational interpreter or translator, it is important to find out if the school district or the schools you interpret for have a particular code of ethics, and perhaps standards, that they expect you to follow.

Note that in December, 2023, AAITE released a code of ethics and standards of practice for both interpreters and translators.[16]

---

[16] https://aaite.memberclicks.net/assets/docs/AAITE_%20CoE_Interpreters_v1.0.pdf

As a 2023 review makes clear (Allen et al., 2023), the eight ethical directives or tenets mentioned earlier are largely agreed on around the world, while three other tenets that can be found in some of the codes for educational interpreters are far more controversial—and risky.

However, two codes for spoken language interpreters listed above (NAETISL, 2022, and University of Minnesota and Minnesota Department of Education, 2015) are closely based on a national code of ethics for interpreters in healthcare (NCIHC, 2004). All three include ethical tenets that are considered highly controversial both in the U.S. in other specializations—for example, in legal, conference or remote interpreting—and also around the world.

But are they risky for U.S. educational interpreters? Let us briefly examine the risky ethical practices.

☛ Potentially risky ethical practices

Sign language interpreting

As reported in the international review of codes of ethics (Allen et al., 2023), three general ethical tenets are somewhat uncommon but included in some codes. They address whether to or how to:

- Manage communication breakdowns.
- Engage in cultural mediation.
- Perform advocacy.

The national NAIE code of ethics for U.S. sign language interpreters in education does not appear to recommend the latter two practices. Here is how that code addresses certain aspects of potential communication breakdowns, either managing or preventing them:

- Interpreters contribute language, communication, and access-related observations and concerns to the IEP or 504 team.
- Interpreters clarify their role and responsibilities to school personnel as needed.

—NAIE, 2021

In addition, the NAIE code contains a number of recommended practices to support its seven tenets that are quite specific to education and not to other specializations, such as:

- Interpreters facilitate all communication in the school environment, both in and out of class (e.g., extracurricular activities).
- Interpreters explain and model developmentally appropriate options for interpreting services to students and staff and encourage students to make decisions.
- Interpreters find resources they may provide to the educational team that encourage positive identity development.
- Interpreters are familiar with lesson objectives and prepare appropriately for effective interpretation.

—NAIE, 2021

Confidentiality

The following aspects of confidentiality are particularly specific to U.S. educational interpreting and critically important:

Interpreters maintain confidentiality of information pertaining to their work.

Core Values: Interpreters value Deaf student's privacy and ownership of their personal and academic information.

>3a. Interpreters adhere to the federal, state, and local laws governing educational settings (e.g., HIPAA, FERPA,[17] mandatory reporting, ADA, IDEA).

>3b. Interpreters maintain confidentiality of all IEP or 504 plan information.

>3c. Interpreters adhere to school and district policies and procedures for professional conduct.

>3d. Interpreters use professional discretion when posting on social media to maintain the confidentiality of all parties involved.

---

[17] HIPAA is the Health Insurance Portability and Accountability Act. FERPA is the Family Educational Rights and Privacy Act. ADA is the Americans with Disabilities Act.

6b. Interpreters inform the student's IEP or 504 plan coordinator in writing and in a timely manner of situations that affect their ability to provide effective interpreting for students due to perceived or actual conflicts of interest.

—NAIE, 2021

Before engaging in any of the practices discussed above, make sure to discuss them with the school staff to be sure you understand the ethical practices that you will ideally support—and how to do so.

Spoken language interpreting

Just prior to the printing of this book, AAITE has released its long awaited National Code of Ethics and Standards of Practice for Interpreters in Education.[18]

Meanwhile, the NAETISL code of ethics supports two highly controversial practices, but a careful reading of the text shows that if you verify first with school staff to make certain the practices are acceptable, and then follow the NAETISL code's guidance[19], you may avoid some potential risks.

The two controversial areas in question are cultural mediation and advocacy. Regarding cultural mediation, here is some of what the code of ethics states.

> **Cultural awareness**
>
> **Translators and spoken language interpreters in education promote and respect for the cultural beliefs and practices of educators, families and colleagues.**
>
> Educational interpreters and translators need to be aware of the unique cultural dynamics of those they serve. It should be noted that educational institutions have their own unique cultural norms and expectations. Translators and spoken language interpreters in education shall:
>
> - Strive to understand cultural differences within the language groups they serve such as traditions, practices and beliefs. If a particular recommendation conflicts with cultural practices, the interpreter addresses the issue when meeting with school staff outside of the interpreted encounter without many generalizations, without stereotyping and without making assumptions of a family in a particular culture.
>
> - Share cultural understandings and impressions as members of the multidisciplinary educational team (preferably during the pre or post meeting with school personnel) without explaining culture on behalf of the family.
>
> - Mediate to point out a break in communication due to a cultural difference. The mediation must be conducted in a sensitive manner in order to maintain the flow of communication. The spoken language interpreters can make a statement such as the following in both languages: "The interpreter needs to step out of the interpreting role to clarify cultural differences."

---

[18] https://aaite.memberclicks.net/assets/docs/AAITE_%20CoE_Interpreters_v1.0.pdf

[19] https://storage.googleapis.com/production-constantcontact-v1-0-8/668/757668/OS7KV81J/a7e881dcbc144a46ab3c50c8f1011af3?fileName=NAETISL%20-%20Code%20of%20Ethics%20-%20Rev%208-2022.pdf

- Be a source of cultural information but not consider themselves cultural experts in a particular culture nor convey this misinformation to other members of the multidisciplinary team.
- Ensure that dialectal and cultural differences are addressed in the special education process.

Regarding advocacy, which is quite rarely permitted in any codes of ethics for interpreters around the world, here is what the NAETISL code of ethics states:

Advocacy

When the student's health, well-being, or dignity are at risk, or when student educational access and outcomes are compromised, translators and spoken language interpreters in education may be justified in acting as advocates.

Advocacy is understood as taking action on behalf of an individual that goes beyond facilitating communication, with the intention of supporting good educational outcomes. Interpreters serve to facilitate communication between parties who speak two different languages. Steps to advocate for any party should only be undertaken after careful and thoughtful analysis. If other less intrusive actions have not resolved a well-defined and specific problem, the interpreter may intervene if the situation is urgent and has not been noticed by other parties. For example, the interpreter may intervene on behalf of a life-threatening allergy if it has been overlooked by the other parties. This can be done by making a statement such as the following in both languages: "The interpreter needs to step out of the interpreting role to share information about the student's life-threatening allergy."

—NAETISL, 2022, p. 9

While any life-threatening situation requires moral action, other situations (such as a school staff member who behaves abusively toward a student or family) might be more confusing for an interpreter to address.

Before engaging in advocacy, discuss with the school or the district whether you are permitted to engage in non-life-threatening situations of advocacy. Try to give specific examples, such as, "Should I advocate for a student who is not getting services required by the IEP?" or "Should I advocate in situations where a school staff member has insulted a child?"

School employees including staff interpreters and translators are mandatory reporters of child abuse. The Federal Child Abuse Prevention Act (CAPTA) requires each state to have procedures and provisions for requiring certain individuals to report suspected instances of such abuse.

Ethics in remote educational interpreting

Interpreters should strive to follow ethical conduct whether they work on site or remotely. Even though an in-person interaction does not take place when using web conference and other meeting platforms, such as Zoom, Google Meet, Webex or Skype, interpreters can still maintain the required etiquette and ethical conduct.

The section on remote interpreting in Chapter 2 of *The Remote Interpreter* textbook (Allen et al., 2023) discusses how to address ethics in remote interpreting, regardless of which specializations you work in and even if you provide interpreting across regional and national borders.

Here, however, is some basic ethical information to be aware of for remote interpreting.

Seek guidance on ethical practice from any language service you work for.

For controversial ethical practices in face-to-face interpreting, you will need to consult school staff, such as teachers and special education teachers, speech-language pathologists, administrative staff, assessment specialists, such as audiologists, guidance counselors, school-based (therapist) counselors and so forth.

But for remote interpreting that you perform as a contract or staff interpreter for a *language service*, you will need to seek other guidance.

If you work for a language company, a refugee resettlement agency or a nonprofit interpreter service, for example, *before you engage in addressing communication breakdowns, cultural mediation or advocacy*, first check with the language service. Find out if it accepts, encourages or prohibits these practices.

Be aware that a language service may:

- Have a policy on such issues.
- Be at legal risk if you engage in advocacy.
- Prohibit advocacy.
- Ask you to say a special script each time you intervene to address a communication breakdown.
- Permit cultural mediation under certain strict conditions, possibly involving a script.
- Ask you to refer to yourself always as "the interpreter" whenever you intervene. For example, if you interrupt to say, "The interpreter requests that you speak closer to the microphone."

In addition, there may be differences of opinion and cultural nuances related to the ethical requirement of confidentiality, such as:

- How to protect data about students and families that is stored on your computer.
- How to take electronic notes while interpreting and what to do with them after the session.
- How to support federal, state and local privacy laws, such as HIPAA, FERPA, mandatory reporting (that is, knowing when and how to report a suspicion of potential harm by someone to themselves or another person or a suspicion of child abuse), IDEA and so on.
- Specific procedures to maintain confidentiality of personal, IEP and Section 504 information.

Chapter 4 review

Educational interpreters generally abide by eight tenets found in most codes of ethics: confidentiality, accuracy, impartiality, professionalism, professional development, role boundaries, respect, and solidarity. NAETISL and AAITE provide national codes of ethics for spoken language interpreters in the United States whether they work in person or remotely.

Interpreters and translators possess multicultural awareness that allows them to deal with issues concerning traditions, beliefs and practices that are a part of both cultures. They incorporate this knowledge while abiding by the code of ethics that is most suited for their profession. Advocacy comes into play when the health, dignity and welfare of a child is at stake; however, advocacy also may require an interpreter to intervene, but as a last resort. Contract interpreters working for an agency should check with this employer regarding procedures related to advocacy.

Chapter 4 activities

1. List NAJIT's eight ethical principles.

1.
2.
3.
4.
5.
6.
7.
8.

2. Fill in the blanks with the appropriate word.

The National Council on Interpreting in Heath Care (NCIHC) Code of Ethics differs from the legal field by the addition of three requirements.

   a. Treating all people with _____

   b. Development of awareness of one's own and others _____ in the performance of interpreting duties.

   c. Right to act as an _____ when the patient's health, well-being, and dignity are at risk.

3. Discuss the following with a partner.

   A. Provide your understanding or explanation of the eight near universal code of ethics that educational interpreters can adhere to.

   a. Confidentiality
   b. Accuracy
   c. Impartiality
   d. Professional conduct
   e. Professional development
   f. Maintaining role boundaries
   g. Treating all participants with respect
   h. Developing professional relationships

   B. Advocacy means taking action to support good educational outcomes. Share a situation where you might intervene or speak up in order to clarify a linguistic or cultural misunderstanding.

4. List and share.

　A. List some of the cultural nuances you might encounter or have encountered while interpreting for English learner parents at IEP meetings.

　B. Create a list of common regional or dialectical expressions you may encounter or have encountered while interpreting for EL parents.

5. Indicate if these statements are true (T) or false (F).　　　　　　　　T　　F

1. Codes of ethics for educational interpreters have been developed by some departments of education and by some school districts. ___ ___

2. Sign language interpreters don't need to adhere to HIPAA or FERPA mandates. ___ ___

3. The NAETISL code of ethics for spoken language interpreters supports cultural mediation and advocacy. ___ ___

4. NAJIT is a national association for healthcare interpreters. ___ ___

☑ Answer key for Chapter 4 activities

1. List NAJIT's eight ethical principles.
1. Accuracy
2. Impartiality and Conflicts of Interest
3. Confidentiality
4. Limitations of Practice
5. Protocol and Demeanor
6. Maintenance and Improvement of Skills and Knowledge
7. Accurate Representation of Credentials
8. Impediments to Compliance

2. Fill in the blanks with the appropriate word.
a. respect
b. culture
c. advocate

3. Discuss the following with a partner.
A. and B. answers vary

4. List and share.
A. and B. answers vary

5. Indicate if these statements are true (T) or false (F).
1. T   2. F   3. T   4. F

Modes of Interpreting: Consecutive 5

Chapter 5

- Introduction
- Appropriate registers
- Preparing for consecutive interpreting
- Symbols and note-taking
- Skill building for consecutive interpreting
- Chapter 5 review
- Chapter 5 role plays

Introduction

Interpreters work by listening to the source language and transmitting the exact message into the target language. They keep the same meaning, tone and intent of the speaker. There are three ways that this communication can take place. The three modes of interpretation are referred to as consecutive, simultaneous and sight translation.

Consecutive mode means an entire utterance or statement is heard before the interpretation into the target language begins. This follows a pause in the speech of the source language. Concentration, good listening and memory skills play a key role. Proper note-taking skills also assist the interpreter.

With **simultaneous interpretation**, an interpreter follows the speaker in real time and provides a smooth delivery of the message into the target language. For this type of interpretation, the use of microphones and headsets or mobile apps is common, yet when interpreting for a single individual such devices may not be necessary.

With **sight translation**, an interpreter will read a text in the source language and render it orally into the target language. A straightforward translation uses the written format exclusively; the original text is translated into the target language with care and precision. When dealing with written work, good reading comprehension skills are necessary. Time works to the advantage of the translator, because it enables the translator to use online resources and dictionaries in order to convey the exact meaning of the written text.

The following graph conveys the process that takes place when interpreters convey a message from the source language to the target language.

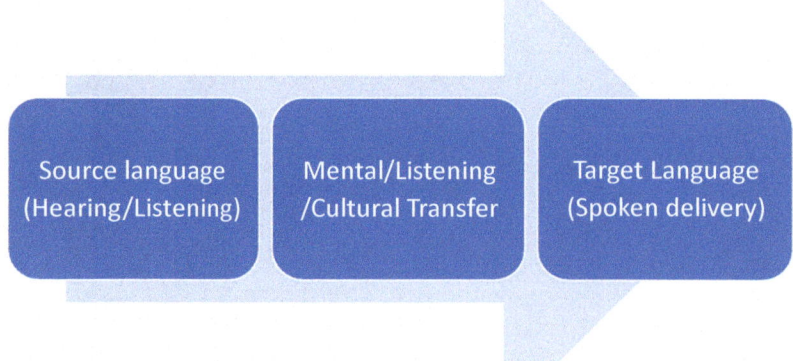

More detailed explanations and samples of the three interpreting modes appear in subsequent chapters.

To summarize, **interpretation** is the transfer of meaning between spoken or signed languages while **translation** is a written activity that typically allows for more time to access resources in order to provide a high degree of accuracy.

Interpretation
- Uses spoken or signed language.
- Works in real time.
- Maintains tone and voice inflections of the speaker.
- Demonstrates skills on the spot.
- Requires good listening skills and concentration.
- Needs extensive in-the-moment vocabulary.

Translation
- Uses written language.
- Works in delayed time.
- Translates, proofs and edits texts for accuracy.
- Uses multiple resources.
- Relies on computer assisted tools.
- Requires sound research skills.

☞ Language registers

The language that we hear in school settings exists across a range of registers. It depends on the level of formality and the attitudes of the speakers in different situations. It means that you, as the interpreter, will be exposed to technical terms that professionals use in their work as well as the basic language used in the home or on the street. Administrators, school specialists and teachers will be using a more standard register at times and a more formal register at other times.

Linguists refer to registers as the way to use language in different circumstances. Language, such as the one used between an administrator and a parent and the one used between a preschool teacher and a child will differ in its register. It may also depend on the type of gathering that is taking place. Consequently, you will be exposed to a number of language registers or levels.

Various language register models exist. A prominent one was developed by the linguist Martin Joos (*The Five Clocks: A Linguistic Excursion into the Five Styles of English Usage,* 1962) for spoken English in which he described five levels of language register.

- **Frozen** language, which focuses on specific language used with certain professions such as doctors, information technology experts, lawyers, teachers, engineers, etc. In schools, this type of language is found in the Pledge of Allegiance, standardized test instructions, acronyms and some special education forms. The vocabulary is precise and consistent.

- **Formal** language refers to one-way participation, such as a teacher's lecture. It can be characterized by exact definitions that are posted on a board or on a PowerPoint presentation. Examples include reports, announcements, agendas and official speeches. Speakers use polite expressions when addressing others.

- **Consultive** or standard register refers to two-way participation using common expressions. A teacher and students exchange information or a principal with a school employee discuss an issue. Most everyday conversations in public settings use standard register.

- **Casual** or colloquial register is commonly used informally with friends and family members in conversations where many are speaking at the same time. It can be dotted with slang. It may even surface in parent-teacher conferences.

- **Intimate** or a low-level variant is found with close friends and family members. It can include vulgar and slang expressions and even dialects.

You will be hearing all levels of language as an interpreter as you navigate from one register to another. Keeping the exact language register while interpreting will maintain the original intent of the message and keep the relationship between the participants at the forefront. As a result, you become aware that there are different ways of addressing and conveying messages between school personnel and parents.

The language and approach you use will have to match the setting and purpose of the topic, and this encompasses the style and context of the source language. The register used will depend on the relationships between the speakers and the listeners. It will also be tied to the topic in question and to the manner of the presentation.

Consecutive interpreting

Consecutive interpretation is a form of interpreting whereby you listen to one or several statements in the source language while taking notes. You, the interpreter, then render the statements into the target language without any additions, deletions or enhancements, keeping the same meaning, tone and intent as the original. It is usually used in smaller meeting spaces. It is frequently used for parent-teacher conferences where a teacher, a parent or guardian, plus the interpreter, meet to talk about a student's progress in school. Oftentimes information on the report card is shared.

Furthermore, teachers reach out to the parent to find out more about the child. Additionally, parents' and teachers' concerns are raised and discussed in order to develop remediation and even commendation strategies. Other school personnel, such as administrative assistants, speech-language pathologists, psychologists, reading specialists, office assistants and administrators will also request the services of an interpreter, especially for IEP meetings, disciplinary meetings and even meetings with the press. Although most meetings take place at the school or the district, interpreters may even accompany school specialists to home visits. There will be times that you may need to switch to either the sight or the simultaneous mode based on the circumstance.

Figure 5.1: Interpreting during an IEP meeting.

As an interpreter, you will keep the information that is shared private and confidential.

- You treat all participants with respect.
- You remain accessible during the entire exchange.
- You interpret all the information that is being shared.
- You do not delete or add any information that the speakers share.

Your Introduction

When approaching the interpretation scenario, you should introduce yourself to the people who do not know you. You may know the teacher or administrator, but you don't know the non-English speaking person. Use the polite form when interpreting in Spanish, that is *usted,* rather than *tú.* If you are interpreting for parents, make them feel comfortable.

A warm smile can help when introducing yourself. Explain your role and the need to pause when speaking in order to capture entire messages. You may be the one to introduce the English-speaking personnel, or they can do so themselves while you act as interpreter. For example, "I am Bob Carpenter, the school principal." You, in turn, will say, "Soy Bob Carpenter, el director de la escuela."

Figure 5.2: Interpreting consecutively during an in-person meeting.

Dress professionally. Avoid T-shirts, especially ones that display controversial messages or images. Find out if the school has a dress code and dress accordingly.

A parent should sit across from the person doing the talking in English, usually the teacher or the principal. This is a way for them to maintain eye contact. You could sit next to the parent or teacher or between the two. If there are more than two English speakers, you could sit slightly behind the parent or parents.

Remember that your role is to convey messages from one person to the other in a language that is understood. Although you are the communicator, they are the key participants in the exchange of messages, and they are the ones making eye contact with each other. Your role is similar to the one of a performer, yet, as interpreter, you are seldom given a script to memorize and deliver ahead of time.

Preparation

A flawless interpretation may seem effortless to an observer. This does not mean that no preparation has taken place. On the contrary, when interpreting flows easily, this is most likely a result of much practice, exposure to similar topics and mastery of some basic interpreting techniques. Even a seasoned interpreter may on occasion draw a blank when hearing a certain word. However, a close approximation may come to mind. Later, as an interpreter, you will look up the problematic word and make sure that it becomes a part of your working vocabulary.

Interpreters need to develop a keen understanding of how English words are pronounced by speakers of another language, especially proper nouns, street names, book and song titles, etc. When pronounced by the non-English speaker, they may not sound like their English equivalent (the same of course is true of English speakers pronouncing words in other languages).

Being mindful of the context can help determine what has been said.

Should one person say they'd like to practice their second language skills by communicating in the language preferred by the other person, you should politely indicate that you are there to interpret for both participants. Avoid, if possible, this type of scenario. It is not helpful to either person and may cause confusion.

Because consecutive interpretation is the most difficult mode to master for most, you, as the interpreter, will need to train and practice this skill extensively. It is a cognitively demanding task. Being well prepared and comfortable with this type of interpreting is critical. Ideally, you should be able to know ahead of time what type of information is going to be shared. Therefore, when explaining what is on a report card, you should have been able to carefully study the vocabulary on the form prior to explaining it to the parent.

The more exposure to this type of assignment, the better you will be at it. Some school districts have already translated the forms into Spanish, Vietnamese, Cantonese or another language, thus making the interpretation session flow with ease. You could check the websites for the district or school where you will be working and locate any of these forms that are available.

Information about assessments of student performance and progress, for example, is usually available in several languages and teachers are encouraged to share available links with parents interested in assisting students at home. The California assessment, for example, can be found at https://www.cde.ca.gov/ta/tg/ca/parentguidetounderstand.asp

If the forms have not been translated, then you should make every attempt to view them ahead of time and become familiar with the vocabulary, because this is information you will be sharing repeatedly, with some variations. It is true that many times you will not know in advance what specific information will be shared at a meeting. Not all children are the same, and parents will come up with different concerns and questions.

Arrival protocols

If possible, try to arrive at the location of the meeting a few minutes ahead of schedule. You may use this time to talk to the teacher, other staff members, and the individuals needing your services to find out what is going to be addressed and what forms, documents or work samples may need to be translated. If the teacher is busy and the parent has arrived, introduce yourself to the parent and describe your role and the procedures that will be followed.

Once inside the meeting room, it's best to remind all present that you are the interpreter and that you will be interpreting everything that is said, including side conversations that can be distracting. You may want to suggest that if participants will be using acronyms to please explain what they mean. Recommend the use of shorter sentences and to pause frequently so that you can interpret everything that is being said without omitting any information. Long statements can be problematic and can test and stress you, especially when speakers do not pay attention to signals that indicate a pause. Also agree as to the type of signal you'll be using when requesting a pause. An introduction that includes a statement about the need to pause after three or four chunks of information or statements will serve all participants well. As a result, your performance as an interpreter will flow much more smoothly and the meaning will not be distorted.

Pausing

It is important to have one person speak at a time so as not to leave out any information. Speaking over each other is distracting and leads to confusing messages. Generally, the rendering of the message follows a pause in the flow of speech. When a question or answer becomes lengthy, the rendition into the target language may be inaccurate if you are not skilled at this type of interpreting.

Furthermore, if the speakers forget to pause, you may want to remind them about the use of the agreed upon gesture in order to stop the flow of the language and thus "catch up" with the message that is being conveyed.

To ensure the interpretation flows smoothly, you are well advised to take notes and know how to use them. Why take notes? It helps to recall what the speakers are saying and activates your listening skills. As a result, accuracy increases, even when you are faced with a long string of thoughts.

Problematic expressions

Should you encounter an expression, acronym or word that you are unfamiliar with, you may indicate that you want to consult a glossary or dictionary in order to convey an accurate meaning. Idiomatic expressions are often hard to interpret; you should attempt to find an equivalent expression in the target language or consult an online reference. Expressions like "the cat is out of the bag" or "that's the way the cookie crumbles" need to be interpreted with expressions that convey the same meaning, avoiding a literal interpretation.

If you cannot come up with an equivalent expression, you could use one that comes closest in meaning. If the correct expression comes to you a few seconds later, you could state politely, "Interpreter correction: not [____] but [____]." Great interpreters correct their mistakes. A similar problematic area is jokes; these don't always translate well, because they are often culturally specific.

Note-taking

When interpreting consecutively, carry with you a notepad and pen or pencil, or a tablet and a stylus so you can take notes. Some interpreters have switched to using a note-taking app. You also have to make sure to bring the right stylus, because some of them only work specifically with certain tablets. Some interpreters prefer tablets, but this will require a certain amount of practice to use them effectively. Using a finger instead of a stylus will not be possible since the notes you take will not be legible. There are several apps that allow you to use a stylus to write your notes, others give you the option of using the keyboard.

One currently popular app is Notability. This app allows the user to record the dialogue and to see the written script on the screen. Other apps you might want to try include Noteshelf, Goodnotes or Notion. Apple Notes allows you to take notes by hand or by using the keyboard. Drawings and signs can be included. You can experiment with any one of these apps to find out if this approach works for you.

What is the best way to take notes? This depends on the interpreter. You might only need to write down problematic words or keywords, dates, numbers, names, acronyms and book or exam titles. Others may prefer to write as much as possible, fearing that they will forget some of the words. Conjunctions or linking words are important and you could create shorter versions of words, such as because, although, but, in order to, etc. At some point you will develop your rhythm and note-taking style. Remember: writing more is not always better. As long as the notes are meaningful to *you* and not a distraction, they should aid with the retention of the passages being exchanged.

Notes can either be written in the source language or the target language. Which do you choose? This may also depend on your preference. Some interpreters will automatically want to interpret the words from the source language to the target language as they hear them, while others will prefer to keep the original or source language in their notes.

Dividing the notebook page with one or two vertical lines might be helpful as you take notes starting on the left side of the page and continuing in a downward fashion. You may want to designate one row or entry for one speaker and another parallel one for a second speaker. Drawing horizontal lines between the chunks of meaning that you interpret helps to separate statements. Arrows are a useful tool to maintain the proper sequence of events. Always remember that it is of most importance to transmit and convey the exact message.

Signs and symbols

It will become useful for you to use a set of signs and/or symbols to represent keywords, directions, gender, positive and negative statements, etc. The symbols you use should be unambiguous, meaningful and consistent. They provide a quicker way to convey a concept or word. It is of vital importance to use the same symbol consistently when referring to an item or idea. If you have shorthand training, you can use symbols from that system. There is no need to write entire words. The first two letters in a word often suffice. Acronyms are helpful. Keywords, such as nouns and verbs, can be abbreviated and will save you space on your paper. These are also faster to write and shorter. The use of arrows, numbers, geometric figures, crosses and other symbols aid in remembering the message.

Common symbols include: #, −, +, <, >, x, $, %, Rx, ≠, =, OK, w, w/o, &. You could create your own symbols to represent various concepts such as before, after, go, stop, man, test, etc. It is important that you use your own symbol or drawing for words that you commonly hear, such as school, reading, math, thank you, want, say, book, etc. Keep using your own symbols consistently, in the same manner, and your job will become easier and smoother.

Here are these common symbols with their equivalents:

Symbol	Meaning	Symbol	Meaning
#	Number	"	Repetition; ditto
+	And, plus, more	X	Placed on word; negates it
−	Less, minus	%	Percentage
=	Is, are, was, equals	Rx	Prescription
≠	Isn't, not equal	w	With
>	Greater than	w/o	Without
<	Less than	&	And
∴	Therefore	OK	Agreed
@	At	?	Unknown; missing
↓	Decrease, down	⟶	Results in, causes, leads to
↑	Increase, up	*	Important
~	Approximately		

Active listening

Active listening is vitally important in consecutive interpreting. This means listening carefully to not only the words but the *messages* in order to accurately convey the meaning into the target language with ease and confidence and without having to ask for repetitions. The acquisition of the message through active listening leads to an accurate rendition of the message.

Concentrating while paying close attention to the meaning of the exchanges is key to rendering a precise interpretation. If the passages become too long for you, requesting a repetition of the portion that you missed is much better than allowing a significant chunk of the message to go untranslated.

Interpreter fatigue

Another challenge faced by interpreters is interpreter fatigue. Studies have shown that interpreter fatigue can set in after 30 minutes of work. Assignments of one hour or more, particularly for simultaneous interpreting, can certainly benefit from a team approach; however, that may not be possible within most educational scenarios. It must be recognized that interpreting is a challenging task that requires a great deal of concentration. It can be stressful. The mind needs a rest after a certain amount of time. (ASL interpreters work in teams and switch every 15 to 20 minutes.) If you interpret for parent-teacher conferences, for example, you should be allowed to take a short break between meetings.

The majority of school interpreters have adapted to solo work, and districts may not be willing to deal with the extra cost of hiring a second interpreter for the same assignment. It is important to bring your own water to stay hydrated and protect your voice. There may be times that you, the interpreter, may be perfectly familiar with the terminology being used and feel comfortable with your interpreting techniques, yet the interpretation may not flow as smoothly as you would like. This may be a result of an unusually long assignment, particularly those over two hours. The key is to attempt to be fully engaged in the task at hand—mentally, physically and emotionally. Don't hesitate to request a five-minute or ten-minute break if the situation warrants it.

Consecutive or simultaneous mode with or without VRI?

Interpreters who work remotely use either a computer, a tablet, such as an iPad, or a smartphone to connect with teachers and English learner parents on a screen using Zoom, Webex, Google Meet, VoiceBoxer or Skype. These platforms allow you to use the consecutive mode when all the speakers are present. It is certainly helpful to see all participants. Having the cameras on will allow you to see facial expressions. You will also be able to increase or decrease the speaker's volume to a level that is comfortable for you.

Some interpreters provide simultaneous interpretation services for many parent-teacher meetings, without worrying about omitting any information that might be lost if the more memory-taxing consecutive mode were used. You, as interpreter, may prefer to use the consecutive mode for parent-teacher conferences. With the simultaneous mode, details are less likely to get lost as long as you are well-versed in the technique and the platform used allows for such an approach. This mode also provides a speedier delivery. There may be times when you start an interpretation session using the consecutive mode and then switch to the simultaneous mode. This may be the case once you realize who is doing most of the speaking and at what speed.

Some interpreters prefer to also use the app WhatsApp or a smartphone to communicate with the EL parent on a one-to-one basis while still seeing all participants on the screen in one of the other platforms. This hybrid VRI and OPI approach can be effective. At times a parent may request a VRI meeting, especially for an IEP meeting. You will need to explore what approach works best for a given situation and for all participants involved.

It is important to note that video remote interpreting (VRI) has gained in popularity and this is likely to continue. VRI fills a gap between over-the-phone interpreting (OPI) and onsite interpreting. All participants can be seen on a screen although some may choose not to turn on the camera. It can be a useful means of communicating for those unable to attend an in-person meeting.

Some common distractions

Those unfamiliar with interpretation protocols may start their statements by saying "Tell them that…" You, as interpreter, may want to state that it is easier to use the first person. Usually the other participants will use the first person and therefore will be able to model such behavior. However, even if the interpreter instructs participants on the way the conversation should be handled, they may not always follow the interpreter's directions nor the modeling provided.

Another possible distraction for an interpreter is when one of the speakers uses the target language within an utterance rather than the source language. This is often the case when Spanglish is used, but it can happen with other languages. This may distract you. Nevertheless, you can still render the entire utterance or passage that you hear into the target language. If this takes you off guard, rather than admonishing the speaker, you should just continue the flow of the conversation by acting professionally and rendering all that is heard into the target language.

There are times that outside noises disturb or distract the interpreter. This could be loud music, outside traffic, use of blowers or vacuum cleaners, mowers, children screaming, air conditioning units humming, airplane noise, a meeting next door, announcements through the loudspeaker, etc. Closing doors or windows may offer a quick fix. Or simply wait a moment for the noise to cease or subside. If these measures don't work, you may want to request locating to a quieter place, if one is available. Consecutive interpretation requires concentration, and the aforementioned distractions will, most likely, interfere with your accuracy.

Sometimes a parent will bring along more than one child to a meeting. It is not your responsibility to bring toys or games to entertain children. Teachers may foresee these situations and are usually ready to deal with such distractions. You are there to make the parent feel at ease and to be the voice of those who are present. If you happen to have a children's book with you, by all means share it with the family.

☞ Additional protocols

At times the individuals needing interpreting services want to talk over you, even when passages haven't been interpreted in their entirety. They may not be used to working with an interpreter. Although this may be frustrating, rendering the missed passage or words during the next exchange will enable you to convey the message in its entirety. Use a gesture, such as raising your hand, to stop the flow of language in these situations when you may need to catch up. Based on what you specified in your introduction, the participants should be aware that exchanges need to be interpreted fully and without deletions.

Some interpreters forget to turn off their cell phones before the session begins. With experience, you will remember to set the cell phone to mute or simply turn it off when interpreting. There are times, though, when you may need to look up the meaning of a problematic word using an online reference. In that case, you will need to use that electronic device to access your glossary or dictionary in order to locate the meaning of that specific word or expression.

If you do need to access your device, you should briefly state that you are looking for the most appropriate and accurate definition of a word. However, this should not become a frequent occurrence because of its distracting nature. It also makes it appear that you are not well prepared for the task.

When you start to interpret consecutively, be ready with your notepad and a pen or pencil. Running out of paper or ink will seem unprofessional and distracting. Bring along a second or third pen/pencil and more than enough paper. If you will be using an iPad or tablet with an interpreting app, bring along the corresponding stylus. These aren't always interchangeable.

☞ Impartiality when interpreting

At times you may be tempted to add a comment or interject your ideas about a situation that the speakers are discussing. You may have an opinion about the situation that you want to share. Avoid the temptation. There is no need to share your story. Such comments detract from the exchange and are not recommended. You should avoid adding personal comments to your interpreting task.

You need to maintain impartiality. If one of the speakers asks you a specific question and seeks your advice, by all means comply with the request. But you should not be giving advice when others are in a better position to do so, such as a school specialist, a psychologist or an administrator.

Keep in mind that your primary role is to interpret from one language into another and thus facilitate the communication between the participants. Remember that you are an impartial communicator and the communication that takes place at these meetings is confidential and is not to be shared with those outside the meeting. Keep firmly in mind the ethical guidelines from Chapter 4.

☞ Memory researchers and authors

Jean-François Rozan developed principles that relate to consecutive interpretation. He suggested taking fewer notes and promoted the use of symbols and abbreviations in order to render the message with accuracy.

Andrew Gillies, a well-regarded researcher and interpreter, is the author of *Note-Taking for Consecutive Interpreting: A Short Course* (2005). He writes about the memory-taxing consecutive mode used frequently in conference interpreting. You can read his insightful analysis of this mode of interpretation. Also helpful is his *Consecutive Interpreting: A Short Course* (2019).

George Miller, Harvard professor and psychologist, studied short-term memory and came up with the concept of numerical limit of capacity (*Psychological Review 63,* 1956, pp. 81-97). He targeted the number seven, plus or minus two, when determining that roughly seven items could be recalled by normal adults. He also offered the concept of chunk, or unit of information, suggesting that the human mind can recall up to about seven chunks.

Alan Baddeley, a neuropsychologist, created a model for working memory. In his 1975 study (Baddeley et al., 1975, Word Length and the Structure of Short-Term Memory, *Journal of Verbal Learning and Verbal Behavior 14*, pp. 575-589), Baddeley concluded that pronunciation time rather than number of items determined the capacity of short-term memory. His model focused on short-term retention and the manipulation of information.

Stanislaus Dehaene, a cognitive neuroscientist, in collaboration with Laurent Cohen, studied brain activity in a small region of the brain that they called the "visual word form area," one that targets written words and is activated during reading activities.

Alan Baddeley, Hazel Emslie, and **Ian Nimmo-Smith** created a memory test titled "Doors and People" (1994), which assesses short-term memory using both verbal and visual recall and recognition. It is composed of four main categories: doors, people, shapes and names. The people category asks test takers to verbally recall the names of four different people both instantaneously and following a delay. It is easy to administer but rather limiting in scope.

👉 Helpful applications

Some common and helpful applications that can aid you in interpreting unfamiliar words are the following:

Google Translate is a popular app that can be used for a large number of language pairs.

Linguee offers two-way translation of words across a range of languages.

Microsoft Translator (what used to be Babel Fish and Bing Translator) can quickly access the translation of a word or phrase, yet it does not cover as many language pairs as Google Translate.

WordReference offers two-way translations for most European languages, plus Korean, Japanese, Turkish and Arabic. It includes a large repository of advice and questions about language usage and allows you to ask questions about specific expressions.

Computer Aided (or Assisted) Interpretation (CAI) is a computer software tool that can benefit you in preparing for a job. Some examples of software support for managing terminology are: InterpretBank, Interpreters' Help, LookUp, Intragloss and The Interpreter's Wizard. Although software tools can make your job easier, you should not become too dependent on them. They may not be easily accessible during a live encounter. These are best used *before* you begin an assignment as long as you know what topic will be covered by the assignment.

👉 Skill building for consecutive interpretation

How can you prepare to become a competent educational interpreter? You, as a talented, bilingual individual may not know anyone who is experienced in this field, someone who can give you feedback on your performance. Nevertheless, you can observe other interpreters' performances on YouTube or in school settings where an interpreter is working.

You need to remember that in order to be a good interpreter you also have to be a good listener, one who is not easily distracted. When practicing to become an interpreter, you need to use memorization techniques. Try to visualize what is being said. You may want to tie what is being said to your own experiences. Here are some activities that you may find helpful. The goal is for you to gradually improve your consecutive interpreting skills and your concentration.

1. **Record what you hear.** You can go to a store looking for a certain product. You seek out a store clerk. You turn on your cell phone recorder as you ask for details about a particular product. This could be anything: a printer, a shredder, a computer, a light fixture, a specific plant, etc. Shortly afterward, try to restate the key points of this conversation using the same language that you heard. Later you will be able to check for accuracy by listening to the original version of the exchange and taking note of any details you may have missed. It is OK to reuse a recording for practicing a specific skill and then moving on to another skill.

2. **Find key points.** After listening to a speech, a short lecture, a sermon or a presentation, try to determine the key points in the language that you heard. Write these down after hearing the message. Try it in either of your working languages without having to interpret. Simply state the main idea and add supporting details. You will be testing your memory skills.

3. **Check your memory.** Have someone read you the names of seven items. These could be names of schools, cities, students, animals, different numbers, brands of cars, states, food, etc. Without taking notes, repeat these names in the order they were provided. You can progressively increase the number of items to be read. For a greater challenge, you can do this not just forward but backward!

4. **Repeat lists.** Another option is to have your reader mix the items and include different categories of items. Repeat the items in the order you heard them. This will certainly help with your concentration.

5. **Retell.** Listen to a passage from a talk show or a dialogue between teachers and note keywords to help you remember what is being said. Maintain the same tone of voice. Then repeat as much information as possible using the same language as the speaker. Use a voice recorder to check what you recalled.

6. **Follow a model.** One of the most effective ways to learn this skill would be to listen to a seasoned interpreter model a consecutive session. This can be easily accessed through YouTube. After you've heard the interpreter's rendition of an exchange, try it on your own by first listening to the speaker of the source language, muting the interpreter you heard earlier, and then taking on the interpreter's role yourself. Your rendition need not be identical to the one you heard, but should convey the exact meaning and retain the same register.

   Here is a sample YouTube parent-teacher conference:
   https://www.youtube.com/watch?v=bzP5XoGssz4

7. **Participate in training courses.** Free training workshops for consecutive interpreters are available, and you could take advantage of this option. Check out note-taking courses online. You may not need to enroll in an expensive training program. Look up what is available online and use the information to improve your own skills.

8. **Practice with YouTube videos.** Access a YouTube video that allows you to practice consecutive interpretation. Although most of these cover medical or legal exchanges, there are a few that include IEP meetings. These exchanges or dialogues serve as a useful tool that allows you to improve your consecutive techniques. You may want to listen to the first speaker in the exchange, probably an English speaker, take notes, and then deliver your first rendition into the target language. You will do the same with the second speaker, the English language learner individual. You may want to pause the exchanges when they become too lengthy because you can select the play, pause and stop options. You can create pauses in the exchange that you deem necessary before rendering the interpretation. Start with shorter exchanges, using pauses, and gradually increase your listening time. With practice comes improvement.

9. **Review acronyms.** Create notecards on the computer or on cards with frequently used educational acronyms such as LD, LEA, ELL, OPI, BI, CTOPP, ATA, etc. Write out what these stand for in English. If the participants only use the acronym in their talk, you may not need to interpret all the words the acronym stands for, unless they use the words that correspond to the acronym—for example, LD is learning disability.

10. **Train with helpful links.** Practice on your own by using relevant materials, such as the following link to address listening skills, consecutive note-taking and consecutive practice.
    http://www.orcit.eu/resources-shelf-en/story.html
    https://interpretertrainingresources.eu

📖 Chapter 5 review

There are three modes of interpretation: consecutive, simultaneous and sight translation. Chapter 5 focused on consecutive interpreting. This is the most common mode used by interpreters in educational settings.

This chapter reviewed how to keep the exact language register, tips for creating an effective introduction, as well as steps to prepare for an assignment and protocols to maintain when interpreting. Chapter 5 also reviewed note-taking with signs and symbols, along with active listening. This chapter covers helpful applications to aid with unfamiliar words in addition to key points for skill building, concentration and activities that aid in retaining information.

✍ Chapter 5 role plays

The role plays that follow are meant to be practiced with partners. There is a Spanish and a Korean sample. (The interpretation has been provided.) You will be taking on the role of the interpreter in all the role plays as you listen to two speakers read the part of the English speaker and that of the Spanish or Korean teacher.

You, as interpreter, will not be reading these exchanges. You will be taking notes as you listen to the exchanges. Deliver your interpretation after a speaker has finished reading their part. If the reading becomes too lengthy for you, use a hand gesture in order to have the reader pause the reading of the passage.

If you do not have two speakers available to read the exchange in front of you, you may want to have the conversation recorded by one or two speakers. Later, you will be able to practice your interpretation. If that happens, although not entirely ideal, it will be up to you to pause and render your interpretation following a natural pause in the exchange. You should not pause after each sentence for fear that you will forget the remaining information provided by one speaker.

Practice this exchange more than once, and each time lengthen what you hear before you render your interpretation.

Sample consecutive interpretation role play: School enrollment (Spanish)

Person	English	Spanish	Interpretation
Office Staff	Good morning. May I help you?		Buenos días. ¿Le puedo asistir?
Parent		Sí. Quisiera matricular a Lidia, mi hija, en esta escuela.	Yes. I'd like to enroll my daughter, Lidia, in this school.
Office Staff	That's fine. We will need your address.		Está bien. Necesitamos su dirección.
Parent		Vivo en la Calle Soledad, el número 4327, apartamento F.	I live at 4327 Soledad Street, apartment F.
Office Staff	I will have to verify your address. Did you bring a utility bill or any official document that shows your address?		Tendré que verificar su dirección. ¿Trajo un recibo de una empresa de servicios públicos u otro documento oficial con su dirección?
Parent		Sí. Aquí tengo mi contrato de renta con la firma del dueño.	Yes. Here is my rental agreement with the owner's signature.
Office Staff	Thank you. I see that it has the owner's phone number. Here are the forms that you will need to fill out.		Gracias. Veo que tiene el número de teléfono del dueño. Aquí están los formularios que tendrá que llenar.
Parent		El intérprete me va a tener que ayudar con el papeleo.	The interpreter will have to help me with the paperwork.
Office Staff	Of course. You will need to complete the application form, the emergency card, the lunch application and a home language survey.		Por supuesto. Ud. va a completar el formulario para matricularla, la tarjeta de emergencia, la solicitud para el almuerzo y la encuesta sobre el idioma del hogar.
Parent		Gracias. ¿Podemos completar todo esto aquí en el mostrador?	Thank you. Can we complete it all here on the counter?
Office Staff	For sure. We will have to request a CUM folder from her previous school. What grade is she in?		Seguro. Tenemos que pedir su carpeta cumulativa de su escuela anterior. ¿En qué grado está?
Parent		Estaba en el segundo grado.	She was in second grade.

Sample consecutive interpretation role play: School enrollment (Korean)

Party	English or Korean	Korean	English
Office Staff	Good morning. May I help you?	안녕하세요. 무엇을 도와드릴까요?	
Parent	네, 제 딸 Lidia를 이 학교에 등록시키고 싶습니다.	.	Yes. I'd like to enroll my daughter, Lidia, in this school.
Office Staff	That's fine. We will need your address.	네, 좋습니다. 등록하려면 거주지 주소가 필요합니다.	
Parent	4327 Soledad Street, 아파트 F호에 살아요.	.	I live at 4327 Soledad Street, apartment F.
Office Staff	I will have to verify your address. Did you bring a utility bill or any official document that shows your address?	저희가 거주지 주소를 확인해야 합니다. 공공요금 납부통지서나 거주지가 명시된 다른 공식 서류가 있으세요?	
Parent	네, 집주인의 사인이 들어간 임대 계약서가 여기 있습니다.		Yes. Here is my rental agreement with the owner's signature.
Office Staff	Thank you. I see that it has the owner's phone number. Here are the forms that you will need to fill out.	감사합니다. 임대계약서에 집주인의 전화번호도 있네요. 여기 이 서류들을 작성하시면 됩니다.	
Parent	통역사가 서류 작성하는 것을 도와 주셔야 하는데요.		The interpreter will have to help me with the paperwork.
Office Staff	Of course. You will need to complete the application form, the emergency card, the lunch application and a home language survey.	물론이죠. 입학신청서, 비상연락 카드, 점심 신청서, 그리고 가정 언어 설문조사를 작성하시면 됩니다.	
Parent	감사합니다. 여기 카운터에서 서류를 모두 작성해도 될까요?		Thank you. Can we complete it all here on the counter?
Office Staff	For sure. We will have to request a CUM folder from her previous school. What grade is she in?	네, 그럼요. 저희가 따님이 다니던 학교에 CUM 폴더를 요청해야 하는데 따님이 몇 학년이죠?	
Parent	이학년이에요.		She was in second grade.

#1 Consecutive interpretation role play: Parent-teacher conference (K–grade 1)

Hello Mrs. García. I was expecting you. Please have a seat over here next to me. I have two adult chairs for you and the interpreter. As you can see, almost all the chairs in this room are for our small children. How are you?

Muy bien gracias, maestra. No traje a Ramona. Se quedó en casa con mis otros hijos.

I am glad you were able to come. Ramona is a very bright girl. She is responsible and pays attention in class. It is a real pleasure to have her in my class.

Qué bien. Es un poquito tímida, pero eso sí, le gusta mucho venir a la escuela.

Her English is pretty good. She doesn't talk a lot with her classmates, but she understands all instructions and is able to respond to questions that I ask her in our small groups.

Habla inglés con sus hermanos mayores, pero conmigo habla español. ¿Ha comenzado a leer con Ud.? Sé que le encantan los libros que trae a casa.

She has now learned to recognize and name all uppercase and lowercase letters of the alphabet. We work with letters and words every day. The children have memorized songs that have to do with the letters of the alphabet.

La he oído cantar en inglés en la casa. ¿Ud. cree que ya puede leer algunos libritos?

She is beginning to combine two or three phonemes or sounds in order to create words with meaning. This is a very important step in learning how to read. She can read some of the early literacy books we have in our classroom library.

Qué bien. A veces la llevo a la biblioteca del barrio. Ahí les leen libros a los niños los sábados por la tarde.

That's a good idea. Well…We are now working on very simple one-syllable words to make new words, such as cat, pat, sat, mat. She is also capable of reading common high-frequency words.

¿A qué palabras se refiere?

Words such as the, a, she, of, you, to.

¿Y cómo quiere Ud. que le ayude en la casa?

A good idea might be to have her categorize objects. This will help with her math skills.

You can choose three different items, such as beans, peanuts or popcorn. You can have her sort three types of coins—quarters, pennies and nickels—or anything you have around the house. She can count up to twenty now.

¡Qué padre! Muy buena idea. Gracias por la sugerencia. Con eso se puede entretener.

#2 Consecutive interpretation role play: Parent-teacher conference (grades 2–3)

Please come in. You must be Evaristo's parents. I'm Rob Morgan, his teacher.

Mucho gusto, Sr. Soy Pedro Gómez Ardiz. Mi esposa, María Dolores.

Please have a seat. Let me pull up another chair.

Mil gracias.

We're going to be assisted by Dora, our interpreter. I'm sorry that I do not speak Spanish. Let's take a look at his report card, so that I can explain to you what he is doing in class.

Gracias. ¿Alcanzas a ver la hoja, vieja?

Sí, está bien.

Let's look at these four areas first: language arts, math, social science and science.

¿Qué significan estas letras?

O stands for excellent, S for satisfactory, I for shows improvement, and H having difficulties. Evaristo does satisfactory work in reading; he is reading at grade level and that is why he received an S. His math skills are also at the satisfactory level.

Muy bien. Me he dado cuenta que sabe contar dinero. Si lo mando a comprar algo en la tienda sabe cuánto le van a devolver. Y el muy listo a veces se quiere quedar con la feria.

¿Y qué pasa con estas otras áreas?

We don't spend a lot of time on social science or natural science. Probably one day per week. He is also doing satisfactory work in social science. As far as science, we've been working on health and nutrition this month. He received an I and that is because he did not complete two of his assignments.

Ud. nos llamó hace una semana para decirnos que no se estaba portando bien.

That's right. This is what worries me the most: his social skills. His behavior needs to improve. He gets distracted very easily, and then he starts bothering other kids. He pokes them with a pencil or he'll throw little wads of paper at his classmates when he thinks I am not looking.

Yo lo castigo y lo dejo encerrado en un cuarto cuando no se porta bien. Jálelo de las orejas aquí en clase. Eso no le gusta y le aseguro que le va a hacer caso.

We do not use that type of punishment. We have been dealing with his behavior. I have moved him to the front of the room so that I can keep a better eye on him. He knows that if he gets three warnings before recess, he will not be able to play outside. At home, you could take away something he enjoys doing, such as a video game.

Ese muchacho siempre ha sido muy travieso. Espero que eso cambie uno de estos días.

Me too. We are doing what we can. When you get home, please remind him that we expect him to behave better in class. On a positive note, I'm happy to report that he is not falling behind in his academic development.

Muchas gracias, profe. Vamos a hablar con él.

#1 Consecutive interpretation role play: Parent-teacher conference (K–grade 1)

Hello Mrs. García. I was expecting you. Please have a seat over here next to me. I have two adult chairs for you and the interpreter. As you can see, almost all the chairs in this room are for our small children. How are you?

Fine, thank you, teacher. I did not bring Ramona. She stayed home with my other kids.

I am glad you were able to come. Ramona is a very bright girl. She is responsible and pays attention in class. It is a real pleasure to have her in my class.

That's great. She's little shy, but oh yes, she loves coming to school.

Her English is pretty good. She doesn't talk a lot with her classmates, but she understands all instructions and is able to respond to questions that I ask her in our small groups.

She speaks English with her older brothers, but she speaks Spanish with me. Has she started reading with you? I know she loves the books she brings home.

She has now learned to recognize and name all uppercase and lowercase letters of the alphabet. We work with letters and words every day. The children have memorized songs that have to do with the letters of the alphabet.

I've heard her sing in English at home. Do you think that she can now read some little books?

She is beginning to combine two or three phonemes or sounds in order to create words with meaning. This is a very important step in learning how to read. She can read some of the early literacy books we have in our classroom library.

Great. Sometimes I take her to our neighborhood library. They read books to the kids Saturday afternoons.

That's a good idea. Well…We are now working on very simple one-syllable words to make new words, such as cat, pat, sat, mat. She is also capable of reading common high-frequency words.

What words are you talking about?

Words such as the, a, she, of, you, to.

And how would you like me to help her at home?

A good idea might be to have her categorize objects. This will help with her math skills.

You can choose three different items, such as beans, peanuts or popcorn. You can have her sort three types of coins—quarters, pennies and nickels—or anything you have around the house. She can count up to twenty now.

Super! A very good idea. Thank you for the suggestion. She can have fun with that.

#2 Consecutive interpretation role play: Parent-teacher conference (grades 2–3)

Please come in. You must be Evaristo's parents. I'm Rob Morgan, his teacher.

Pleased to meet you, sir. I am Pedro Gómez Ardiz. My wife, María Dolores.

Please have a seat. Let me pull up another chair.

Many thanks.

We're going to be assisted by Dora, our interpreter. I'm sorry that I do not speak Spanish. Let's take a look at his report card, so that I can explain to you what he is doing in class.

Thank you. Can you see the paper, honey?

Yes. It's fine.

Let's look at these four areas first: language arts, math, social science and science.

What do these letters mean?

O stands for excellent, S for satisfactory, I for shows improvement, and H having difficulties. Evaristo does satisfactory work in reading; he is reading at grade level and that is why he received an S. His math skills are also at the satisfactory level.

Very good. I realize that he knows how to count money. If I send him to the store to buy something, he knows how much he'll get back. He's very bright and sometimes he wants to keep the change.

And what's going on with these other areas?

We don't spend a lot of time on social science or natural science. Probably one day per week. He is also doing satisfactory work in social science. As far as science, we've been working on health and nutrition this month. He received an I and that is because he did not complete two of his assignments.

You called us a week ago to tell us that he wasn't behaving well.

That's right. This is what worries me the most: his social skills. His behavior needs to improve. He gets distracted very easily, and then he starts bothering other kids. He pokes them with a pencil or he'll throw little wads of paper at his classmates when he thinks I am not looking.

I punish him and I lock him up in his room when he does not behave. Pull him by his ears in class. He does not like that and I assure you that he's going to pay attention to you.

We do not use that type of punishment. We have been dealing with his behavior. I have moved him to the front of the room so that I can keep a better eye on him. He knows that if he gets three warnings before recess, he will not be able to play outside. At home, you could take away something he enjoys doing, such as a video game.

That kid has always been very mischievous. I hope that changes one of these days.

Me too. We are doing what we can. When you get home, please remind him that we expect him to behave better in class. On a positive note, I'm happy to report that he is not falling behind in his academic development.

Thank you, teacher. We're going to talk to him.

Modes of Interpreting: Simultaneous 6

Chapter 6
- Introduction
- Familiarization with SI technique
- Skill building for simultaneous interpretation
- Chapter 6 review
- Chapter 6 role plays

Introduction

Simultaneous interpretation (SI) is the mode used to render an oral message from a source language to a target language in real time without disrupting the flow of delivery. To an observer, it looks like you are talking at the same time as the person delivering the message. As a simultaneous interpreter, you keep up with the language flow of the speaker while listening carefully to what is being said. Everything that is said by the speaker is interpreted.

There is naturally a slight time lag between the listening of the message in the source language and the delivery of the message into the target language. This particular time gap is called *décalage* and refers to the slight delay that takes place. This gap enables you to understand the full meaning of a thought or idea before you render your interpretation. It takes processing time to understand the full message as you determine how you will render it into the target language.

This slight delay calls for the use of all your expertise and language knowledge as you almost instantaneously deliver a version of the message that is as close to the original as possible. Your rendition might require a different syntax or word order and that is why sometimes a slightly longer décalage will enable you to render a better version of the original speech. A longer delay and poor listening skills can make you lose your train of thought.

Stay focused while avoiding any distractions. Some interpreters get into a trance-like state in this mode in order to become totally focused on the task. When interpreting information that includes lists, numbers and many names, it is convenient to maintain a shorter décalage so that you do not miss any of the information being shared.

If the delay between hearing the source language is too long, your delivery into the target language could be put in jeopardy if you are forced to catch up quickly to the rest of the message. Always attempt to have a natural sounding voice free of awkward pauses. Clarity and accuracy are important as you render complete thoughts.

SI is frequently used in United Nations conferences. In educational settings, it is used to interpret for both large and small gatherings. If you are interpreting for a larger group, adequate equipment, such as receivers, microphones and headsets, should be requested and made available to you. A few school districts may have this equipment already.

Some interpreters or agencies already own this type of SI equipment and interpreters will bring it to their work assignment. Most equipment accommodates from one to about thirty participants, but some vendors are now able to provide equipment to much larger groups. (This same type of equipment is commonly used by tourists when listening to an interpretation provided by a guide.) Audio resource groups can provide isolation booths for the privacy of interpreters should these be requested.

Check the audio equipment carefully prior to using it, especially when this equipment is new to you. When you are not meeting in person, online platforms like Zoom, Google Meet or Webex are effective. Zoom includes a feature that allows for SI delivery to a significant number of EL listeners once it is activated in the account. The participants in the Zoom meeting must be invited by a host and granted access in order to participate. The host is the only one who can activate this language interpretation option by clicking on the globe-like icon at the bottom of the screen. Hosts then add the interpreter's email and select the language combination.

Remote SI eliminates the use of booths and can be accessed using other platforms. You can learn about different platforms for remote interpreting through the IT representative in your school district. Understandably, some parents may be reluctant to use remote interpreting without proper instructions and guidance. School sites can partner with agencies, contract interpreters and staff interpreters to make this process easier to use and to enable families needing interpretation services access to online platforms.

SI, with or without its technological features, is often used for conferences, board meetings, awards ceremonies, in-services, training or any large or small gatherings where the audience of English speakers and English learner participants is there to listen to a presentation.

Soundproof booths for educational interpreters can be provided through specialized audio resource technology companies but are seldom ordered or utilized. When meeting in person in small groups SI may be performed in a whispered fashion so as to not disrupt the other participants. Some refer to this as a subcategory of the simultaneous mode, although the techniques are the same. This type of SI is also referred to as *chuchotage*, a French word for whispering.

Even if you don't go into a full whisper, you should lower your voice volume slightly when interpreting for EL parents or families. At the same time, you must make sure that your listeners clearly hear your rendition of what the English speaker is saying. Rather than sitting next to the EL parent, you can provide them a headset while you use a microphone to render the message into the target language. The use of a wireless microphone and headsets for the listeners is effective and unobtrusive. Remember that listeners will need to turn to a specific channel and be shown how to adjust the volume as needed.

Figure 6.1: Interpreting a meeting simultaneously via wireless headsets.

And you, as the interpreter, double-check you have the microphone turned on! When not interpreting, turn it off so that the listeners don't get distracted if you should carry on a side conversation. Oftentimes, you will be interpreting information from several experts, especially when taking part in an IEP meeting. In these types of meetings, where detailed plans and assessment results are discussed, you will most likely interpret primarily from English into the English learner's native language, rather than the other way around. However, any responses, comments or questions that the parent may have will be rendered into English.

☞ Familiarization with the SI technique

For a novice interpreter, the most problematic area in SI is the acquisition of the technique. As a novice, start by familiarizing yourself with shadowing exercises by repeating what a speaker is saying, using the same language but maintaining a slight lag in speed. Once you feel comfortable with this technique, try interpreting short passages from English into the target language. With sufficient practice you will be able to keep up with the speaker.

Acquiring and becoming confident with the technique does not guarantee that you will give a flawless performance. Your job as a simultaneous interpreter is difficult and requires a great deal of concentration. You must focus on rendering everything that you hear with accuracy and without deleting or adding any information. Your rendition must mirror the speaker's message. Your delivery must emulate its tone and intent. You should neither omit information nor add enhancements in order to make the message sound more pleasing. The most common problems in SI are when interpreters omit, add, make inaccurate statements or distort longer passages.

☞ Recommendations

You do not have time to take notes in SI. If you encounter a problematic word, all you can do is write it down and quickly look it up on an app when there is a pause, assuming you are working by yourself without a partner. Unfortunately, by the time you find the exact meaning of a particular word, you will probably be interpreting statements that are quite a bit beyond that word. An educated guess or an explanation of a problematic word is better than omitting it altogether.

Figure 6.2: Include backup devices in your toolkit for remote interpreting.

It is always helpful to know ahead of time how long you will be interpreting. Some informational meetings may take as little as half an hour or up to one hour. Alternatively, there will be times when you interpret at school board meetings where your time commitment may not be predictable. It is not unusual for some board meetings to last three to four hours, especially when the issues that are being addressed are controversial. If an agenda is provided ahead of time, try to access it so that you can be better prepared to handle the topic. This will enable you to look up terminology that might be used by the speakers.

There are times that you will have to interpret a letter or document as it's read aloud. You will need to adjust the speed of your rendition. Reading usually happens faster than speaking. Keeping up with the reader will test your SI skills.

You will benefit by having a partner with you when you are asked to interpret simultaneously for more than two hours. This way you can take turns every twenty to thirty minutes. When switching, wait for a pause or a change of speakers and do not make any comments or noises. If you are using a transmitter, hand it over carefully.

Breaks give you an opportunity to recharge yourself. If a meeting is three or more hours long, covers complex topics and addresses a unique audience, it is recommended that you use team interpreting. You can suffer from mental fatigue if forced to interpret on your own for over two hours. Nevertheless, requesting a second interpreter may not be an option in many school settings. Requests for a second interpreter need to be made ahead of time and funding should be allocated for this.

Some interpreters like to stand as they deliver their rendition of a speech, while others feel more comfortable and grounded sitting down. If you are interpreting for a large group with a headset and the use of microphones, you may want to move around the room, as long as you do not distract the participants. However, if you are interpreting for one or two people, it is best to position yourself next to them, In that case you will be using the chuchotage technique or a microphone, and therefore need to sit close to the main speaker.

Furthermore, make sure that you can see the screen if one is being used in a PowerPoint presentation. If possible, face the speaker when interpreting. You will benefit by seeing facial expressions, lip movements and gestures. If that is not possible, then make sure you are in the same room as the speaker or that you see the speaker on a screen.

SI experts

Should you want to learn more about simultaneous interpretation, consider exploring a series of research articles compiled by Sylvie Lambert and Barbara Moser-Mercer in a book titled *Bridging the Gap—Empirical Research in Simultaneous Interpretation,* 1994.

Andy Gillies, a conference interpreter and trainer, offers practical YouTube videos that you may also want to investigate.

The skill-building exercises that follow are particularly useful for the development of your SI skills, but skills and activities that are presented in Chapters 5 and 7 also address these same mental tasks.

Skill building for simultaneous interpretation

1. **Shadow a speaker.** Shadowing or parroting can be used for self-training. You can use it with or without an instructor and with or without any recording equipment. You can listen to a speech given by an educator, a principal or a professor. These can be found online. You may want to listen to a TED talk on education. As you listen to the talk, and while lagging slightly behind, repeat exactly what the speaker is saying in the language you hear. Keep your voice at a low volume, almost at a whisper, so you can better hear the speaker.

2. **Dual task outside a passage.** As you become familiar with the shadowing technique, try adding another task as you listen while shadowing the speaker. You can dual task by using a notepad to draw or to write numbers in ascending and then descending order as you continue to shadow a speaker. You may even want to draw something at the same time. This will help you build your concentration.

3. **Dual task within a passage.** A different type of dual task to use with the shadowing technique is to write down any acronym, problematic word, number or names that you hear as you shadow the speaker. Try not to get distracted by this other task. Later, you can listen to the talk a second

time to see if you missed any of these words. Choosing talks related to education will also firm up your vocabulary in this area.

4. **Paraphrase.** Paraphrasing is another good technique as you hone your SI skills. While listening to a speech given by a superintendent, principal or teacher, repeat the message by changing some of the wording using only the source language. Make sure you do not alter the meaning. This difficult exercise will test your language flexibility, mental agility and alertness. It will also help you with speed control and concentration.

5. **Locate a mentor.** Another way to improve your interpretation skills is to locate a mentor, an experienced interpreter who has been doing the job for a long time. By accompanying that person on their assignment you will naturally pick up valuable tips and techniques for improving your simultaneous interpreting.

6. **Do more simultaneous interpreting.** Once you become comfortable with the shadowing technique, begin interpreting simultaneously from the source language into the target language. First select online talks in the education field that are not too difficult nor too fast (100 to 120 words per minute).[20]

7. **Become an observer.** Continue your simultaneous interpretation practice by attending district board meetings, preferably where you can observe working interpreters. Write down any problematic terminology or expressions as you listen to the exchanges. Many of these board meetings are recorded and later linked on the school district website; that allows you to access later and practice interpreting into the target language in the comfort of your home.

8. **Anticipate.** This is a skill that will enable you to predict what hasn't yet been said. Listen to a recording of a speech or a video and pause it at certain instances while shadowing what you hear. Then predict and state what you believe will come next in the speech. It may be one word or several words or phrases. Continue with this activity for several minutes, pausing at appropriate times. This will help you tap into your ability to anticipate and help you keep up during real-life SI.

9. **Prepare to practice.** Locate a speech in the source language and read it silently while writing down problematic words or expressions and looking them up. Then record the speech aloud and, as you play it back, interpret it into the target language. Afterward, listen to the recording of your interpretation while checking the speech in the source language. Repeat this exercise more than once until you are satisfied with the result, making sure that the message in the source language is being conveyed correctly into the target language.

10. **Watch training videos.** Take advantage of online training videos in SI. Although many are geared toward the medical, legal, political and community fields, the techniques used in SI are the same and will assist you when working in educational settings. Check out some of the training videos for interpreting students from the European Commission: https://ec.europa.eu

---

[20] To determine the speaking rate of words per minute, there are two ways to measure. Manually count the words as you listen back to the audio and time one minute. Or upload the recording to a speech-to-text platform.

Chapter 6 review

There are three modes of interpretating: consecutive, simultaneous and sight translation. Chapter 6 focused on simultaneous interpreting. As an SI interpreter you will need to grasp the nuances and precise meaning of the source language. Almost instantaneously, you will be processing and delivering, through a transfer process, the same meaning into the target language. This rendition should be clear, accurate and free of additions.

In many situations when interpreting for groups you may need to use equipment such as microphones, headsets and a receiver. Become familiar with their use and the way you can assist listeners who use the equipment, such as participants at a meeting who are relying on headsets.

When rendering a message, avoid distorting its meaning or omitting pertinent information. Try to find out ahead of time how long you will be required to interpret. For longer sessions such as board meetings, it is advisable to work with a partner so that you can take breaks and avoid fatigue. Your job is cognitively demanding and requires concentration. Practice the skill building exercises, including shadowing, anticipating messages, dual tasking and paraphrasing. These will help you become more familiar and adept at the SI technique.

Chapter 6 role plays

Simultaneous interpretation role plays

The following simultaneous sample role play texts are for your practice. These can be utilized in two ways. First, you can work with a partner who reads the material while you interpret. If that is not possible, you or someone else can record these texts. Afterward, listen to the recording as you interpret from the source into the target language.

Keep in mind the speed of your recording. You may need to keep it at about 100 to 120 words per minute at first. Increase the speed gradually and rerecord the material until it reaches about 200 words per minute. When listening to a recording, you may want to wear a headset to maximize your concentration and to drown out noises.

Sample simultaneous interpretation in English: Raffle announcement

Thank you all for coming to this meeting. I am J. T., the president of the PTA. I would like to announce that on October eleventh, the PTA will start selling raffle tickets. Your children will receive the tickets on that very day. We will ask the students to sell these tickets to family members and friends. We do not want door-to-door sales. Tickets will cost five dollars each or three for ten dollars. The ticket stubs and the money should be turned in to a PTA representative prior to October twenty-second. These funds will be used to pay for field trips to our Museum of Natural History and the Aquarium.

This raffle is one of the most important events we have to collect funds. We will be raffling a stay for four people at the famous Ocean Hotel, a bicycle, an iPad, and other fantastic prizes.

The student who turns in the most tickets will receive a forty-dollar gift card from their favorite store. Winners will be announced during the Spring Carnival that takes place on Saturday, October twenty-third from eleven A.M. to three P.M. It is going to be a lot of fun, and I hope you can all participate. Any winners not present will still be able to collect their prizes later.

The money and the ticket stubs can be turned in any day until October twenty-second to Miss Ofelia Short, our PTA treasurer. She will be here in the cafeteria from seven-thirty A.M. to nine A.M. every morning starting October twelfth until October twenty-second.

If you would like your child to participate and sell tickets, please sign the form that we are passing around now and return it to your child's teacher or leave it with me once this meeting is over. I will be standing by the exit door. Are there any questions? Thank you all very much.

Sample simultaneous interpretation into Spanish: Anuncio de una rifa

Gracias por asistir a esta reunión. Soy J. T., presidente de la organización de padres y maestros. Quisiera anunciar que el once de octubre, la PTA comenzará a vender boletos para una rifa. Sus niños recibirán los boletos ese mismo día. Les vamos a pedir a los estudiantes que les vendan los boletos a su familia y a sus amigos. No queremos ventas de puerta en puerta. Los boletos costarán cinco dólares cada uno o diez dólares por tres.

Los comprobantes de los boletos y el dinero se le entregará a un representante de la PTA antes del veintidós de octubre. Los fondos se utilizarán para pagar por las excursiones al Museo de historia natural y al acuario.

La rifa es uno de los eventos más importantes para recaudar fondos. Vamos a rifar una estancia para cuatro personas en el Hotel Ocean, una bicicleta, un iPad y otros premios extraordinarios. El estudiante que venda el mayor número de boletos recibirá una tarjeta regalo de su tienda favorita por cuarenta dólares. Los ganadores serán anunciados durante el carnaval de primavera que se llevará a cabo el sábado, veintitrés de octubre desde las once de la mañana hasta las tres de la tarde. Va a ser muy divertido, y espero que todos participen. Los ganadores no tendrán que estar presentes.

El dinero y los talones de los boletos se podrán entregar cualquier día hasta el veintidós de octubre a la Srta. Ofelia Short, la tesorera de la PTA. Ella se encontrará aquí en la cafetería cada mañana entre las siete y media hasta las nueve de la mañana, desde el doce de octubre hasta el veintidós de octubre.

Si desea que su hijo participe y venda boletos, por favor firme el formulario que estamos repartiendo ahora y devuélvaselo al maestro de su hijo o déjelo conmigo cuando se termine esta reunión. Estaré parado junto a la puerta de salida. ¿Hay algunas preguntas? Muchas gracias a todos.

Sample simultaneous interpretation into Arabic: Raffle announcement

شكرا لكم جميعاً على حضوركم هذا الاجتماع. أنا -----جي تي-----، رئيس جمعية أولياء الأمور والمعلمين. أود أن أعلن أنه في الحادي عشر من أكتوبر ستبدأ جمعية أولياء الأمور والمعلمين بيع تذاكر اليانصيب. سيتلقى أطفالكم التذاكر في ذلك يوم عينه. سنطلب من الطلاب بيع هذه التذاكر لأفراد العائلة والأصدقاء. لا نريد بيع التذاكر من خلال طرق الأبواب. ستكلف التذكرة خمس دولارات للتذكرة الواحدة أو ثلاثة تذاكر مقابل عشر دولارات. يجب تسليم أجزاء التذاكر والمبلغ المالي إلى ممثل أولياء الأمور والمعلمين قبل الثاني والعشرين من أكتوبر. سيتم استخدام هذه الأموال لدفع تكاليف الرحلات المدرسية إلى متحفنا التاريخ الطبيعي وأحواض السمك.
هذا اليانصيب هو أحد أهم الفعاليات لجمع الأموال. سنقوم بسحب القرعة على جائزة إقامة لأربع أشخاص في فندق المحيط الشهير، وعلى دراجة هوائية، وجهاز آيباد، وجوائز أخرى رائعة.
الطالب الذي يسلم أكبر عدد من التذاكر سوف يحصل على بطاقة هدية بقيمة ٤٠ دولار من متجره المفضل. سيتم إعلان سوف يُعلن عن الفائزين أثناء مهرجان الربيع يوم السبت ٢٣ أكتوبر من الساعة ١١:٠٠ صباحا إلى ٣:٠٠ مساء. وستكون متعة كبيرة، وآمل أن تشاركوا جميعا. ولا يشترط أن يكون الفائزون موجودين. ويمكن تسليم المال وأجزاء التذاكر في اي يوم لغايه ٢٢ أكتوبر إلى السيدة أوفيليا شورت، مسؤولة الخزان في جمعية أولياء الأمور والمعلمين. وستكون متواجدة في الكافتيريا من الساعة ٧:٣٠ صباحا إلى ٩:٠٠ صباحا كل صباح من ٢١ أكتوبر حتى ٢٢ أكتوبر. إذا كنت ترغب بأن يشارك طفلك في بيع التذاكر، يرجى توقيع النموذج الذي نمرره الآن وإرجاعه إلى مدرس طفلك او تسليمه لي عند انتهاء هذا الاجتماع. وسأكون واقفاً بالقرب من باب الخروج. هل هناك أسئلة؟ شكرا جزيلا للجميع

#1 Simultaneous interpretation role play: Principal's welcome to school

Good afternoon, everyone. Welcome to our school! For those of you who don't know me, I am S. L. Robertson, the school principal. I'm very pleased to see you all here today. What a fantastic turnout! We are providing interpretation services in Spanish for those of you who need it. Madam interpreter, can you please identify yourself? Thank you. Please raise your hand if you need this service. Everyone have a seat, please. There are a few empty chairs here in the second row.

Today you will have an opportunity to visit our classrooms and meet the teachers and counselors who work so hard in preparing your children for future challenges. Let me first introduce you to this group. Teachers, please identify yourselves.

Very soon you will be able to visit your son's or daughter's classrooms. A map of our school layout is on our district website. If you did not download it, we also sent all parents a map of our campus so that you'd be able to easily find the classrooms and restrooms. All classrooms have a number and that should help you locate the one you're looking for. If you get lost, just ask any of the teachers you encounter or look at this enlarged map that is located on the wall to my left. We have placed another one next to the front office for your convenience.

I will now dismiss our teachers so that they can get their classrooms ready for your arrival. Meanwhile, you will be hearing from the president of the PTA. It is not too late to join this dedicated group of parents. They have been able to provide us with that extra support and funds that benefit all our students. The president of the English Learners Advisory Committee (ELAC) will also share some important information.

I would now like to point out that our school was built around a center courtyard. As you stroll by this courtyard, take a look at all the work that has gone into planting vegetables and flowers. Our National FFA Organization has done an extraordinary job at beautifying our school. You will also be seeing the long-stemmed sunflowers as you walk by that area. These students have researched and written about the importance of our local crops. This very dedicated group has shown us that we depend on agriculture, especially in this area of the county.

The Debate Club is another student organization that has been very active and has sent six members to the Model UN this fall. Please encourage your son or daughter to join a club of their choice.

Our athletes have been training very hard. If your son or daughter plays a sport, please go to the gym to hear from the coaches. They will provide you with details about past and future games. Later on in the semester, we will be scheduling awards ceremonies for our deserving athletes.

I would now like to introduce you to K. C., the PTA president.

#2 Simultaneous interpretation role play: Teacher's presentation

Good afternoon, parents. I hope you're in the right classroom. This is room seventeen. I am Mrs. Hardingrass, a sixth-grade teacher. Welcome. I'm glad to see so many of you today.

I would like to explain to you some of the procedures I have in place that relate to the education of your child. Keep in mind that at this school we have developed a well-balanced curriculum and course of study that prepares students for their continued education beyond the sixth grade. I will be working hard to teach your child the importance of academics and collaboration toward others.

I expect my students to follow the classroom rules and procedures and to get along with classmates and teachers in a respectful way. I strive for good quality in our educational programs, and I expect my students to strive for high quality on their school work as well. I will work hard to foster positive attitudes to help your child have successful experiences this year.

Let me explain my homework policy so that you know what to expect. All of my students are assigned library books to read at home for at least thirty minutes each night. I create individual reading contracts for everyone. Every student has to read a certain number of pages in these books from Monday to Thursday. Additionally, any school work that is not completed in the classroom becomes homework for that evening and must be turned in the following day after arriving at school.

Occasionally students will have to complete special assignments, enrichment activities or remediation practice, depending on the need of the student. Special assignments will be in the area of social studies. Students will be studying early civilizations of Mesopotamia, Egypt, Ancient Greece, India, China and the Roman Empire. A minimum of half an hour per evening during the week for homework should be a good guide as to the amount of time students might be spending on homework. The students who complete all their assigned work in the classroom will naturally have less homework at home.

Every Friday, a letter and a folder containing school papers completed by your child during the week will be sent home for your review. The letter must be signed by a parent or guardian and the letter must be returned on Monday along with the folder. Here is a sample folder so that you can see what it looks like. All completed papers must be kept at home and the folder will be turned in to me along with the signed letter. This weekly communication will ensure your involvement and knowledge of your child's ongoing progress during the year.

If you have any questions for me throughout the year, you can post your question on our school's website under my name, or you can simply call me at school after the students leave for home. You can even send me a handwritten note. I am available for an hour after the bus leaves, except for Mondays when we have our staff meeting. I hope I have explained my homework policy well. I'd be happy to answer any questions.

Modes of Interpreting: Sight Translation 7

Chapter 7

- Introduction
- Types of forms, documents or requests
- Preparation
- Delivery
- Skill building for sight translation
- Chapter 7 review
- Chapter 7 exercises

Introduction

Sight translation involves the reading of a text in the source language and delivering it orally into the target language. This mode incorporates both the written word, one that is visible but not heard, and also the spoken and oral interpretation. Of the three modes of interpreting, sight translation is the least studied.[21]

Our present focus is the use of sight translations in educational settings. You may be called upon to sight translate everything from legal documents (such as a birth certificate) from a home country, vaccination records, consent forms, report cards, letters of recommendation, school certificates or awards, assessment results, disciplinary reports or adoption papers.

Teachers and special school personnel may have you translate exam descriptions or instructions, classroom rules, individual learning plans, and behavior expectations. Occasionally, the front office receives restraining orders, police reports or other legal documents. Although a number of forms have been translated into non-English languages, there are many that have not. Translated documents are especially rare for languages of lesser diffusion.

By no means will you be dealing exclusively with formal documents. You may have to translate notes that are delivered to the office or to any staff member in the parent's first language (L1). You will be asked to interpret or translate these into English. Many deal with excuses for absences, explanations about an illness, reasons why a student needs to attend or not attend a certain event, questions about a specific requirement, etc. If these notes are in the parents' L1, there will be times when the spelling might be unconventional or illegible, and you may have to decipher them. These types of texts may not follow standard rules of grammar or punctuation.

Many teachers prefer that parents ask questions through email. However, not all parents have access to electronic devices to write emails. Some parents prefer to send notes written on paper to teachers or school staff.

For parents who do send emails in their L1, you will then translate these messages, including the teacher's response. Some school districts use a website called Parent Square, a platform that schools use to communicate with parents. Parents must send a request to the school to be added to this platform. Their email or phone number needs to match the contact details in the school's database. Communication with schools happens through emails, cell phones, texts or the app. If EL parents send a message in their L1, you would have to interpret it for the English-speaking recipient. If these parents send direct email messages to the school office, you will most likely assist the staff member with the sight translation and with a written response in the parent's L1.

You may be asked to do a sight translation while participating in a parent-teacher conference. A teacher might ask you to read and translate a questionnaire, rules regarding certain activities or events, homework requirements, a certain description, assessment results and even student essays.

---

[21] For further reading on the processes involved in sight translation, consider A.L. Jakobsen and K.T. Jensen. (2008). *Eye Movement Behaviour Across Four Different Types of Reading Task. Copenhagen Studies in Language 36*, pp. 103-124 or read G.M. Shreve, I. Lacruz and E. Angelone. (2010). Cognitive Effort, Syntactic Disruption, and Visual Interference in a Sight Translation Task. *Translation and Cognition,* pp. 63-84.

You may also encounter EL parents who are illiterate and unable to read what is provided or translated into their native language. In some cases, you may have to sight translate school-related documents from English into the parent's home language or merely read the translated information in the home language. For IEP meetings, this type of sight translation or reading is critical to ensure parents needing interpreting services clearly understand the steps, procedures and recommendations suggested by school experts.

Figure 7.1: Sight translating a document during a meeting.

☛ Types of forms, documents or requests

- Questionnaires
- Parent consent forms
- Behavior expectations
- Report cards
- Language proficiency assessment reports
- IEP assessment results
- Program modification forms
- Disciplinary reports

- Handouts
- Flyers
- Legal documents
  - Birth certificates
  - Adoption papers
  - Restraining orders
  - Police reports
- Vaccination records
- School certificates or awards
- Exam instructions and/or descriptions
- Parents' notes
- Teacher's requests

Preparation

When you are told that you will be doing a sight translation at a certain place and time, ask if you can see the materials that are to be translated ahead of time. Many times you can. This will allow you to preview the content and look up any unfamiliar words. Most often, however, you will be given a text to sight translate on the spot. When you scan a sight translation document for the first time, determine its subject matter, the main idea and its key points. Also pay attention to the context, the style and its purpose.

Count the number of pages that need to be translated. This will give you a good idea as to how much time you will spend on it. You may ask if you need to translate the entire text or just parts of it. As you read, pay close attention to any problematic words and acronyms, including any you should look up before you start to sight translate. Make sure you understand the abbreviations and acronyms. Take notes in the margins, if that is possible, or on a separate pad or paper.

You must also keep in mind while translating from English into the target language that you need to jump ahead in your reading as you deliver the target language version. For example, when translating between English and Spanish, English usually uses qualifiers before a noun while Spanish adds most of its qualifiers after a noun. Concentrate on one unit of meaning at a time.

Delivery

When delivering your sight translation, you should speak without hesitation, keeping a level voice, not too loud or too soft. Avoid awkward and lengthy pauses as you search for the right terminology. Long pauses and sudden stops can be distracting to a listener. Remember that your tone of voice should not cast doubt on what you are saying. Keep it neutral. Maintain a steady pace. There is no need to rush your delivery. When speaking in front of a group, project your voice so that all listeners can hear you. Your delivery can be done in either a sitting or a standing position, depending on the circumstances.

If you are with one or two individuals, your volume should not be above your regular speaking voice. If a larger audience needs to hear your sight translation, you may need to use a microphone. Some interpreters prefer to use a microphone regardless of the size of the group, because they find it more professional and hygienic.

You will need to judge for yourself if the sight translation will be delivered in a formal or informal setting. More formal settings will likely require the use of a microphone. After you have completed sight translating several school documents, you should quickly find your comfort level.

Figure 7.2: Delivering a sight translation to a parent.

☞ Observer's reflective analysis for sight translation

Those observing and listening to a sight translation should:

- Allow the interpreter time to briefly review the text to make note of any difficult terminology.
- Encourage all participants to read in advance the text in the source language before they start listening to the interpreter.
- Follow along with the text and mark with a pen or pencil any place the interpreter came up with a particularly good solution or where they struggled.
  - Note where the interpreter is backtracking (starting a sentence over again), using fillers or staying silent for extended periods and note the pace (too slow, too fast). Delivery is particularly important for sight translation.

☞ Skill building for sight translation

1. **Read aloud.** Face a mirror while you read passages from a school document, such as announcements, exam instructions, graduation requirements or classroom rules. Analyze your speed and tone of voice. Read the passage in the source language with care, maintaining clear pronunciation.

2. **Record yourself.** It is also a good idea to videotape yourself so that you know what you look like and what you sound like. Select a short passage to sight translate first. Use your cell phone's video to record yourself. View the recording, and, if you don't like what you see, make the necessary modifications. For instance, you may need to adjust your pitch, tone, projection, enunciation, expression and even posture. With practice, this will all become second nature. Seeing yourself on a video or a camera will also reflect how others see you on a screen should you have to work remotely.

3. **Summarize.** After reading a short story, a newspaper article, an obituary, a poem or other short piece of writing, try to summarize what you read in one sentence. This will help you focus on the main idea rather than on individual words.

4. **Paraphrase.** First select a paragraph or two from a letter, story or newspaper in either your first or second language. Read it out loud while recording yourself. Then read it a second time. This time change the wording in a way that does not change the meaning. This activity will help you develop flexibility with syntax and will increase your breadth of vocabulary.

5. **Translate visuals.** You can also practice your sight translation skills by actually translating what you see around you: signs, announcements, ads. You may already have done this in your everyday life, such as when you go to a restaurant with a non-English speaking friend. Practice sight translating the food choices and the descriptions that appear on the menu. Should you find a problematic word, look it up in one of your apps.

6. **Condense.** To get at the main idea of a text, try to read the entire text out loud and then condense it into a summary paragraph. You will not be translating, but use either one of your two languages, L1 or L2, to create the summary.

7. **Expand.** Now try the opposite. As you read a passage out loud, you will add words that carry the same meaning as the original message. This expansion helps you with vocabulary development and mental agility. For example, "I thought about going to the park by following this trail" could be changed to "It occurred to me that in order to reach the park I would be able to follow this path." Keep in mind that when you actually sight translate from one language to another, you will be keeping the same register and the same meaning as the original text.

8. **Chunk.** It's helpful to mark off meaningful units within the text. This is called chunking and is done by separating or dividing chunks of meaning with a diagonal line. This can be done as follows: "New York City's population / is fast becoming / a mirror of the linguistic and cultural diversity / of the world outside the United States. / New York is home / to many native speakers / of languages other than English."

Dividing the text into chunks enables you to better analyze its meaning. Select a text, such as a paragraph from a children's short story or an interesting article, and use the chunking technique as you prepare to render your sight translation into the target language. Then render the sight translation, keeping the units of meaning in mind. This will help you better learn to hear messages in terms of units of meaning rather than individual words.

9. **Locate documents to translate.** Find sample documents in the parents' native language, such as birth certificates, proof of vaccinations or report cards. Visually scan the documents and pick out any problematic or technical terminology. Look up the meaning of these words and add them to your own vocabulary list. You will most likely be using them in an educational setting.

10. **Read.** Read as much as possible in either working language, preferably in both. Read on a variety of topics. Good literature abounds in every language. Reading will broaden your exposure to a variety of styles and topics. Read texts in their original languages rather than translations.

Chapter 7 review

There are three modes of interpretation: consecutive, simultaneous and sight translation. Chapter 7 focused on sight translation. Sight translation is commonly used when there is a need to translate legal documents, consent forms, report cards, assessment results or any school related information on the spot. The scenarios can take place in person at IEP meetings, meetings at the school office, at parent-teacher conferences or through electronic means, such as when parents send messages from a computer or other device in their home language. A lis of the types of documents that you might be asked to sight translate is included in the chapter.

If possible, take a few minutes to preview the materials you need to sight translate in order to grasp the main idea, determine the length of the material, and look up any problematic terminology. Your delivery should be smooth and free of awkward pauses.

You are provided with skill building exercises that will help in the development and improvement of your sight translation skills.

Chapter 7 exercises

Sight translation exercises

For each sight translation exercise, first preview the material while paying close attention to any problematic terminology. The first time you sight translate the text, start by skimming over the material and then deliver your sight translation without looking up any words. The second time you sight translate the text, write the problematic expressions or words on a separate sheet of paper. Look up two or three of these, but no more than that. You'll want to begin your rendition of the text without spending an excessive amount of time preparing for this task since preparation time is normally limited in real-life scenarios.

Sample for sight translation—IEP information

There are two main aspects in developing a student's IEP.

1. A meeting must be held where the parent and the school staff members decide on an educational program that meets the needs of the student.
2. The document that is developed at the meeting is signed and serves as a written contract. It lists what services and forms of support the student will be receiving.

The development of an IEP starts with a meeting of experts from the school staff. The IEP meeting is somewhat formal. By law, certain people must attend. People sign in to show who is there. Lots of papers are looked at and passed around. People present will talk about the student's needs and strengths, and what type of educational program would be appropriate. Parents should participate and ask questions and offer suggestions. IEP team members will also want the parent to understand what steps will be taken in planning and recommending specific programs.

A parent and the school representative agree on where and when to meet about the IEP. Usually meetings take place at school during regular school hours; however, a meeting could take place before, during or after a regular school day. Parents are notified in writing about the reason for the meeting, as well as the time and the place of the meeting. The school must inform the parent the following in writing:

- The purpose of the IEP meeting.
- The time and place of the meeting.
- Who will be present.
- The possibility of inviting other individuals or experts who know the student.

Furthermore, the school needs to have the meeting to develop the IEP within a period of 30 calendar days from the time the student becomes eligible for special education services.

If English is not the parent's first language, or if the parent communicates using sign language, the law states that the school must be prepared to provide an interpreter.

Información para los padres acerca del IEP (Programa Educacional Individualizado)

Hay dos aspectos importantes para desarrollar el IEP.

- Se tiene que llevar a cabo una reunión para que los padres y los miembros del personal de la escuela decidan qué programa educacional le conviene al estudiante.
- El documento que se desarrolla en la reunión se firma y sirve como contrato escrito. Enumera los servicios y los apoyos que recibirá el estudiante.

El desarrollo del IEP comienza con una reunión de expertos del personal escolar. La junta del IEP es algo formal. Según la ley, ciertas personas deben asistir. Las personas firman para indicar que están presentes. Se miran muchos papeles y se hacen circular. Los presentes hablan de las necesidades y de los puntos fuertes del estudiante y qué tipo de programa sería el apropiado. Los padres deberían participar y hacer preguntas y ofrecer sugerencias. Los miembros de la junta del IEP quieren que los padres entiendan los pasos que se seguirán al planear y recomendar programas específicos.

Un padre y un representante de la escuela se ponen de acuerdo acerca de dónde y cuándo tendrán lugar las reuniones. Generalmente las reuniones tienen lugar en la escuela durante el horario regular de la escuela. Esto significa, sin embargo, que la reunión podría ser antes, durante, o después del día escolar regular. La escuela les debe notificar a los padres por escrito acerca de lo siguiente:

- el propósito de la reunión
- la hora y el lugar de la reunión
- quién estará presente
- la posibilidad de invitar a otros individuos o expertos que conocen al estudiante

Además:

La escuela debe fijar una reunión para desarrollar el IEP en un plazo de 30 días, comenzando con la fecha en que se determinó que el estudiante necesitaba servicios de educación especial. Si el inglés no es el primer idioma de los padres, o si el padre se comunica con señas, la ley indica que la escuela debe proporcionarle un intérprete si es que el padre lo necesita.

Sample Sight Translation: IEP information in Mandarin Chinese

個別學習計畫家長會相關信息示例

關於個別學習計畫的制定：

· 家長和學校輔導員必須一起開會，會議中雙方將制定出一個能滿足學生教育需求的個別學習計畫

· 會議中擬定的個別學習計畫將作為一個正式的書面契約，學生從學校獲得的各種支援與服務都會寫明在契約上。

個別學習計畫制定前，學校的專業輔導員必須和家長開會溝通其內容與細節。個別學習計畫籌備會議算是一個正式的會議，按照法律規定，特定人士必須到場與會並簽到。 會議中，大家會審閱一些相關文件，分析學生的強項和特殊需要，討論並決定什麼樣的教育方案是最適合該學生的。個別學習計畫專案團隊會向家長說明他們將採取那些具體的步驟來設計並制定個別學習計畫。會議中，家長應積極參與，提出任何疑慮和建議。

個別學習計畫籌備會議舉行的時間和地點

家長和學校代表將共同商議會面的時間和地點。籌備會議的地點通常是選在學校，時間一般來說是在上課的時段內舉行，但有時候也會定在學生上課前或放學後舉行。學校會以書面形式通知家長開會的原因，時間和地點。學校必須以書面形式通知家長以下細節：

開會的目的

開會的時間和地點

與會人員

邀請其他了解學生情況的人士或專家與會的可能性

此外，學生獲得特殊教育服務資格30個日曆天之內必須召開籌備會議以制定其個別學習計畫。

如果家長的母語不是英語或者家長使用手語溝通，按照法律規定，如果家長有需要的話，學校必須提供一名口譯員。

#1 Sight translation role play: Parents' notes

Estimada profesora,

Mediante la presente quisiera informarle que mi hijo Rodrigo no podrá presentarse a clase desde el 15 de octubre hasta el 30 de octubre. Mi familia, mi marido, mis otros dos hijos, tendremos que viajar a México para el funeral de mi papá, que en paz descanse.

Si Ud. pudiera darle alguna tarea a mi hijo, se lo agradecería mucho. Aunque estaremos algo ocupados con otros miembros de la familia, Rodrigo tendrá tiempo para completar lo que Ud. le pueda enviar. No quisiera que se atrasara con sus estudios.

Muchas gracias y que Dios la bendiga, Sra. Ema Sánchez de Lara

---

Ola maestra ay disculpe crero saber cuando tengo sita con ute, mijo me trajo la nota otro dia pelo no la pude leer. grosia

---

Aca lemando latortillas qe pepare pa la fiesta de lata de no puedo ir poqe oy travajo todo el dia y qeria qe eten frescas pa qe alo niños le guste aber si mi comadre mando lo frijole qe tamvien etan mui ricos mucha bendisione paute maestra

#2 Sight translation role play: Report card in Spanish

Areas	Idioma nacional	Estudios sociales	Matemá-ticas	Estudios de la naturaleza	*Responsa-bilidad*	*Relaciones personales*	*Hábitos de estudio*
	-Rendimiento intelectual -				- Conducta -		
No. 1	9	9	6	7	MB	B	MB
No. 2	7	7	6	7	B	B	B
No. 3	8	8	6	7	MB	B	B
No. 4							
No. 5							
Promedio anual							

Alumno: Roberto López de Lujano

Nota	Equivalente	Concepto
9 y 10	Excelente	E
7 y 8	Muy bueno	MB
5 y 6	Bueno	B
3 y 4	Regular	R
1 y 2	Necesita mejorar	NM

Maestro del grado escolar:_____ DEPARTAMENTO DE

EDUCACION

Director escolar:_____

Written Translation in School Settings 8

Chapter 8

- Introduction
- Recommendations for school translators
- Resources for translators
- Applications, software and dictionaries
- Voiceover
- Closed captioning
- Chapter 8 review
- Chapter 8 exercises

Introduction

Translations convert the written source language into a written target language. In schools and school districts, translations are used to facilitate the exchange of information and messages to English learner parents and guardians. Meaningful written communication helps families understand myriad forms, applications, announcements, agendas, messages, etc. Requests for translations in school settings are often made last-minute.

Some of the more important announcements appear on a district's web page, and parents or guardians can easily access these by clicking on the desired language from a list of options. Most districts have now been able to include this option on their web sites. The use of Google Translate or Microsoft Translator on websites is convenient, however, it may be beneficial for districts to add a disclaimer to their sites regarding this service. Districts may want to include a disclaimer such as "This translation was created using Google Translate [or Microsoft Translator] and may not be a completely accurate version of the original message."

In school settings, announcements are frequently sent home with the students. These can relate to the following: disciplinary actions, recommendations for various programs, parent-teacher conference appointments and reminders, workshops for parents, calls for volunteers, field trip information, back-to-school night, minutes from board meetings, volunteer appreciation events, winter or spring concerts, homework reminders, PTA meetings, school site council meetings and special education requests. Other documents that may be translated include flyers, certificates, reports, testing materials, medical records and health-related announcements.

Some larger district and county and regional offices of education have full-time translators who translate documents and announcements for all schools in the district. This can be a time-consuming task. Unlike interpreters, translators have more time to find the exact wording for a particular document. By no means is this an easy job, even though dictionaries and online resources are readily available.

Deadlines will force you to expedite the translation. It is best to translate into your dominant language in order to maintain its integrity and authenticity. If, for example, you are a non-native English speaker, it might be wise to have a native English-speaking person proofread your translation before it is delivered or posted. In dual immersion schools, which are gaining in popularity in the states of California, Washington and Texas, particularly with a Spanish/English focus, bilingual teachers collaborate in sending translated notices to parents.

Recommendations for school translators

As translator, you have to know the best way to word a document by using appropriate sentence structures, precise terminology and culturally relevant expressions. You need to have excellent writing skills, particularly in the target language. You will also need to navigate with ease a word processing program, such as Microsoft Word. This enables you to use proper formatting, fonts, and the required layout. Formatting should mirror the original document. Use the same font and layout as the source document. If you find an error in the original document, you can add the word in brackets when translating.

The material translated needs to be made understandable and bear the intended meaning of the original. If you should find a word or passage that is illegible, write the word illegible in brackets, like this: [illegible]. If the original is handwritten, use italics for your translation. Translate everything that is presented to you, unless there is an indication to omit a certain section.

When dealing with stamps or seals on a document, you can try to read any written text, while including where applicable the name of the office, the city and the county in brackets. For signatures, you can write the word signature in brackets, like this [signature]. At times, materials translated include figures, data and charts; these must also be translated into the target language and formatted identically to the original.

As translator, you need to keep the same tone and register as the original text throughout your translation. A statement such as "She was canned," which uses a low register, is translated differently than the more formal statement: "She was fired," or "She was let go." In Spanish, maintaining the polite form of address, usted, is more appropriate than the familiar tú. The usted is preferred when sending notices or messages to a parent.

Figure 8.1: Looking up a word in an online glossary.

Once you translate the material, you need to spend some time proofreading it and making it free of any misspellings, odd sentence structures, improper punctuation or problematic terminology. Also double-check any numbers on charts, addresses and dates.

Familiarize yourself with the Track Changes tool in Microsoft Word. If necessary, take a Microsoft formatting course. Make sure that when you use a certain term, you use the same term throughout your translation; for example, use "solicitud de empleo" to translate "job application," rather than any other option.

There have been instances when well-meaning school employees or volunteers decide to bypass the services of a professional translator and use an online translation application. This is not advisable, although translation applications do serve a purpose. Should you need to translate large volumes in a short time, you may consider getting assistance from an online translation tool, such as DeepL. You may also try Trados, a computer-assisted software tool. However, you will still have to review and edit the translated text thoroughly before it is distributed.

Once you have edited, proofread and finalized the translation of your document, it is best to save it as a PDF document to preserve its integrity. When a document is saved as a PDF, the contents cannot be easily changed. You may want to use Microsoft Word's Save a Copy feature to save as a PDF or use the Adobe PDF converter when saving your document. If additional security is required you may also password-protect the PDF.

Resources for translators

Should you want to learn more about the topic of translation, a valuable read would be Jeremy Munday's book, *Introducing Translation Studies: Theories and Applications,* 4th edition, 2016. It provides basic material related to translation studies and is useful to trainers and trainees who want to analyze text types and explore an extensive bibliography related to the topic.

Another recommended book for school translators and freelance translators is Corinne McKay's *How to Succeed as a Freelance Translator,* 3rd edition, 2015.

Applications, software and dictionaries

Translation memory software is a helpful tool that aids translators by creating bilingual glossaries that can then be reused. Most of these programs divide your document into smaller units, such as clauses, sentences and even paragraphs. When a unit is ready for translating, the program will find a match, which will help you with a faster translation.

Current leaders in this market are Trados, SDLX and Déjà Vu. These are not free programs. Your school district may cover the cost if translators will be using them. Translators will benefit from training sessions in order to use these software tools, especially with Trados, one that is well rated. However, free translation software that may not be as sophisticated as the aforementioned ones is available. OmegaT (http://omegat.org) and WordFisher for MS Word (https://www.wordfisher.hu/wordfisher-2/) are popular and relatively easy to use. You may also wish to use DeepL, a free online translator that uses artificial intelligence to create translations.

Remember that if you use the Google Translate, the Microsoft Translator or the DeepL applications, the computer-created translation may not be free of errors and will require careful review. At times, the software creates some rather odd and curious expressions that are not what an educational translator would want to use or send to a parent, teacher or administrator. The translation app must be used with caution. It's best suited for travelers who are not familiar with a country's language. It is unlikely that machine translations will replace human translators, though familiarizing yourself with the current translation technology can help you remain efficient in your work.

Meanwhile, AI is a tool that people can use for instant translation. It is being approached with caution by many translators and interpreters, fearing that it could be used to replace them. Nothing can take the place of the human brain and human emotion. AI would not be able to catch body language nor feelings. Furthermore, people in general are more comfortable working with humans. AI translation could be used in emergency situations. When translators rely on it, a disclaimer should appear indicating that the translation is computer generated. The end product will still need to be reviewed and edited by a human translator.

There are recommended apps that you, as an educational translator can use successfully. All of these can be found online. You can rely on bilingual dictionaries, but with practice you will most likely find it easier to look up words and expressions using a well-known and reliable website or app.

For both the most common languages and a number of languages of lesser diffusion, try:

- WordReference
- Linguee
- Collins Picture Dictionary

Alternatively, there are a number of well-known dictionaries that can aid you in finding the right wording in English and Spanish:

- *Merriam-Webster's Spanish-English Visual Dictionary,* with over 22,500 technical and everyday terms.
- *Larousse Unabridged Dictionary: Spanish English,* with 250,000 words and phrases.

- *Collins English-Spanish Dictionary.*
- *Oxford Spanish Dictionary,* with more than 300,000 words.
- *Simon & Schuster's International Spanish Dictionary,* with over 200,000 entries.

If you are looking for an excellent Spanish-only dictionary, you have a choice of these top three that rank as the best in this area.

- *Diccionario de la Lengua Española*
- *María Moliner, Diccionario de Uso del Español*
- *Duden Español: Diccionario por la Imagen,* dictionary with illustrations

Apart from Google Translate, here are some other common translation apps for a quick reference when language assistance is necessary for a staff member who does not understand a certain word or phrase:

- iTranslate
- TripLingo
- SayHi
- Papago
- Microsoft Translator
- Hola
- Waygo
- iTranslate Voice

Despite having these resources at hand, not all translators want to also work as interpreters. Administrators may not realize that there is a big difference in the performance, delivery and preparation of these separate tasks. Many translators prefer to strictly work with the written word while others like the variety that both roles offer.

Should you want to read about the latest news in the field of translation, visit https://slator.com/ or https://multilingual.com/. Those who work as educational translators may also be assigned work in related subcategories, namely voiceover or captioning.

Voiceover

A voiceover translation is a technique whereby one records translated audio overtop the original narration. It is not done in real time and one can still hear in the background the sound of the original language at a low volume. Having good diction and native pronunciation are of vital importance. Voiceovers are most common in the movie and advertising industries. They may also be a part of news reports.

In school settings, voiceovers are rare, yet they may be requested for printed materials, video clips or PowerPoint presentations. If these are requested, you are usually allowed to preview the narration before embarking on the voiceover. If you do not feel comfortable handling these types of translations, and or believe it's outside the scope of your job duties, the district or school should reach out to a company that specializes in this type of translation.

Closed captioning

Closed captioning is a technique that displays on a screen a text rendition of the audio, either matching the source language or translating to another language. If the audio and text are in the same language it's called a transcription. When a translation is required, the translator renders the words into a target language. This can be done in real time or in edited or delayed mode. The difference between closed captioning and open captioning is that closed captioning must be activated by the viewer through a menu option or a remote control. Open captioning means that the text and descriptors are displayed for all viewers. This also includes a description of any music or sounds that may be heard.

Either type of captioning is helpful and necessary for maintaining the accessibility of the original content. Same language captioning is aimed mainly at individuals who are Deaf or Hard of Hearing, although there are many people who like to read the captions as they view a program or a movie. Programs for the Deaf and Hard of Hearing use open captioning and are of great value in special education departments.

YouTube offers captioning services in videos. There are also professional caption vendors in the United States. If captioning is needed for video presentations in school districts it's best to go with a professional company. School translators should be aware that captioning can assist English learner populations and, in particular, students who are enrolled in schools for the Deaf or Hard of Hearing.

As a freelance or contract translator, you can choose what jobs to accept and reject, but as a school district employee, that choice may not be available. Seldom are voiceovers or captioning tasks listed as a job requirement for a school translator.

Here are some ways you can continue to enhance your translation skills.

☞ Skill building for written translations

1. **Read.** Read extensively in the source language and the target language. This will help you expand your vocabulary and expose you to various styles of writing. Choose books, novels, newspapers or magazines that interest you. Do not choose translations of original works. Select the writings of respected authors, especially those who write about teachers and students.

2. **Watch programs.** Watch television programs, movies, the news or YouTube clips in the target language. Pay careful attention to idiomatic expressions and technical words.

3. **Play word games.** Play games to challenge your language skills, such as crossword puzzles or semantic games. You can play by yourself through an app or else find a friend or family member who might enjoy playing with you.

4. **Travel.** If possible, take a trip to where the target language is spoken. While there, take time to read the local newspapers, signs, labels, anything you see posted on walls, billboards, buses and public buildings. Language is constantly changing and evolving and being exposed to these changes is beneficial. Don't isolate yourself. Interact with various people.

5. **Translate.** When encountering signs and instructions, translate them wherever you are. These can appear in unpredictable places. Make this into a game. Consider keeping a journal of "random translations" you enjoyed creating.

6. **Train yourself.** Participate in free translator training courses, or take a class to improve your own writing skills.

7. **Take an exam.** Take the practice exam from the American Translators Association. It is reasonably priced and will provide you with an idea as to the expectations required of a professional translator. It will also alert you as to any weaknesses you might have when translating.

8. **Review picture dictionaries.** Study illustrated dictionaries, such as the *Larousse Ilustrado* or *Duden español: Diccionario por la Imagen*.

9. **View style manuals.** Check out *Chicago Manual of Style* for formatting and style guidelines.

10. **Create glossaries.** Create your own glossary or template of your most frequently used words. Continue to add problematic terminology and their translations as you encounter common and uncommon expressions.

📖 Chapter 8 review

A translation converts the written source language into a written target language. Translations are used to convey information to English learner families and help them understand forms, applications, announcements, agendas, messages, flyers, reports, etc. Translators work with administrators, teachers, office staff and specialized personnel. The work of an educational translator is detail-oriented. You may wish to use translation apps such as Google Translate or Microsoft Translator or a translation tool like DeepL or Trados to assist your work.

When completing a translation using computer-generated assistance, it is essential to review and edit the final product with care. Before sending it off, change it to PDF format. Online resources, applications, software and books are very helpful to a translator, but should always be double-checked before creating the finished product. The related subcategories of voiceovers and closed captioning are seldom used in educational settings, yet translators need to be aware of their use. You should keep your skills in constant check by engaging in skill building activities for written translations.

✏ Chapter 8 exercises

Sample written translation: PTA announcement in English

PTA News

The PTA would like to invite all of its members to the final general membership meeting and volunteer potluck dinner on Wednesday, May 25. The potluck dinner will begin at 6:00 P.M. with the general membership meeting beginning at 7:00 P.M. This meeting is the most important one of the year with voting to be held on two key issues:

1. Next year's PTA Executive Board

2. Recommendations of the Allocations Committee

If you plan to attend the dinner, please bring a main dish to share if your last name begins with the letter A through M. Please bring a salad or a dessert if your last name begins with the letter N through Z.

Call Justin Landloy at 880-000-0000 if you have any questions about the May 25 meeting.

Sample written translation: Anuncio de la PTA en español

Noticias de la PTA

La PTA quisiera invitar a todos los miembros a la última junta general de miembros y voluntarios en la que se compartirá comida, el miércoles, 25 de mayo. La cena comenzará a las 6:00 P.M. y la junta general de miembros comenzará a las 7:00 P.M. Esta junta es la más importante del año ya que se votará sobre dos asuntos claves.

1. La junta directiva de la PTA del año entrante

2. Las recomendaciones del comité de distribución de fondos

Si piensan participar en la cena, por favor traigan un plato principal para compartir si su apellido comienza con la letra A hasta la M. Por favor traigan una ensalada o un postre si su apellido comienza con la letra N hasta la Z.

Llamen a Justin Landloy al 880-000-000 si tienen cualquier pregunta acerca de la junta del 25 de mayo.

Sample written translation: PTA announcement in Russian

Новости Ассоциации родителей и учителей (АРУ)

АРУ хотела бы пригласить всех своих членов на итоговое общее собрание членов и обед для волонтёров в среду 25 мая. Ужин начнется в 18:00, а общее собрание членов начнется в 19:00. Это собрание является самым важным в году, и голосование будет проводиться по двум ключевым вопросам:

1. Исполнительный совет АРУ в следующем году

2. Рекомендации Комитета по распределению средств

Если вы планируете присутствовать на ужине, принесите горячее блюдо, если ваша фамилия начинается с букв от А до М. Пожалуйста, принесите салат или десерт, если ваша фамилия начинается с букв от Н до конца алфавита.

Позвоните Джастину Лэндлою по телефону 880-000-000, если у вас возникнут вопросы о собрании 25 мая.

Sample for Translation: Recruiting for a Sports Activity

Dear parents and guardians,

Your child has the opportunity to play soccer for the ABC school team this September. This soccer team will be open to boys and girls who are 8 or 9 years old. There will be ten Saturday soccer games at the Expo fields and your child will get to keep the game uniform which will be provided through PTA funds. We will practice on Mondays, Wednesdays, and Fridays from 2:00 P.M. to 3:30 P.M. at our school.

The registration for the soccer team will begin tomorrow and end this Friday, August 8th. The ABC School's PTA has offered to pay $25 of the $50 fee for each player. If you are interested in having your child join the ABC soccer team, please fill out, sign, and return the interest sheet below along with a $25.00 check. If you write a check, please make it out to the "Fair Game Recreation Center."

I look forward to coaching your child in soccer this September. I can answer any questions you may have. You may send me a note or call me at ABC School.

Sincerely,
Coach Goals

Sample for Translation: Volunteer Appreciation Day

Dear_____,

Friday, May 20th has been designated as Volunteer Appreciation Day at ABC School. We have planned a special program to honor you and show our appreciation for your generous contributions to our students' educational development. In order to not interrupt parents' work schedule, the Volunteer Appreciation Program is scheduled from noon to 1:00 P.M. in the school's courtyard. The program will consist of the following:

12:00 to 12:15: Music Tribute to ABC Volunteers by Advanced Band Students

12:15 to 1:00: Social Gathering for School Volunteers

Food, coffee, tea and punch will be provided.

We hope you can join us as we salute you and the many volunteers who are assisting us in creating the most successful students in our town.

Respectfully,
Principal Hope Sunrise

Language Proficiency and Certification 9

Chapter 9

- Introduction
- Language proficiency
- ACTFL proficiency levels
- ILR Scale
- Certificates vs. Certification
- Types of interpreting and translation certifications
- Job descriptions
- Chapter 9 activities
- Answer key for Chapter 9 activities

Introduction

How can language proficiency be measured? Interpreter's language proficiency can be determined by testing, using one of the two most valid assessment tools that are commonly used in academic settings, the American Council on the Teaching of Foreign Languages (ACTFL) proficiency rating scale or the Interagency Language Roundtable (ILR) Scale. An interpreter's English language proficiency can be determined by using the free Education First Standard English Test (EF SET).

In order to improve or hone your interpreting skills, you can participate in college courses or training sessions for interpreters and translators. These may offer certificates of attendance, but should not be confused with certification through organizations like American Translators Association (ATA), the U.S. federal courts, the Certification Commission for Healthcare Interpreters (CCHI), or the National Board of Certification for Medical Interpreters (NBCMI).

Keep in mind that when applying for a position as an educational translator or interpreter, you will most likely be performing a number of clerical functions as well. You will be reading about the requirements for this type of position in this chapter.

Language proficiency

Language proficiency has often been measured using various assessment tools. The most well-known among educational settings are the ACTFL proficiency rating scale and the ILR Scale. The ACTFL rating scale has been incorporated in language courses since 1986 and was revised in 2012. (See ACTFL.org.)

ACTFL proficiency levels

Developed from the federal government's ILR Scale by ACTFL, the ACTFL proficiency rating scale has five levels (novice, intermediate, advanced, superior, distinguished). The first three levels are each subdivided into three sublevels (low, mid, high).

The ACTFL proficiency rating scale provides a great deal of definition, especially at the lower levels of proficiency usually achieved in language learning. It is widely used in many arenas, but particularly in academia. Within each level there are four language skills: listening, speaking, reading and writing. An oral proficiency interview (OPI) determines the speaker's level.

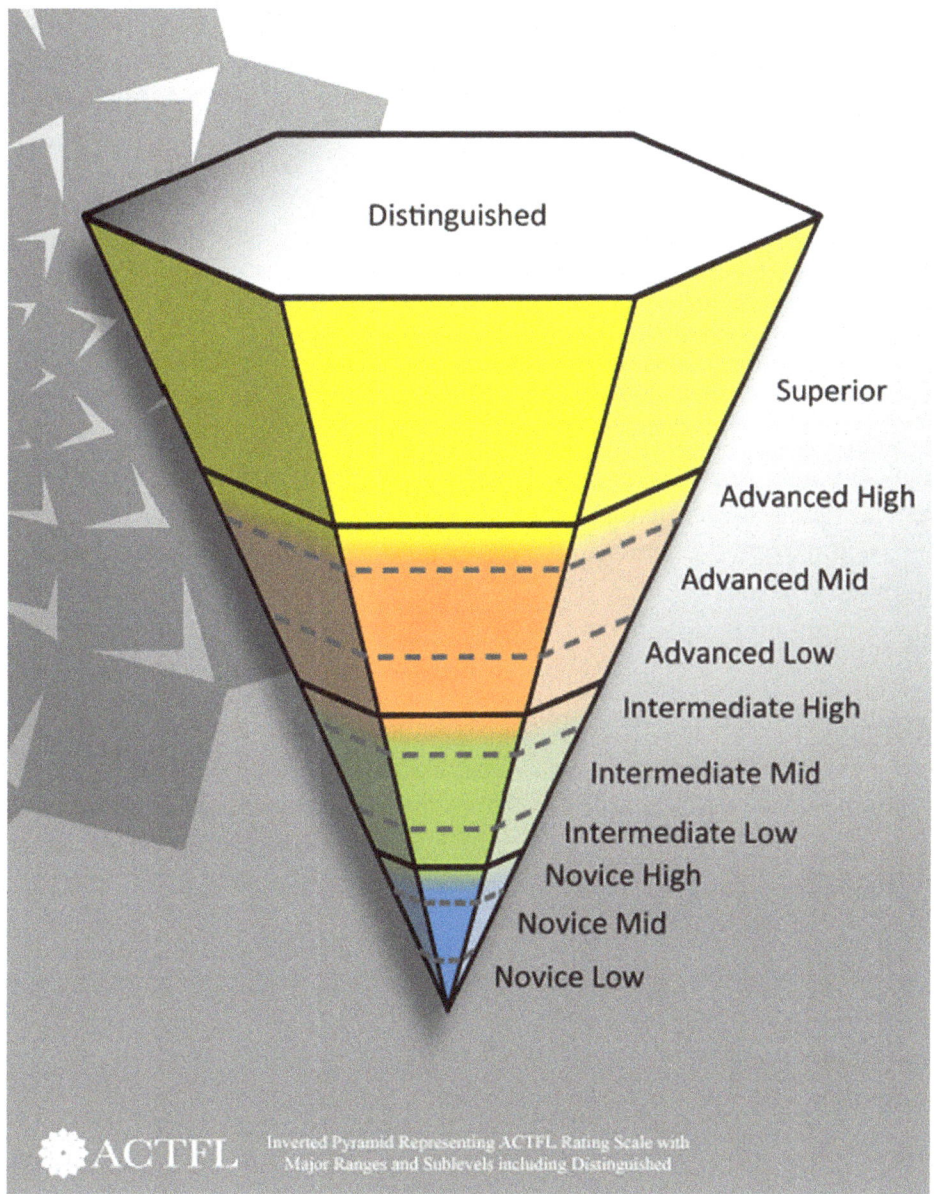

Figure 9.1: ACTFL Proficiency Rating Scale.

Speaking ability is described as follows according to the ACTFL guidelines.

Distinguished

Speakers at the Distinguished level are able to use language skillfully, and with accuracy, efficiency, and effectiveness. They are educated and articulate users of the language. They can reflect on a wide range of global issues and highly abstract concepts in a culturally appropriate manner. Distinguished-level speakers can use persuasive and hypothetical discourse for representational purposes, allowing them to advocate a point of view that is not necessarily their own. They can tailor language to a variety of audiences by adapting their speech and register in ways that are culturally authentic.

Speakers at the Distinguished level produce highly sophisticated and tightly organized extended discourse. At the same time, they can speak succinctly, often using cultural and historical references to allow them to say less and mean more. At this level, oral discourse typically resembles written discourse.

A non-native accent, a lack of a native-like economy of expression, a limited control of deeply embedded cultural references, and/or an occasional isolated language error may still be present at this level.

Superior

Speakers at the Superior level are able to communicate with accuracy and fluency in order to participate fully and effectively in conversations on a variety of topics in formal and informal settings from both concrete and abstract perspectives. They discuss their interests and special fields of competence, explain complex matters in detail, and provide lengthy and coherent narrations, all with ease, fluency, and accuracy. They present their opinions on a number of issues of interest to them, such as social and political issues, and provide structured arguments to support these opinions. They are able to construct and develop hypotheses to explore alternative possibilities.

When appropriate, these speakers use extended discourse without unnaturally lengthy hesitation to make their point, even when engaged in abstract elaborations. Such discourse, while coherent, may still be influenced by language patterns other than those of the target language. Superior-level speakers employ a variety of interactive and discourse strategies, such as turn-taking and separating main ideas from supporting information through the use of syntactic, lexical, and phonetic devices.

Speakers at the Superior level demonstrate no pattern of error in the use of basic structures, although they may make sporadic errors, particularly in low-frequency structures and in complex high-frequency structures. Such errors, if they do occur, do not distract the native interlocutor or interfere with communication.

Advanced

Speakers at the Advanced level engage in conversation in a clearly participatory manner in order to communicate information on autobiographical topics, as well as topics of community, national, or international interest. The topics are handled concretely by means of narration and description in the major times frames of past, present, and future. These speakers can also deal with a social situation with an unexpected complication. The language of Advanced-level speakers is abundant, the oral paragraph being the measure of Advanced-level length and discourse. Advanced-level speakers have sufficient control of basic structures and generic vocabulary to be understood by native speakers of the language, including those unaccustomed to non-native speech.

Intermediate

Speakers at the Intermediate level are distinguished primarily by their ability to create with the language when talking about familiar topics related to their daily life. They are able to recombine learned material in order to express personal meaning. Intermediate-level speakers can ask simple questions and can handle a straightforward survival situation. They produce sentence-level language, ranging from discrete sentences to strings of sentences, typically in present time. Intermediate-level speakers are understood by interlocutors who are accustomed to dealing with non-native learners of the language.

Novice

Novice-level speakers can communicate short messages on highly predictable, everyday topics that affect them directly. They do so primarily through the use of isolated words and phrases that have been encountered, memorized, and recalled. Novice-level speakers may be difficult to understand even by the most sympathetic interlocutors accustomed to non-native speech.

—ACTFL Proficiency Guidelines, 2012

STAMP

Avant STAMP (Standards-Based Measurement of Proficiency) is an internationally recognized web-based test that assesses language proficiency in 45 languages. STAMP 4S was created in 2001 by a team of experts from the University of Oregon. It consists of four areas: reading, writing, listening and speaking. The test questions are based on real everyday situations. It can be used in grades 7 and higher, with university students and adults. The scores are aligned with the ACTFL Proficiency Guidelines. The highest level that can be attained is the Advanced High, which is the expected level for interpreters. The test does not assess the distinguished nor the superior levels where many interpreters belong.

ILR Scale

The ILR Scale is used primarily by federal employees and includes six base levels, with corresponding sublevels.

0—no proficiency. This means that knowledge of the language is nonexistent or only a few words.

1—elementary proficiency. Demonstrating this level of fluency means you know how to structure basic sentences, which may include common questions and answers typically used by tourists.

2—limited working proficiency. Level two means you're able to have limited social conversations and understand basic commands.

3—general professional proficiency. Level three means you understand the language well enough to contribute greatly in the workplace, though you may exhibit an obvious accent and need help with advanced terminology.

4—advanced professional proficiency. Having level four skills is what most employers want to see. It means that you can have conversations at an advanced level and have a firm understanding of the language, though you may have some misunderstandings or occasional mistakes.

5—functionally native proficiency. Level five means you are entirely fluent in a language. You were raised speaking the language or have spoken it long enough to become proficient in it. Your accent is either nonexistent or barely recognizable.

Here is a visual to see how the levels of these two scales compare.

ACTFL Proficiency Rating Scale	ILR Scale
Superior	5 Functionally Native Proficiency 4+ Advanced Professional Proficiency, Plus 4 Advanced Professional Proficiency 3+ General Professional Proficiency, Plus 3 General Professional Proficiency
Advanced High Advanced Mid Advanced Low	2+ Limited Working Proficiency, Plus 2 Limited Working Proficiency
Intermediate High Intermediate Mid Intermediate Low	1+ Elementary Proficiency, Plus 1 Elementary Proficiency
Novice High Novice Mid Novice Low	0+ Memorized Proficiency 0 No Proficiency

👉 How do these scales relate to translators and interpreters?

By examining the descriptors for the various ACTFL proficiency rating scale, most language experts would agree that interpreters' language skills in the two languages they command would fall under the superior or advanced high, certainly with regard to their speaking and listening skills. Some certificate programs require that students enter with at least an advanced high level in oral proficiency while others may accept students in the advanced mid level.

Superior level speakers

Speakers at the Superior level are able to communicate with accuracy and fluency in order to participate fully and effectively in conversations on a variety of topics in formal and informal settings from both concrete and abstract perspectives. They discuss their interests and special fields of competence, explain complex matters in detail, and provide lengthy and coherent narrations, all with ease, fluency and accuracy. They present their opinions on a number of issues of interest to them, such as social and political issues, and provide structured arguments to support these opinions. They are able to construct and develop hypotheses to explore alternative possibilities.

When appropriate, these speakers use extended discourse without unnaturally lengthy hesitation to make their point, even when engaged in abstract elaborations. Such discourse, while coherent, may still be influenced by language patterns other than those of the target language. Superior-level speakers employ a variety of interactive and discourse strategies, such as turn-taking and separating main ideas from supporting information through the use of syntactic, lexical and phonetic devices.

Speakers at the Superior level demonstrate no pattern of error in the use of basic structures, although they may make sporadic errors, particularly in low-frequency structures and in complex high-frequency structures. Such errors, if they do occur, do not distract the native interlocutor or interfere with communication.

Advanced high speakers

Speakers at the Advanced High sublevel perform all Advanced-level tasks with linguistic ease, confidence and competence. They are consistently able to explain in detail and narrate fully and accurately in all time frames. In addition, Advanced High speakers handle the tasks pertaining to the Superior level but cannot sustain performance at that level across a variety of topics. They may provide a structured argument to support their opinions, and they may construct hypotheses, but patterns of error appear. They can discuss some topics abstractly, especially those relating to their particular interests and special fields of expertise, but in general, they are more comfortable discussing a variety of topics concretely.

Advanced High speakers may demonstrate a well-developed ability to compensate for an imperfect grasp of some forms or for limitations in vocabulary by the confident use of communicative strategies, such as paraphrasing, circumlocution and illustration. They use precise vocabulary and intonation to express meaning and often show great fluency and ease of speech. However, when called on to perform the complex tasks associated with the Superior level over a variety of topics, their language will at times break down or prove inadequate, or they may avoid the task altogether, for example, by resorting to simplification through the use of description or narration in place of argument or hypothesis.

Professional translators prefer to work from Language B into Language A, their native or mother tongue, the one they have been schooled and educated in. Educational translators' skills would need to be in the distinguished, superior, and at a minimum, high advance levels in reading and writing skills in both languages since they will be translating from Language A into B, and from Language B into A. There could be some very competent interpreters whose reading and writing skills would correspond to either distinguished and high advanced levels, while the skills of translators in the speaking and listening categories would match the distinguished, superior, and high advanced levels. The description of the Superior level in writing from the ACTFL guidelines follows:

Superior Writers: classified at the Superior level are able to produce most kinds of formal and informal correspondence, in-depth summaries, reports and research papers on a variety of social, academic and professional topics. Their treatment of these issues moves beyond the concrete to the abstract. Such writers demonstrate the ability to explain complex matters and to present and support opinions by developing cogent arguments and hypotheses. Their treatment of the topic is enhanced by the effective use of structure, lexicon and writing protocols. They organize and prioritize ideas to convey to the reader what is significant. The relationship among ideas is consistently clear, due to organizational and developmental principles (e.g., cause and effect, comparison, chronology). Superior writers are capable of extended treatment of a topic, which typically requires at least a series of paragraphs, but can extend to a number of pages. Writers at the Superior level demonstrate a high degree of control of grammar and syntax, of both general and specialized/professional vocabulary, of spelling or symbol production, of cohesive devices and of punctuation. Their vocabulary is precise and varied. Writers at this level direct their writing to their audiences; their writing fluency eases the reader's task. Writers at the Superior level do not typically control target-language cultural, organizational or stylistic patterns. At the Superior level, writers demonstrate no pattern of error; however, occasional errors may occur, particularly in low-frequency structures. When present, these errors do not interfere with comprehension, and they rarely distract the native reader.

As an educational translator you will not need to "explain complex matters, and to present and support opinions for developing cogent arguments and hypotheses" as mentioned above, however, you will need to have a solid control of the grammar and syntax of your native language, one that corresponds to the Distinguished level. As a translator you will have more time to select precise terminology and sentence structures that match what is written in the source language.

Here are the descriptors for the ILR 4+ and 5 levels that correspond to the speaking abilities of a highly skilled educational interpreter:

Speaking 4+ (Advanced Professional Proficiency Plus): Speaking proficiency is regularly Superior in all respects, usually equivalent to that of a well-educated, highly articulate native speaker. Language ability does not impede the performance of any language-use task. However, the individual would not necessarily be perceived as culturally native. Examples: The individual organizes discourse well, employing functional rhetorical speech devices, native cultural references and understanding. Effectively applies a native speaker's social and circumstantial knowledge; however, cannot sustain that performance under all circumstances. While the individual has a wide range and control of structure, an occasional nonnative slip may occur. The individual has a sophisticated control of vocabulary and phrasing that is rarely imprecise, yet there are occasional weaknesses in idioms, colloquialisms, pronunciation, cultural reference or there may be an occasional failure to interact in a totally native manner.

Speaking 5 (Functionally Native Proficiency): Speaking proficiency is functionally equivalent to that of a highly articulate well-educated native speaker and reflects the cultural standards of the country where the language is natively spoken. The individual uses the language with complete flexibility and intuition, so that the speech on all levels is fully accepted by well-educated native speakers in all of its features, including breadth of vocabulary and idiom, colloquialisms and pertinent cultural references. Pronunciation is typically consistent with that of well-educated native speakers of a non-stigmatized dialect.

By combining these high level speaking proficiencies with the skills required for interpreting, an interpreter can perform her or their job successfully. One must keep in mind that interpreting is a complex task and a solid command of two languages is a prerequisite to an interpreter's performance. Interpreting is a skill that can be acquired with training, practice or both. Since educational interpreting takes place in a number of settings, such as formal board meetings, parent teacher conferences, school offices or homes, the interpreter must become adept at switching language levels from very formal discourse to street talk. That is why flexibility and adaptability are often associated with interpreters. A sound knowledge of idioms and colloquialisms in both languages, including specialized educational terminology, also comes into play. Furthermore, the interpreter should be familiar with the cultural context of the source message in order to deliver an accurate and faithful rendition into the target language.

☞ EF SET

The EF SET (https://www.efset.org) is a free standard reliable and valid English test developed in 2014. It was developed for adults and covers all levels from beginners to advanced. It is aligned with the Common European Framework of Reference for Languages (CEFR), www.coe.int/lang.

EF SET	CEFR
1–10	< A1
11–30	A1 Beginner
31–40	A2 Elementary
41–50	B1 Intermediate
51–60	B2 Upper Intermediate
61–70	C1 Advanced
71–100	C2 Proficient

☛ TOEFL exams

The Test of English as a Foreign Language (TOEFL) or Internet-based Test of English as a Foreign Language (TOEFL-iBT) (www.ets.org) exams measure four language skills: listening, speaking, reading, writing. These are essential tests that prepare individuals for entrance into university courses.

Here is a comparison table with the CEFR. The highest proficiency belongs in the B2 and C1 levels, which are the levels that typically correspond to university admission requirements.

CEFR level	Reading (0–30)	Listening (0–30)	Speaking (0–30)	Writing (0–30)	Total (0–120)
C2	29	28	28	29	114
C1	24	22	25	24	95
B2	18	17	20	17	72
B1	4	9	16	13	42
A2	n/a	n/a	10	7	n/a

Certificates vs. Certification

Community colleges, public and private universities and a number of private institutions provide coursework in translation and interpreting. Some offer certificates of completion once all requirements—usually a series of courses—have been satisfied. Certificates may be issued after the completion of one or two courses. Note that not all courses are taught by experienced interpreters or translators, nor by those who hold a valid state or federal court certificate. Some school districts have even created their own certificate programs.

These types of certificates, however, do not compare with the certificates that assess interpreting skills using a valid and reliable testing metric, or by taking a minimum of four introductory courses that address all modes of interpretation, including practicum experiences in all three modes as well as at least one translation course. This education and training will set a future interpreter on the right path. Such courses provide essential information for potential interpreters planning to become certified in the medical, legal or educational fields.

A movement is currently underway to establish certification standards for educational interpreters across the United States. It is being spearheaded by the American Association of Interpreters and Translators in Education (AAITE).

You may also consider attending a community college or university to enroll in a certificate program specializing in translation and interpreting. Here is a description of an introductory course for translation:

> Students perform introductory translation assignments from Spanish to English and vice versa. They develop an understanding of translation theory through reading and class discussion and come to understand communicative translation and compare it to a direct, word-for-word approach. The grammar of Spanish is reviewed in detail.
>
> —Monterey Peninsula College, California

A number of community colleges, private providers or agencies and universities, oftentimes through extended learning opportunities, offer courses in translation and interpreting. They also grant certificates to students who complete the program requirements. Potential educational interpreters or translators benefit by participating and completing one of these programs. Language proficiency testing is usually required to enroll. At a minimum most programs require an advanced proficiency level on an oral proficiency interview.

You may not need to apply to a university for admission but rather can enroll in courses leading to a certificate in translation and interpreting by applying directly to the program through an open university system. Many courses are offered online, and some give you the option of participating asynchronously on your own schedule without real-time interactions. Although these programs give more emphasis to the legal, healthcare and community interpreting fields, valuable information and practicum make the courses meaningful and practical for educational interpreters.

The certificate may take up to a year or two to complete and can range from 18 to 40 credits, but it takes less time to complete than a college degree. At a minimum, you should complete 40 lecture hours—preferably many more. Participation can range from 30 hours of lectures and discussions to 450 contact hours. Some programs are language neutral, but the majority focus on English/Spanish, English/Cantonese or English/Korean combinations. Most certificates cover translation and interpretation theory, simultaneous interpretation, consecutive interpretation, sight translation, ethics, a course in the legal field and/or the healthcare field and plenty of practicum experience.

Advanced degrees in translation and/or interpreting are currently available in the following states: Arizona, California, Florida, Massachusetts, New Jersey, New York, Nevada, North Carolina, Ohio, Oregon, Pennsylvania and Texas. The top graduate level program is offered at Middlebury Institute of International Studies in Monterey, California. (https://www.middlebury.edu)

Rutgers, The State University of New Jersey, (https://span-port.rutgers.edu) offers a certificate in translation and interpreting but provides the following notice on its website.

> It is important to recognize that the **Certificate in Spanish-English Translation and Interpreting does NOT indicate that a student is a certified translator or interpreter.** The certificate provides a strong foundation in translation and interpreting which can enhance further specialization in those areas.

Currently valid certifications at the national and/or state levels are found through the following associations: American Translators Association (ATA), Certification Commission for Healthcare Interpreters (CCHI), National Board of Certification for Medical Interpreters (NBCMI) and state boards that rely on the National Center for State Courts (NCSC) for certifications. These are the most sought-after certifications and passing their rigorous exams is proof that an interpreter or translator has the necessary skills to perform a specialized interpreting or translating assignment.

Interpreting certificates from colleges or private providers could provide you with an excellent foundation to pass any of the previously mentioned exams. You should be aware that certifications must be renewed every two to three years by presenting proof of continuing education courses or training. It is important to not let the certification lapse because that would force you to reapply for certification and most likely retake the rigorous exam.

At school district levels, particularly larger ones with a substantial number of English learner parents, interpreter training and workshops are often provided for interested bilingual staff members, including current staff interpreters who need to refresh their bilingual skills and keep up to date on any new developments in the field of interpretation. Some districts, with the assistance of experts or practitioners in the field, have created and administered proficiency exams for bilingual staff who show interest and promise in working as interpreters or translators.

After successfully completing the training sessions or coursework approved by the district and having received passing scores on the required language assessments, bilingual staff members may be deemed ready for interpreting tasks in educational settings. They may be interviewed for district level positions similar to the job description that appears later in this chapter. By no means are these qualifications and courses on par with the certifications described previously, but they are well worth pursuing as doorways to interpreting and translating in schools.

However, community college or university certificates specializing in translation and interpreting may offer a better option for many candidates, especially those who are new to the field or who reside in districts that do not offer in-house training programs.

Types of interpreting and translation certifications

In the United States, there are a range of certifications for interpreters and translators at the national and/or state levels for medical, legal or court settings.

Valid certifications for interpreters and translators are complex. They encompass various language combinations, Spanish/English being the most needed and administered. The common trends in the U.S. include the following.

- Many language combinations.
- Distinct specializations (medical, legal, conference, educational, business, community, etc.).
- Frequent integration into the industries where translators and interpreters work.
- May lack universal roadmap to skill acquisition (through training or academia).

Proven qualifications and a solid skill set for interpreting are critical for stellar interpreter performance. Most interpreters keep in their portfolio proof of education, training, language proficiency, testing skills, testing specialties and certifications.

Here are samples of the certificates currently available in the U.S. for translators and interpreters.

Federal Court Interpreters Certification

Consists of two phases: a written exam and an oral exam in two languages: Spanish and English. The written exam is computer corrected and must be passed before the oral exam can be taken. The oral examination tests the ability to effectively perform the three modes of court interpreting: sight translation (one legal and one with low registers), one simultaneous passage and one consecutive interpretation for a witness and a legal representative. All of these must reflect the intent of the speaker while demonstrating the authentic interpreting functions encountered in federal courts.

Accordingly, the candidate is required to demonstrate the ability to effectively carry out these functions bidirectionally, keeping in mind the registers, style, tone and intent of the discourse. Test items include both formal and informal/colloquial language, technical and legal terminology, and special vocabulary or other specialized language use, which is part of the active vocabulary of a highly articulate speaker. The Federal Court Interpreter Certification Exam is offered only for Spanish/English, because that is the primary interpreting need in the federal judiciary system. Practice tests are available, allowing candidates to prepare for all phases of this rigorous exam. Find more information at https://www.uscourts.gov/services-forms/federal-court-interpreters

State Certification

Most states have reciprocity agreements that allow interpreters to work in another state after passing that state's exam. The National Center for State Courts (NCSC) is the central resource for state courts. This nonprofit organization provides potential interpreters information about each state's certification process. You can obtain information about available exams by visiting the website at ncsc.org. Interested interpreters can contact the Language Access Services Section (https://www.ncsc.org/consulting-and-research/areas-of-expertise/language-access) to obtain more information about each state's requirements.

In order to become a state-certified spoken language court interpreter in Oregon, for example, a certificate will be awarded to an interpreter who fulfills the following credential steps.

- Passes a criminal history check.
- Achieves a passing score on the Written Examination.
- Attends the Orientation and the Ethics Orientation conducted by CLAS.
- Achieves a passing score on the Court Interpreting Oral Examination.
- Achieves a passing score on the Ethics Examination.
- Completes and submits documentation of 20 hours of court interpreting services or court observation during the 12 months prior to application in courts of record in Oregon or Consortium member states, federal courts of record, or where the interpreter is sworn in and the record can be presented into evidence.
- Completes the application process.
- Takes the Interpreter's Oath administered by an Oregon state court judge.

—NCSC, Oregon Minimum Certification Requirements

To become a certified court interpreter in California, candidates must pass the Oral Proficiency Exams in English and the other working language, along with the English-Only Written Exam, and the Bilingual Oral Interpreting Exam, which consists of four parts. Besides Spanish, other languages also require certification status. The format is similar to the federal court interpreters' exam.

The oral interpreting exam consists of four parts, which are based on actual transcripts or other court documents and simulate actual court interpreting. The four parts of the exam are:

1. Sight translation of a document written in English interpreted orally into the non-English language.
2. Sight translation of a document written in the non-English language interpreted into oral English.
3. Consecutive interpreting from English into the non-English language and from the non-English language into English.
4. Simultaneous interpreting from English into the non-English language.

To pass this exam, you will need a score of 70 percent or higher in each of these sections.

Additional information about language access and court interpreting for other states can be found by visiting the Resources for Court Interpreters page on the NCSC website.

American Translators Association (ATA)

The ATA certification assesses comprehension of the source-language text, translation techniques, and writing in the target language. This is one of the most respected and sought-after certificates for translators. The exam can be taken online or in person with proctors. You must become a member of ATA to enroll. The exam consists of three passages, each 225 to 275 words in length. Two of these passages must be translated. Once certified, translators will need to present proof of continuing education credits in order to maintain their certification. Furthermore, translators pay an annual fee to keep their certification active.

This particular certification is the most valued and recognized by translators throughout the United States. Because of its rigor, it has a low passing rate of 20 percent. It is a three-hour exam that does allow the use of dictionaries. You must check the ATA website to determine administration dates. Those who want to take the ATA exam should see the Guide to ATA Certification at https://www.atanet.org/certification/guide-to-ata-certification/. The exams are available in 15 languages translating into English and 17 languages translating from English. For a relatively low fee, you can also take a practice test to determine if you are ready to pass the certification exam. The practice exam will be returned to you with helpful comments.

Certification Commission for Healthcare Interpreters (CCHI)

This type of certification is used primarily by individuals seeking to interpret in medical settings. According to the CCHI website, the individual most suited for this field is:

> A person who is able to perform the functions of a healthcare interpreter **competently, independently,** and **unsupervised** *in any setting* and *in any modality* where health care is provided, with the knowledge, skill, and ability required to relay messages accurately from a source language to a target language in a culturally competent manner and in accordance with established ethical standards.
>
> —Healthcare Interpreting Is a Career, CCHI

Proper certification is required and CCHI offers three national certifications for medical interpreters of any language: the Core Certification Healthcare Interpreter™ (CoreCHI™), the CoreCHI-Performance™ (CoreCHI-P™), and Certified Healthcare Interpreter™ (CHI™). To become a CCHI interpreter, candidates must meet specific prerequisites, such as completing a high school diploma, proving linguistic competency in English and a second language, and completing a minimum of 40 hours of professional training before taking the certification exam. You can find more information at https://www.cchiinterpreters.org.

The National Board of Certification for Medical Interpreters (NBCMI)

This certification is aimed at individuals who want to work in medical settings. In order to receive this type of certification, candidates must pass written and oral exams. Candidates need to meet certain prerequisites prior to taking the rigorous exams, including 40 hours of medical interpretation training through coursework. The exams may be taken at testing centers or from home through ProctorU. Certification is available in Cantonese, Korean, Mandarin, Russian, Spanish and Vietnamese. See http://www.certifiedmedicalinterpreters.org:

- The written exam focuses 61 percent on medical knowledge, 15 percent on code of ethics and the remaining 24 percent focuses on roles of the interpreter, cultural awareness and legislation and regulations.

- The oral exam focuses 35 percent on medical terminology within the context in two languages, 30 percent on linguistic knowledge in English and the target language, 25 percent on consecutive interpreting and sight translation from English to the target language and 10 percent on cultural awareness.

Job descriptions

Here is a typical composite listing of the job requirements for a position as an interpreter/translator based on job postings from school districts in the states of Washington and California.

Qualifications for interpreter/translator

High school diploma, or an equivalent, supplemented by college-level coursework in English language, Spanish language or a related course; two (2) years of experience performing clerical duties involving extensive document writing, data/record management and public contacts; and at least one (1) year of professional experience translating written documents and providing simultaneous oral interpretation services.

Personnel staff may consider other educational preparation as acceptable to qualify for participation in the examination process resulting in an eligibility list.

1. Written examination—to assess basic competency in math, English grammar usage and spelling, reading comprehension and clerical skills.

2. Bilingual assessment—to assess fluency and ability to read, write and translate from English to Spanish and Spanish to English.

3. Structured oral interview—to assess technical knowledge and experience, oral interpretation from English to Spanish and Spanish to English and general fitness for successful performance in the position.

> Note: Interpreters/translators working in schools often have additional duties on top of translating and interpreting. This is reflected in the following list of responsibilities that appear in this fictional but realistic job listing for an educational interpreter/translator.

Responsibilities of the interpreter/translator

- Translates district-wide written materials of educational and technical nature for use by the district, school staff, parents and the public in a designated second language.
- Provides interpretation services from English to a designated second language and vice versa, during official district meetings, workshops, conferences and special events, including but not limited to individualized education program (IEP) meetings, parent-teacher conferences and interviews.
- Provides language assistance in the designated second language and English to callers, parents and other staff members at school sites.
- Coordinates interpreting services for English learner families during back-to-school events and during parent-teacher conferences.
- Assists special school personnel in assessing EL students' language skills.
- Translates written materials for various school sites, including official documents, forms, letters, notes, reports, presentations, announcements and special events from English to a designated second language and vice versa.
- Uses current translation applications and resources to determine the most accurate meaning of the material to be translated.
- Proofreads and edits translations from one language to another in order to produce material that is accurate, readable and conforms to the style of the original text.
- Takes notes and writes minutes during and following school meetings as necessary.
- Maintains confidentiality of sensitive information encountered during interpreting and translating duties.
- Provides information to EL families regarding school activities, programs, assessments, practices, objectives, policies and procedures.
- Informs EL families about programs and community resources as appropriate.
- Assists the office staff with clerical duties, such as establishing and maintaining student records.
- Inputs data into the school's database system and retrieves student information when necessary.
- Administers, under the supervision of the teaching or resource staff, standardized educational assessments in the designated second language to students.
- Performs other job-related duties as assigned.

Such job descriptions may overwhelm potential candidates by indicating that the role will include the duties of assistant, greeter, telephone operator, counselor, data entry clerk and test administrator.

In reality, the day-to-day job is not as haphazard as the description makes it sound. In these types of positions, most work is between six to eight hours daily. If the interpreter is needed to interpret at an evening board meeting, the interpreter's schedule could be adjusted to accommodate this need by modifying the overall hours for that day.

If the interpreter/translator is expected to work during evening meetings, their schedule would need to be flexible unless that employee is allowed to receive overtime pay for any hours worked beyond the regular workday. Another option would be for the district to hire an ad hoc or contract interpreter or translator from an agency for a meeting scheduled outside regular hours.

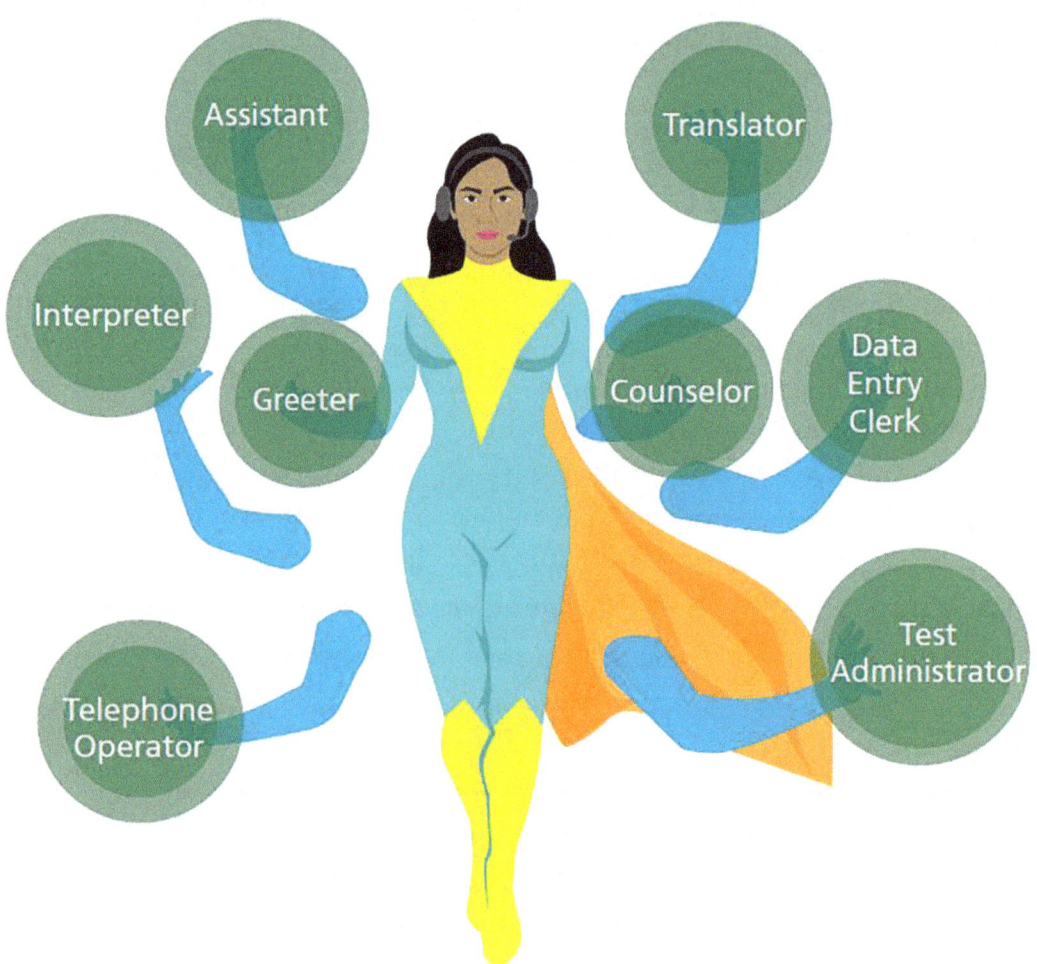

Figure 9.2: The many tasks of an interpreter.

As mentioned in the certificates vs. certification section of this chapter, there is a movement within education toward certifying educational translators and interpreters at the national level so that standards and expectations can be addressed across all states. A reliable and valid assessment instrument for educational interpreters is currently being developed by the American Association of Interpreters and Translators in Education (AAITE). This is a nonprofit professional association for interpreters and translators who work in educational settings, along with interested stakeholders and other allies.

The association is working to create a valid and reliable tool to nationally assess interpreters' skills. Regardless of the format that will be used, this will be a big step in the right direction. National certification standards would guarantee there is a pool of competent and qualified professionals that school districts can access within a district, county or across the United States.

If you are considering a career as a full-time interpreter/translator for a school or school district, consider obtaining a university or community college certificate in translation and interpreting. It is not necessary for you to be a native speaker of one of the two languages. The qualifications that are essential include:

- A broad vocabulary in both languages.
- Excellent memory and concentration skills.
- Ability to keep up with the speakers of the first language.
- Awareness of the tone and inflection of the speakers.
- Ability to maintain neutrality between the participants.
- Awareness of cultural nuances.
- Thorough knowledge of idiomatic and technical expressions in both languages.
- Proper certification, where available, to verify language proficiency.

📖 Chapter 9 review

This chapter offered information about the language assessment tools offered to individuals using the ACTFL proficiency rating scale, the ILR Scale and the EF SET. These metrics, along with language testing instruments developed by bilingual experts in school districts, can determine the proficiency level of students and interpreters. There are valid pathways to certification available for translators, court interpreters and medical interpreters thanks to ATA, the Federal Court Interpreting Certification Examination, the CCHI and the NBCMI. The exams are rigorous and address the needs of these professions.

Novice educational interpreters benefit from taking a series of courses in translating and interpreting from community colleges, online interpreting programs, open university programs and, when available, through their school districts.

When applying for a position as an interpreter or translator for a school, keep in mind that such positions often include other types of responsibilities, mostly clerical in nature.

Chapter 9 activities

1. Multiple choice

Circle the letter that corresponds to the best response.

1. Language proficiency can be accurately measured using any of the following except:
   a. ACTFL proficiency rating scale.
   b. ILR Scale.
   c. An interview with a school principal.
   d. The EF SET.

2. Most certificate programs require attendees to have:
   a. Advanced High Proficiency
   b. Advanced Mid Proficiency
   c. Advanced Low Proficiency
   d. Intermediate High Proficiency

3. First language can be defined as:
   a. Your preferred language.
   b. Your native language.
   c. A language that your parents speak.
   d. A language that you learned in high school.

4. Superior writers, as defined by ACTFL:
   a. Demonstrate some deficiencies in controlling grammar.
   b. Can usually control target-language patterns.
   c. Possess precise and varied vocabulary.
   d. Demonstrate some patterns of error.

5. The oral proficiency interview (OPI) measures:
   a. EF SET levels.
   b. ILR Scale.
   c. CEFR proficiency levels.
   d. ACTFL proficiency levels

6. Community college interpreting certificate programs:
   a. Are sometimes offered online.
   b. Do not usually require proof of language proficiency.
   c. Mostly address educational interpreting.
   d. Are only taught by interpreters with a valid certification.

7. The most prestigious and valid translation certification is offered by:
   a. CCHI.
   b. NBCMI.
   c. NCSC.
   d. ATA.

2. Indicate if these statements are true (T) or false (F).   T   F
   1. Valid certifications exist in order to interpret in the healthcare field. ___ ___
   2. NBCMI requires 30 hours of medical interpretation training. ___ ___
   3. Job descriptions for educational interpreters do not include clerical duties. ___ ___
   4. A movement has begun to certify educational interpreters through AAITE. ___ ___
   5. School interpreters may need to work in the evenings, particularly when board meetings take place. ___ ___

3. Share with a partner.
   A. Discuss the differences between the various certifications: ATA, CCHI, NBCMI, NCSC.
   B. Create a realistic job description for an educational interpreter. Share it with a partner.

☑ Answer key for Chapter 9 activities

1. Multiple choice

1. C. 2. A. 3. B. 4. C. 5. D. 6. A. 7. D.

2. Indicate if these statements are true (T) or false (F).

1. T. 2. F. 3. F. 4. T. 5. T.

3. Share with a partner.

A. Open ended discussion will vary.

B. Written answers vary.

Legal Requirements in Educational Settings 10

Chapter 10

- Introduction
- Legal requirements
- Language access
- No Child Left Behind (NCLB)
- Every Student Succeeds Act (ESSA)
- English Learner Tool Kit
- Noncompliance with Laws
- Chapter 10 review
- Chapter 10 activities
- Answer key for Chapter 10 activities

Introduction

In this chapter we will cover the federal laws that are enforced in schools by the U.S. Department of Education, specifically by the Office for Civil Rights. These laws ensure that English learner families can access information related to their children in a language they understand. This access and intervention can start as early as the birth of the children, especially for those born with disabilities or impairments.

In order to facilitate communication between the schools and these parents, many districts have created language access plans. Such plans provide equal access and fair opportunities for EL parents with regard to the education of their children. Guidance to set up such plans can be obtained from the U.S. Department of Education and from state level educational departments. These plans help coordinate and facilitate meetings between you, the interpreter, and the parents or guardian who need your services.

Legal requirements

Why provide interpreting services to English learner parents and/or guardians whose children attend schools in the United States? Providing interpretation and translation services to parents and school staff is mandated by laws set forth by the federal government.

This provision has been included in the Common Core State Standards and addresses the fact that parental involvement and engagement leads to greater success for students. Therefore, it is of vital importance for school districts to take necessary measures to ensure effective communication between parents and school staff.

The Common Core State Standards represent academic benchmarks for what students should know about English language arts and math from kindergarten through 12th grade. They include parental involvement. As of May 2023, 40 states have adopted the Common Core State Standards. Five states adopted the standards but later repealed them, choosing to adopt their own standards. One state partially adopted the standards. Four states never adopted the standards.

☞ Civil right laws affecting English language learner parents

Title VI of the Civil Rights Act of 1964 prohibits the exclusion of individuals from federally funded activities on the basis of race, color and national origin. Many such activities or programs involve schools. About 10 years after the passage of this act, on January 21, 1974, in the case of Lau v. Nichols, a group of Chinese students argued that language differences prevented equal access to federally funded educational programs. The United States Supreme Court clarified the provisions of Title VI in this landmark case. It prohibited actions that would have a negative effect on individuals with limited proficiency in the English language, because such conduct represented discrimination. On August 24, 2000, the William Clinton presidential administration clarified that the prohibition against discrimination extended to languages.

☛ Civil rights

The **Civil Rights Division** of the U.S. Department of Justice enforces laws that mandate English learner parents of public school students receive equal access to information about school matters, such as communication with teachers and administrators regarding events and meetings that take place throughout the school year. Schools must strive for inclusiveness for all parents, regardless of their primary language.

Schools must communicate with English learner parents in a language they can understand to provide information about programs, services or activities that parents of students should know. This includes, but is not limited to, the following topics and information:

- Registration and enrollment in school and school programs
- Grievance procedures and notices of nondiscrimination
- Language assistance programs
- Parent handbooks
- Report cards
- Gifted and talented programs
- Student discipline policies and procedures
- Magnet schools and charter schools
- Special education and related services
- Meetings to discuss special education
- Parent-teacher conferences
- Requests for parent permission for student participation in school activities

School districts should ensure that interpreters and translators have a solid foundation in two working languages. They should also have knowledge of any specialized terms or concepts to be used in the communication of an issue and be trained on the role of an interpreter and/or translator, along with the ethics of interpreting and translating.

The **Office for Civil Rights** of the U.S. Department of Education enforces several federal civil rights laws that prohibit discrimination in programs or activities that receive federal funding. There are 12 enforcement offices throughout the United States. Representatives are sent to school districts to make sure compliance standards are being met. Districts, in turn, prepare for these reviews, provide the required documentation, arrange for school visits and receive feedback and recommendations from the team of government representatives.

The **Elementary and Secondary Education Act** (ESEA) of 1965 of the U.S. Department of Education was reauthorized in 2001 as No Child Left Behind and addresses parental involvement in Sec. 1118.

Parents need to participate in decision-making that affects school matters. However, it is up to the school districts to take the necessary steps to make this possible. All parents, regardless of their primary language, should be allowed to participate. School districts cannot receive funds unless there is proof that parents are involved in decision-making at their child's school. Therefore, schools are incentivized to include, involve and train parents in a language they understand. This way they become participants, or stakeholders, in educational decisions related to programs, assessments and other educational activities.

When necessary, interpreting and translation services must be provided. This involvement includes participation in all types of meetings: Parent Teacher Association (PTA), Parent Teacher Organization (PTO), English Learner Advisory Committee (ELAC), School Site Council (SSC), special education such as the individualized education program (IEP) and any mandated meetings where parents or guardians are invited or required to participate.

ESEA requires parents to receive notification of their child's school performance. Interpreting for EL parents at parent-teacher conferences makes this possible. (See https://www.ed.gov.)

The **Individuals with Disabilities Education Act**[22] (IDEA) was originally named Education for All Handicapped Children. It was reviewed and renamed in 1990. The Office of Special Education Programs of the U.S. Department of Education provides financial support to assist states and school districts in its role as an administrative body to support IDEA.

Part A lays the foundation for the act and outlines general provisions, including the purpose of IDEA. It addresses and serves students ages 3 to 21.

Part B of the act addresses the need for special services and the creation of individualized education programs. It ensures that EL parents are able to participate in the decision-making process through the interpretation and translation of vital information. Interpreters will need to have a strong grasp of special education terminology in order to skillfully perform their services.

Part C ensures that eligible children with disabilities from birth to two years old (up to 36 months) receive early intervention services. Families receive an Individualized Family Service Plan (IFSP) that addresses the concerns and priorities of the family. Interpreters and translators assist parents as needed. Interpreters must manage the delicate task of explaining assessments, interventions and recommendations from the experts.

---

[22] Retrieved from https://sites.ed.gov/idea/

Language access

Language access is directly related to the Civil Rights Act of 1964 and to ESEA, Title 1, Part A, because it defines the actions a school district or organization must take to provide timely and accurate communication to all relevant parties. That most certainly includes EL parents or guardians of schoolchildren.

Title VI of the Civil Rights Act of 1964 states that "No person in the United States shall, on the ground of race, color, or national origin, be excluded from participation in, be denied the benefits of, or be subjected to discrimination under any program or activity receiving Federal financial assistance."[23]

If there is a need for in-person interpretation, video remote interpretation, telephonic interpretation, or document translation for parents or guardians, steps should be in place to address these situations. Each district and school will have a different climate and culture, though, and addressing this issue will depend on the number of EL parents needing such services. Furthermore, school districts and schools would need to determine what languages these parents speak. Accessibility to school programs, events and meetings must be provided to all parents, regardless of race or language dominance.

It is the district's responsibility to identify the primary language of the parents. Some districts may have to develop a language access plan, a document that details how to provide services to parents and individuals who are non-English speaking or are English learners. Such a plan would describe the types of interpretation and translation services provided to them.

---

[23] Retrieved from https://www.dol.gov/agencies/oasam/regulatory/statutes/title-vi-civil-rights-act-of-1964

Some districts have set up language access departments to implement this plan and to provide quality interpreting and translation services from a centralized system. In large school districts, a centrally based coordinator or manager works with staff interpreters, freelancers, language banks and interpreting agencies. Language access departments also offer ongoing training for interpreters, as well as managing translation projects. Most important, such departments collect relevant data regarding the work of interpreters and translators.

The U.S. Department of Justice and the U.S. Department of Education, through the Office for Civil Rights, have created a fact sheet to address communication between parents and guardians and schools and school districts. It answers the following question.

What steps must school districts take to provide effective language assistance to English learner parents?

- School districts must provide effective language assistance to [English learner] parents, such as by offering translated materials or a language interpreter. Language assistance must be free and provided by appropriate and competent staff, or through appropriate and competent outside resources.

- School districts should ensure that interpreters and translators have knowledge in both languages of any specialized terms or concepts to be used in the communication at issue, and are trained on the role of an interpreter and translator, the ethics of interpreting and translating, and the need to maintain confidentiality.

- It is not sufficient for the staff merely to be bilingual. For example, a staff member who is bilingual may be able to communicate directly with [English learner] parents in a different language, but may not be competent to interpret in and out of that language, or to translate documents.[24]

For more information about the rights of English learners, visit http://www2.ed.gov/about/offices/list/ocr/docs/dcl-factsheet-el-students-201501.pdf

A language access plan (LAP) for school districts describes the services that are provided to non-English speaking and English learner individuals. Ideally, parents will be made aware that such a plan exists and shown how to access it. The LAP includes guidelines and policies for language access. It also defines the roles of interpreters and translators. A good example of a LAP can be found at https://www.k12.wa.us/policy-funding/equity-and-civil-rights/resources-school-districts-civil-rights-washington-schools/interpretation-and-translation.

On August 11, 2000, President Clinton signed Executive Order 13166, which requires federal agencies to examine the services they provide, identify any need for services to those who are EL parents of school children and develop and implement a system to provide meaningful access to these services. The language access plan should provide meaningful access consistent with, and without unduly burdening, the fundamental mission of the agency.

The Executive Order also requires that federal agencies work to ensure that recipients of federal financial assistance provide meaningful access to their limited English proficient applicants and

---

[24] Retrieved from https://www2.ed.gov/about/offices/list/ocr/docs/dcl-factsheet-lep-parents-201501.pdf

beneficiaries. To assist federal agencies in carrying out these responsibilities, the U.S. Department of Justice issued a policy guidance document, which sets forth the compliance standards that recipients of federal financial assistance must follow to ensure that their programs and activities normally provided in English are accessible to all, including those needing interpreting services.

No Child Left Behind (NCLB)

The No Child Left Behind Act of 2001 reauthorized the ESEA of 1965. In NCLB, Title 1, Part A, in the parent involvement section, it states:

> Studies have found that students with involved parents, no matter what their income or background, are more likely to—

- Earn high grades and test scores, and enroll in higher-level programs;
- Pass their classes, earn credits, and be promoted;
- Attend school regularly; and
- Graduate and go on to postsecondary education.

—NCLB, *Parental Involvement, Title I, Part A, Non-Regulatory Guidance*, A-5, p. 4

According to the NCLB, parental involvement programs must include all families, regardless of their language dominance. Two main goals of the sociology of education are to understand inequalities in education and to design and test programs that yield more equal educational opportunities. Equity is also the stated goal of the NCLB's requirements for family involvement. The law repeatedly stresses that communication with parents must be clear, useful, and in languages that every parent understands. Equal access to school-related matters must include all parents or guardians.

According to Ruby Payne's study, there appears to be a perception that Latino parents are uninterested and uninvolved in school matters. This can be attributed to the cultural deficit model as explained in *A Framework for Understanding Poverty: A Cognitive Approach* (Payne, 2005). According to this study, a disconnect seems to exist between school and home culture due to the following.

- Lack of clear communication.
- Lack of translation/interpretation services.
- School expectations of parents.

It is to be noted that "all parents attributed supportive relationships with school personnel and a bilingual climate as the most important sources of feeling welcome at school" (Durand & Perez, 2013, p. 49).

Every Student Succeeds Act (ESSA)

In 2015, ESSA[25] was passed, replacing NCLB. Many of the provisions were kept, including those that relate to parents. This act now requires states to get input from parents and families as they create state plans. With NCLB, states were not required to include parent input when creating their state plans. With ESSA, the role of parents has expanded. It is worth noting that ELs are concentrated in six states: Arizona, California, Florida, Illinois, New York and Texas. As a result, it is in these states that there is a greater need for interpreters and translators.

It is evident that to help students succeed, teachers and administrators must have effective written and oral communication between parents or guardians. With the assistance of qualified interpreters or translators, teachers and school personnel can communicate effectively with a child's parent and vice versa. The goal is for all parents to better understand the instructional goals, classroom requirements and expectations of the school, and to make their own voices heard in the process.

English Learner Tool Kit

The English Learner Tool Kit from the U.S. Department of Education, specifically Chapter 5, addresses parent involvement and provides schoolwide tools and resources that lead to quality programs and collaboration with newcomer families. See https://ncela.ed.gov/files/english_learner_toolkit/OELA_2017_ELsToolkit_508C.pdf

Noncompliance with laws

A school district may be cited for not providing adequate translation and interpreting services to parents. For example, the Charleston County School District of South Carolina was flagged in March 2021. Fortunately, following the investigation by the U.S. Department of Justice, the district established a plan to address and resolve the cited deficiencies. The district made substantial changes to its policies and thus was able to start providing the necessary training to its personnel in order to rectify the situation.

> "The Charleston County School District should be commended for its cooperation with this investigation and for its commitment to its students, parents and guardians," said Acting

---

[25] Retrieved from: https://www.ed.gov/essa

U.S. Attorney M. Rhett DeHart for the District of South Carolina. "The U.S. Attorney's Office looks forward to [continuing to work] with the school district, as it strives to be a model for other districts in providing full and equal access to information."

The district cooperated at every stage of the investigation and committed to improving its practices through revised policies and professional development. The settlement agreement required the district to use qualified interpreters and translators to communicate with parents about matters essential to their children's education and to cease relying on family members, untrained staff and students for such purposes. The district was able to provide [English learner] parents with access to documents and information about program offerings, including special education services, in a language they understand. The agreement requires the district to provide these interpretation and translation services for [parents and guardians] at each of its 80 schools and programs.

Under the agreement, the district will:

Implement effective policies and procedures and provide employees with training so that schools properly identify and meaningfully communicate with [English language learner] parents and guardians;

Ensure that all parents and guardians knowingly consent to or decline educational programming and services for their children; and

Contact [English learner] parents and guardians prior to holding special education-related meetings in order to notify them of the right to have a qualified interpreter at the meeting and translated special-education related documents, at no cost to the parent/guardian.[26]

In Monterey County, California, the school board of the Chualar Unified School District sent a notice of intent to recall a board member for failing to address discrimination against the Spanish-speaking community. This action stemmed from the lack of Spanish interpretation at board meetings.

Ofelia Flores, who signed the recall notice, says [in Spanish] they now have a translator but the district needs to do more to address parents' concerns. She says questions go unanswered, and their comments to the board are not properly documented…

According to Board member Martha Gallegos, these claims are accurate. "In a community where 99 percent of the population is Hispanic, we still didn't have Spanish translators."[27]

Unfortunately, these types of situations occur in other school districts. Therefore, such situations should be brought to the attention of the school board, addressed and rectified.

---

[26] Retrieved from: https://www.justice.gov/opa/pr/washington-today-justice-department-announced-settlement-agreement-charleston-county-school

[27] Retrieved from: https://www.montereycountyweekly.com/news/local_news/a-recall-campaign-is-underway-against-a-chualar-union-school-district-board-member/article_d6a27ba6-be68-11eb-bd38-674d290b5c64.html

Chapter 10 review

It is important to familiarize yourself with the laws related to parental involvement in education. These laws or mandates exist to ensure that English learner parents have equal access to information related to their schoolchildren. Several civil rights laws have impacted the field of education. These federal laws make it possible for English learner families to access information about their children in a language they understand.

Starting with Title VI of the Civil Rights Act of 1964, discrimination is prohibited based on race, color or national origin. ESEA, particularly Section 1118, addresses and encourages parental involvement. It requires schools to notify parents of a child's performance in a language they understand. Executive Order 13166 clarified the need for these parents to receive information about school events and to participate in the creation of programs, plans or activities related to their children. NCLB addresses equity and accessibility for EL parents. Oversight is handled by the Office for Civil Rights through the U.S. Department of Health and Human Services.

Resources are available to implement these laws through the U.S. Department of Education. It's also worth noting that IDEA employs many interpreters and translators in special education programs. It is important for you as an interpreter to gain a basic competency in navigating this complex field, particularly its specific terminology.

Chapter 10 activities

1. Multiple choice

Circle the letter that corresponds to the best response.

1. Title VI of the U.S. Civil Rights Act:
   a. Created the Common Core State Standards.
   b. Denied federal assistance to schools that discriminated based on race.
   c. Opposed discrimination in schools based on race, color and national origin.
   d. Prohibited the use of languages other than English in public schools.

2. The federal department that enforces laws related to equal access of information for English learner parents in schools is:
   a. The English Learner Advisory Committee.
   b. The Office for Civil Rights.
   c. The Department of Labor.
   d. The Department of the Interior.

3. A language access plan:
   a. Is required for every public school in the U.S.
   b. Is not related to Title VI of the U.S. Civil Rights Act.
   c. Was created by the U.S. Civil Rights Act.
   d. Is recommended for school districts with a high number of English learner parents.

4. A language access plan does not include:
   a. Offering interpretation services at a cost to English learner families.
   b. Identifying languages that need to be serviced.
   c. Informing English learner parents that interpretation services are available.
   d. Providing interpretation services to English learner families.

5. What steps can districts take to provide interpreting and translation services for English learner parents?
   a. Have a language access plan in place.
   b. Identify English learner parents who need such services.
   c. Hire qualified, trained interpreters and translators for schools.
   d. All of the above.

2. Match the years with the appropriate law or mandate.

1.	No Child Left Behind	2015
2.	Lau v. Nichols	1990
3.	Title VI of the U.S. Civil Rights Act	1974
4.	Executive Order 13166	1964
5.	Every Student Succeeds	2001
6.	IDEA	2000

3. Answer the following questions.
1. What types of meetings can EL parents participate in?
2. Can any bilingual person perform interpreting services at schools? Why or why not?
3. What has been proven to happen with students when parents are involved in school affairs?
4. What may be the result when a school district does not provide necessary translation and interpreting service to English learner parents?
5. Where can districts find tools and resources that lead to collaboration with English learner and newcomer families?

☑ Answer key for Chapter 10 activities

1. Multiple choice

1. C. 2. B. 3. C. 4. A. 5. D.

2. Match the years with the appropriate law or mandate.

1. 2001
2. 1974
3. 1964
4. 2000
5. 2015
6. 1990

3. Answer the following questions.

Answers will vary and are open to discussion.

Review Chapter 10 for best responses.

Interpreting for Assessments 11

Chapter 11

- Introduction
- Language and special education assessment
- Language assessment tools for English learners (EL)
- Chapter 11 review
- Chapter 11 activities
- Answer key for Chapter 11 activities

Introduction

This chapter explores assessments for language dominance in English and a first language for English language learner (ELL) students. These assessments determine the type of placement that is best suited for a student. Following this initial testing, some students are classified as Fluent English Proficient (FEP). Others as ELLs. ELL students and FEP students may at times be recommended for special education programs. In that case, they are given additional tests to determine strengths and weaknesses in several academic and non-academic areas. Following these assessments a specialized team meets and recommends the best placement for a student, with the goal of creating the most appropriate and least restrictive school environment. EL parents meet with a team of experts and learn the results of these assessments. They also listen to placement recommendations.

In IEP meetings, parents are given the opportunity to ask questions from special personnel about the assessments. Any points of confusion are explained to parents with the assistance of interpreters. Under IDEA, Part C, for children from birth to five years old, specialists can test and observe children for specific cognitive skills, language, physical development, hearing, gross and fine motor skills and visual impairments. Additional assessments are administered to students in elementary and middle schools. Less frequent assessments take place in high school. At all levels, interpreters and translators must be present to ensure all parents have an equal understanding of the meetings where these assessments are discussed and explained.

Language and special education assessment

- What happens to English learner students when they enroll in schools?
- What forms identify a child as an English learner?
- What information does the school need from the parents?
- What triggers the need to have students tested in their English language skills?
- What tools are used to identify English learner students?
- If a student is tested for language proficiency, are parents notified of the assessment results?
- Are they provided the results in a language the parents understand?

When parents first enroll their child in a public school, they are given several forms to fill out. One of these identifies the home language. The Home Language Survey (part of the English Learner Tool Kit) is a questionnaire that helps schools identify potential ELLs within 30 days of enrollment. The answers provided in the survey trigger English-language assessments.

Home Language Surveys are used in all 50 states and the District of Columbia.[28] The form is available in most languages. However, the questions vary by state. The Office for Civil Rights and the U.S. Department of Justice have approved the following three questions as compliant with the law.

1. What is the primary language used by the student in the home?
2. What is the language most often spoken by the student?
3. What is the language first acquired by the student?

The state of California requires all school districts to collect a Home Language Survey signed by the parent for their child. The information on this survey is used to determine what language students speak at home with their families. It helps identify students who need to be assessed for English language proficiency.

Four questions appear on this survey.

1. Which language did the student learn when they first began to talk?
2. Which language does the student most frequently speak at home?
3. Which language do you (the parents and/or guardians) most frequently use when speaking with the student?
4. Which language is most often spoken by adults in the home (parents, guardians, grandparents or any other adults)?

Parents complete, sign and date the form. Most states limit themselves to three or four questions, but a few add two, three or even more additional questions. One common additional question is "If available, in what language would you prefer to receive communication from the school?" This is an important question. It makes parents aware that interpreting and translation services can be offered at the school.

North Dakota schools ask parents/guardians to identify a child as immigrant, refugee, Native American, Alaskan Native or migrant.

If a language other than English appears in response to any of the four questions listed above, or the three deemed compliant by the Office for Civil Rights, the student is given an assessment of the English language. Students are also assessed in the other language listed on the form if a testing instrument is available.

A student is subsequently tested in English with a language proficiency screening assessment, usually the World-Class Instructional Design and Assessment (WIDA), Assessing Comprehension and Communication in English State-to-State for English Language Learners (ACCESS) or, as is mandated in the state of California, the English Language Proficiency Assessments for California (ELPAC). Interpreters who are trained in the administration of the exam can assess these students. After the student is assessed for English proficiency, an individual student report is sent home to the parent based on the results of the assessments. These are described in the next section.

---

[28] Retrieved from: https://journals.sagepub.com/doi/full/10.1177/23328584211002212#:~:text=Home%20Language%20Surveys%20(HLS)%20are%20used%20in%20all%2050%20states,Second%20Language%20(ESL)%20services.

In California, information about students speaking another language, along with other data about English learners, is submitted to the California Department of Education each year. The R-30 Language Census Report for every school includes the following information.

- The number of ELs by grade level and by language.
- The number of fluent English proficient (FEP), both initially identified FEP students and reclassified FEP students, by grade level and by language.
- The number of ELs in each type of instructional setting.
- The number of ELs receiving which instructional services.
- The number of ELs reclassified since March 1 of the reporting year.
- The number of parental exception waivers received and granted.
- The number of teachers and instructional aides providing primary language instruction or support and in which languages.
- The number of teachers providing English language development and/or specially designed academic instruction in English by authorization.

According to the U.S. Department of Education's National Center for Education Statistics, in the fall of 2019, Spanish was the home language of 3.9 million EL public school students, representing 75.7 percent of all EL students and 7.9 percent of all public school students. Arabic was the second most commonly reported home language (spoken by 131,600 students). English was the third most common home language for EL students (105,300 students), which may reflect students who live in multilingual households or students adopted from other countries who were raised speaking another language but who currently live in households where English is spoken. Chinese (100,100), Vietnamese (75,600), Portuguese (44,800), Russian (39,700), Haitian (31,500), Hmong (30,800) and Korean (25,800) were the next most commonly reported home languages of EL students.

Notably, there were 49.4 million students in the fall of 2022 in grades pre-kindergarten to grade 12 attending school in the United States. Of the ELs, more than half were born in the United States.

Language assessment tools for English learners (EL)

In public school settings, various instruments have been used to determine students' oral and/or written proficiency in English and other languages. The tests are administered by trained personnel, such as bilingual teachers or bilingual paraprofessionals, and oftentimes by trained interpreters or translators. Here is an overview of some of the most common tests used in the past and used presently.

The following three were commonly used in the seventies and eighties and are still used occasionally in some school districts.

Basic Inventory of Natural Languages (BINL). Created in 1977, the exam measures oral and listening proficiency in 32 languages. It is administered individually and uses a variety of language posters to elicit language and determine English-speaking proficiency. (See http://ericae.net.)

Bilingual Syntax Measure I and II (BSMI and BSMII). Developed in 1975, it measures English and Spanish proficiency in grades K–12. The BSMI is for K–2, while the BSMII corresponds to grades 3–12. There is a five-level scoring criteria: 1: No English or Spanish, 2: Receptive English or Spanish, 3: Survival English or Spanish, 4: Intermediate English or Spanish, 5: Proficient English or Spanish. (See http://ericae.net.)

Language Assessment Scales (LAS I and LAS II). Published in 1977 and used in grades K–6 (LAS I) and grades 7–12 (LAS II). Just like the previous two tests, these are used for initial identification, placement and reclassification. Speaking, listening, reading and writing are assessed resulting in designations of non-English speaker, limited English speaker, and fluent English speaker. There is also a reading/writing scale, the LAS R/W.

California English Language Development Test (CELDT). This test was administered primarily between 2000 and 2017 in grades K–12. Its designations corresponded to five levels: 1 is for beginning, 2 for early intermediate, 3 for intermediate, 4 for early advanced and 5 for advanced. The test was aligned with the English language development (ELD) standards. It has been replaced by the ELPAC.

World-Class Instructional Design and Assessment (WIDA) Assessing Comprehension and Communication in English State-to-State for English Language Learners (ACCESS). Following the NCLB Act of 2001, a grant was awarded to three states—Wisconsin, Delaware and Arkansas—to develop the 2004 ELD standards. These then served as the basis for WIDA's ACCESS for the EL test, which is the tool used by states to determine the English language proficiency of K–12 students. The test meets U.S. federal requirements of ESSA for tracking and reporting ELs' progress toward English language proficiency. Unlike some of the older tests, it is aligned to the ELD standards, just like the CELDT and the ELPAC. It also addresses all four domains: listening, speaking, reading and writing. Additionally, school districts can select a testing format based on their needs.

The test comes in an online format or a paper-pencil format. The online format is scored automatically for the listening and reading domains, which include multiple choice questions, hotspot questions (a type of matching), and drag-and-drop responses. However, trained raters, oftentimes interpreters or translators, must score the speaking and writing portions. Helpful practice tests are available. The ACCESS kindergarten for ELLs is paper based and administered individually. There is also an alternate ACCESS for 1–12 grades that is paper based, featuring large print, for students with cognitive disabilities. The results categorize the students into one of six proficiency levels: 1. Entering, 2. Emerging, 3. Developing, 4. Expanding, 5. Bridging and 6. Reaching. To date, this is the most commonly used assessment tool in 41 US states. (See https://wida.wisc.edu.)

English Language Proficiency Assessments for California (ELPAC). This test replaced the CELDT and began to be administered in California in 2017. It is aligned to the 2012 ELD standards. It assesses the four language skills: listening, speaking, reading and writing. The reporting is as follows: a 4 indicates well developed, a 3 moderately developed, a 2 somewhat developed and a 1 beginning to be developed. It consists of a listening and speaking component, administered individually, and a reading and writing component, administered in small groups. (See www.elpac.org.)

These language assessment tests should provide a basis for instructional planning and classroom placement.

Student Oral Language Observation Matrix (SOLOM). SOLOM is an informal assessment instrument that has proven to be of value. Developed by the San Jose Area Bilingual Consortium and the Bilingual Office of the California Department of Education, SOLOM is used to determine oral language proficiency in any language. A qualified individual can administer the exam and determine the results almost immediately.

SOLOM Student Oral Language Observation Matrix

	Level I	Level II	Level III	Level IV	Level V
Comprehension	Cannot be said to understand even a simple conversation.	Has great difficulty following what is said. Can comprehend only "social conversation" spoken slowly and with frequent repetitions.	Understands most of what is said at slower-than-normal speed with repetitions.	Understands everyday conversation and normal classroom discussions without difficulty.	Understands nearly everything at normal speed, although occasional repetition may be necessary.
Fluency	Speech is so halting and fragmentary as to make conversation virtually impossible.	Usually hesitant: often forced into silence by language limitations.	Speech in everyday conversation and classroom discussion frequently disrupted by the student's search (or the correct manner of expression.	Speech in everyday conversation and classroom discussions generally fluent, with occasional lapses while the student searches for the correct manner of expression.	Speech in everyday conversation and classroom discussions fluent and effortless, approximating that of a native speaker.
Vocabulary	Vocabulary limitations so extreme as to make conversation virtually impossible.	Misuse of words and limited vocabulary comprehension quite difficult.	Student frequently uses the wrong words; conversation somewhat limited because of inadequate vocabulary.	Student occasionally uses inappropriate terms and/or must rephrase ideas because of lexical inadequacies.	Use of vocabulary and idioms approximates that of a native speaker.
Pronunciation	Pronunciation problems so severe as to make speech virtually unintelligible.	Pronunciation problems necessitate concentration on the part of the listener and occasionally lead to misunderstanding.	Hard to understand because of pronunciation problems. Must frequently repeat to make himself or herself understood	Always intelligible though one is conscious of a definite accent and occasional inappropriate intonation patterns	Pronunciation and intonation approximate that of a native speaker.
Grammar	Errors in grammar and word order so severe as to make speech virtually unintelligible.	Grammar and word-order errors make comprehension difficult. Must often rephrase and/or restrict himself or herself to basic patterns.	Grammar Makes frequent errors of grammar and word order that occasionally obscure meaning.	Occasionally makes grammatical and/or word-order errors that do not obscure meaning	Grammatical usage and word order approximate that of a native speaker.

Figure 11.1: SOLOM, California State Department of Education.

The SOLOM is a rating scale that teachers, language professionals or interpreters and translators can use to assess a student's oral language. Observations of the student's speech can occur in a variety of school situations, such as interactions with other students, teachers, siblings, interpreters or parents. This tool should be administered by individuals who will score and determine the level for each category in all of the five areas: comprehension, fluency, vocabulary, pronunciation and grammar. It is not meant to be used to assess reading or writing skills.

Teachers can use the SOLOM to assess the oral English language of a student, while interpreters can use it to determine how well a student speaks their first language. It can be an effective way to assess some of the uncommon languages. For the comprehension category, the student is asked to describe a series of pictures or events. For fluency and vocabulary, the student can describe a multistep process, such as making a meal or the rules of a game. To check pronunciation, the student's speech can be recorded. To check grammar, ask questions about what the student has learned in class. Total scores that are above 19, out of a total of 25, are considered proficient.

Special education assessment tools

Assessments are key tools when setting up an individualized plan for a special education student. Specialists on the IEP team often recommend specific assessments in order to create an appropriate program for a child in need of certain interventions. Frequently, interviews with parents and teachers help determine what direction to follow. These interviews can start as early as infancy, when it is determined that a child has special needs. Special education experts such as psychologists and speech-language pathologists may at times require assistance from an interpreter when administering certain assessments or when doing home visits.

The assessments can be based on interviews, formal and informal observations, and criterion-referenced tests. These tests compare a student's abilities and performance against a fixed set of criteria and are distinct from norm-referenced tests, which compare the skills of a student with those of a norm group composed of the averaged results of several thousand students that share the same characteristics.

Teachers give formative assessments throughout the year. These identify strengths and weaknesses in certain areas or subjects. Examples are portfolios, group projects or class discussions. Alternatively, summative assessments inform teachers about a student's understanding of specific areas in the curriculum. These may include final projects, midterms or book reports.

The most commonly used assessments correspond primarily to IDEA, Part C, for children from birth to 36 months old. These early intervention strategies utilize some of the following tools.

Individual Family Service Plan (IFSP). The evaluation is based on the skills a child can perform. The plan is written, as indicated, for children with disabilities from birth to 36 months old. It covers physical, cognitive, communication, social/emotional and adaptive areas, which are explained to parents.

Hawaii Early Learning Profile (HELP). This is a norm-referenced standardized test for children from birth to six years old. It addresses development in the following areas: cognitive, language, gross motor, fine motor, social/emotional and self-help. The instrument covers 685 skills from birth to three years old, and 585 skills from three to six years old. It is approached through observations by professionals, such as psychologists or speech pathologists, and interviews with the parents. The testing materials are published by the Values, Objectives, Resources and Time (VORT) Corporation. (See https://eceteacher.weebly.com.)

SKI-HI. This nationally accepted assessment is for the Deaf and Hard of Hearing child between birth through age five. Every child who is Deaf or Hard of Hearing must be evaluated using the SKI-HI Language Development Scale. It is available in English and Spanish and can be completed by the parent, a caregiver, occupational or physical therapist, a program administrator or a special education teacher. The assessment aids in determining a child's present level of function. It is criterion referenced and easy to administer. (See https://ski-hi.mystrikingly.com/blog/deaf-hard-of-hearing.)

Developmental Milestones Matter! This checklist is based on the US Centers for Disease Control and Prevention (CDC) developmental milestones chart aimed at infants and children from two months to five years. The chart addresses social/emotional, language, communication, movement, physical development and visual motor integration. It is available in English and Spanish and can be accessed in print or app formats.

Other types of assessments administered to children who are more than five years old often address difficulties that involve language processing, speech delays, dyslexia, developmental delay, autism and inappropriate behaviors. These are usually identified in the elementary grades (K–5 or K–6), although it is not uncommon to use them in middle schools (6–8 grades or 7–8 grades). Students with learning disabilities will continue to be monitored on a yearly basis during their middle school and high school years to ensure that appropriate measures are being taken to facilitate learning in the least restrictive environment. (See https://www.cdc.gov/ncbddd/actearly/milestones/index.html.)

Beery-Buktenica Developmental Test of Visual-Motor Integration (BEERY VMI). This test provides information relating to visual perception, motor coordination and hand-eye coordination. In this 10–15 minute test, students reproduce geometric forms using paper and pencil, individually or in a group setting. Tests are available for children and for adults.

Wechsler Intelligence Scale for Children (WISC). This popular test measures intellectual ability for children from ages 6 to 16 and measures intellectual functioning in verbal comprehension, perceptual reasoning, working memory and processing speed. It is oftentimes used to determine the existence of a learning disability or developmental delay, yet it can also identify giftedness.

Woodcock-Johnson IV Tests of Cognitive Abilities (WJ-IV DOG). This is a norm-referenced testing instrument that measures general intellectual ability and specific cognitive abilities. Individually administered, it measures academic achievement in reading, math, written language and other areas of academic skills and knowledge. It is frequently used to identify head injuries, attention-deficit / hyperactivity disorder (ADHD), visual impairment and autism. It also serves to identify gifted students, including those with learning disabilities.

Behavior Assessment System for Children (BASC-3). This norm-referenced system of assessment uses a set of standardized rating scales and forms to inform and understand the behavior and emotions of children and adolescents ages 2 through 21. The methods that are used include observation, self-monitoring, psychophysiology and self-report. Parents, teachers and the child participate. Parent rating scales are available in Spanish and in English. Parents can complete the BASC forms in about 10 to 20 minutes.

Clinical Evaluation of Language Fundamentals (CELF-5). The fifth edition of CELF is a system of individually administered tests that assist speech pathologists in diagnosing a language disorder in children ages 5 through 21. If a disorder is diagnosed, it is described in detail and a plan for treatment can then be created. It can be administered not only by speech pathologists but also by psychologists and special education personnel. Administration takes between 30 and 45 minutes.

Basic Reading Inventory (BRI). This is an easy-to-use, individually administered, informal reading assessment that includes two forms for K–12 students. The BRI assesses, summarizes and develops responsive reading instructions for students.

Kaufman Test of Educational Achievement (KTEA-3). This is a popular, individually administered, in-depth assessment of key academic skills in reading, math, written and oral language. It also measures progress or response to intervention and supports identification of learning disabilities. It is used for ages 4 to 25 and includes a number of subtests. It may take between 15 and 85 minutes to administer.

Peabody Picture Vocabulary Test (PPVT-5). This standardized, norm-referenced test evaluates receptive vocabulary knowledge. This is a point-to-picture task for ages two years, six months, to adulthood. It is usually administered by a speech pathologist or a trained educator. It usually takes between 10 and 15 minutes to administer.

Comprehensive Test of Phonological Processing (CTOPP-2). This test may be used to identify individuals who are substantially below their peers in phonological abilities. It determines students' relative strengths and weaknesses in this area and documents students' progress in specific intervention programs. It can serve as a research tool. It can also identify dyslexia. It addresses students' phonological awareness, phoneme-grapheme correspondences and phonetic decoding skills. Test results help educators focus on those aspects of a child's oral language that may not be systematically targeted in classroom reading instruction. It takes about 40 minutes to administer and is usually administered by speech pathologists or psychologists.

Vineland Adaptive Behavior Scales (VABS). This is a widely used standardized assessment instrument that measures adaptive behavior and diagnosis of intellectual and developmental disabilities, such as autism and developmental delays. It also offers treatment plans. VABS is usually administered by psychologists, occupational therapists, counselors or social workers for children ages three to nine. It takes approximately 10 minutes to administer the shortest form and about 45 minutes when motor skills and maladaptive behavior domains are included.

Slingerland Screening Tests (SST). These tests, for individuals or groups, are used to identify learning strengths and weaknesses in children who may have dyslexia or a specific language disability. All forms contain individual auditory tests to identify those unable to recall or pronounce words correctly or unable to express organized thoughts in their spoken or written language. The results are based on observations of how students process language. The forms evaluate visual-motor coordination, visual memory, visual discrimination, auditory-visual discrimination, auditory memory-to-motor ability, orientation in time and space and ability to express ideas in writing. SSTs are administered beginning in kindergarten and continuing through high school. (See https://www.slingerland.org)

GARS-3 is a school's most widely used autism instrument for the assessment of autism spectrum disorder. It can detect autism and estimate its severity.

Functional behavior assessment (FBA). This involves a pathway that identifies problem behaviors in children. Under the amendments to IDEA, any child who is identified with an emotional or behavior disorder should undergo an FBA to better define and understand undesired behavior. Six steps are involved in the assessment: 1. Collect data for all types of documented negative behaviors. 2. Develop a hypothesis using information from the collected data. 3. Observe the child to confirm the accuracy of the hypothesis. 4. Design a plan to modify circumstances to reduce the problem behavior. 5. Develop specific scripts indicating who is responsible for each part of the behavior support plan. 6. Collect data on the effectiveness of the program and redesign the areas that need improvement.

Behavior intervention plan (BIP). As a result of the FBA, an IEP team can then create and recommend a BIP, a formally written plan that aims to reward good behavior and prevent undesired behavior. Typically, it is made up of four key components: a detailed description of the problem, including a summary statement of the problem; interventions used; behavioral goals and a plan to teach and support the new behavior.

Escalation psychological management plan. This plan is also based on the FBA. It addresses aggressive behaviors and includes data entries that document the type of undesired behavior, its duration and frequency, intervals, intensity/severity, the impact on instruction, students and staff and any other relevant component. Based on the data gathered, the IEP team sets in motion a management plan and strategies that address the misbehavior. Examples of this plan can be found at https://confidentcounselors.com/2018/01/11/de-escalation-strategies/.

By no means is this an exhaustive list of assessments and plans for remediation. However, these are some that are prominently referenced during IEP meetings, where interpreters play a critical role. Other assessment tools may be included as needed for each individual case. Frequently, grade level standards are addressed. IEP team members often refer to teachers' assessments, district standards, yearly testing scores in various areas, primarily in reading and math, and formative and summative assessments. Furthermore, interpreters may need to familiarize themselves with various statewide and districtwide assessments.

All states are required to administer yearly tests in the areas of math and reading in grades 3–8 and once in high school under the current ESSA. Federal law also requires assessments in science in fourth or fifth grade, eighth grade, and once in high school, with an end-of-course assessment in biology. These standardized tests vary by state. (More information can be found at https://ecs.org/50-state-comparison-state-summative-assessments/). Half of U.S. states administer an exit exam that students must pass to receive a high school diploma.

📖 Chapter 11 review

This chapter covered the most utilized language assessments in schools, the ELPAC and the WIDA. These are administered by teachers, assessment experts or trained interpreters to students who speak a home language other than English. A more informal test, the SOLOM, can be used to rate the speaking and listening skills of a student's first language. Special education assessments can begin at birth. The most common assessment for hearing impairment or hearing loss for young children is the SKI-HI.

At IEP meetings, educational experts, such as psychologists, speech-language pathologists, case managers, resource or special education teachers and general education teachers, can recommend appropriate assessments in an attempt to better define a student's deficiency and set in motion remediation strategies. Interpreters must be present to facilitate clear communication between EL parents and the experts explaining the results of such testing.

Elementary school assessments might focus on the BEERY VMI, the Wechsler Intelligence Scale for Children, the Woodcock-Johnson IV, the CELF-5, the BRI and many others. Behavioral assessments are addressed with the FBA and may lead to the creation of an escalation psychological management plan or a BIP.

In your role as interpreter, you should not feel overwhelmed by the complexity of these assessments. You are present at the meetings to convey the information related to the assessments to English language learner families in a language they can understand and interpret any questions they may have.

Interpreting for Assessments — Chapter 11

✏ Chapter 11 activities

1. Multiple choice

Circle the letter that corresponds to the best response.

1. What form is used to help determine if a student must get assessed in the English language?
    a. BIP
    b. HLS
    c. R-30
    d. Registration form

2. Currently, the most widely used English assessment in K–12 schools is the:
    a. WIDA.
    b. ELPAC.
    c. CELDT.
    d. BSM I.

3. Which one of these questions has not been approved on the HLS by the Office for Civil Rights nor by the U.S. Department of Justice?
    a. What is the primary language used by the student in the home?
    b. What is the language most often spoken by the student?
    c. What is the language first acquired by the student?
    d. What is the language most often spoken by adults in the home?

4. Which of these languages does not belong to the top four most commonly reported home languages?
    a. Arabic
    b. Pashto
    c. Spanish
    d. Vietnamese

5. In 2023, the most commonly used English language assessment in California was the:
    a. WIDA.
    b. BINL.
    c. ELPAC.
    d. CELDT.

183

6. All except one of these assessments is aligned with the ELD standards.
   a. LAS I and II
   b. CELDT
   c. ELPAC
   d. WIDA

7. Learning disabilities can be diagnosed and identified administering the:
   a. BASC.
   b. SKI-HI.
   c. ELPAC.
   d. Wechsler Intelligence Scale for Children.

8. Behavioral assessments may lead to the creation of a:
   a. FBA.
   b. BASC.
   c. BIP.
   d. HLS.

2. Classify the following as belonging to IDEA, Part A, or IDEA, Part C.

IFSP, BEERY VMI, HELP, BRI, CELF-5, SKI-HI, Developmental Milestones Matter!, Woodcock-Johnson IV

IDEA, Part A	IDEA, Part C
a.	a.
b.	b.
c.	c.
d.	d.

3. Indicate if these statements are true (T) or false (F).   T   F

1. Interpreters can never administer the WIDA. ___ ___
2. More than half of ELs were born abroad. ___ ___
3. The CELF-5 exams are used to diagnose a language disorder. ___ ___
4. The SOLOM is used to determine oral proficiency in English only. ___ ___
5. The CTOPP-2 can be used to diagnose dyslexia. ___ ___
6. The SKI-HI assessments are used to determine Deafness in infants. ___ ___

☑ Answer key for Chapter 11 activities

1. Multiple choice

1. B. 2. A. 3. D. 4. B. 5. C. 6. A. 7. D. 8. C.

2. Classify the following as belonging to IDEA, Part A, or IDEA, Part C.

IDEA-A	IDEA-C
a. BEERY VMI	a. IFSP
b. BRI	b. HELP
c. CELF-5	c. SKI-HI
d. Woodcock-Johnson IV	d. Development Milestones Matter!

3. Indicate if these statements are true (T) or false (F).

1. F. 2. F. 3. T. 4. F. 5. T. 6. T.

Practice for Interpreting and Translating in School Settings *12*

Chapter 12
- Introduction
- Practice: Consecutive Interpretation
- Practice: Sight translation
- Practice: Simultaneous interpretation
- Practice: Translations

Introduction

The exercises in this chapter are meant to be practiced with partners. You will be taking on the role of the interpreter in all the role plays as you listen to two speakers read the part of the English speaker and the part of the Spanish speaker. You, as interpreter, will not be reading these exchanges. You will be taking notes as you listen to the exchanges. Deliver your interpretation after a speaker has finished reading their part. If the reading becomes too lengthy for you, use a hand gesture to request the reader pause the reading of the passage.

If you do not have two speakers available to read the dialogue in front of you, you may ask one or two speakers to record the passages. Later, you will be able to practice your interpretation. If that happens, it will be up to you to pause and render your interpretation following a natural pause in the exchange. You should not pause after each sentence out of fear that you will forget the remaining information—this is not realistic practice.

Practice this exchange more than once, and each time lengthen what you hear before you render your interpretation.

☛ #1 Consecutive interpretation role play: Parent-teacher conference (grades 4–6)

Hello. I'm Miss Young, Javier's teacher. You must be his mom. Please come in. You can sit right here.

Gracias por atenderme. Javier me ayudó a encontrar su salón. Y disculpe que traiga a mi niña, la pequeña. Es que no tenía con quién dejarla.

That's fine. I am glad you were able to make it. What's her name?

Se llama Rubisol. Así también se llama una tía mía muy querida.

It's a beautiful name. Here. Let me give her a coloring book and some crayons. She can sit right here, not far from us. Javier can sit in the chair next to you. Here is Miss García, she will be your interpreter.

Mucho gusto. Mil gracias. Veo que tiene todo preparado para mi visita. Siéntate ahí mijita. Vas a colorear ese librito.

Javier told me that today was your day off. I am so glad you were able to come. First of all, I'd like to share his report card with you. Let's start with math.

Muy bien. Creo que le gustan mucho las matemáticas.

You're right. He's doing an excellent job in math. Here are the grades he's been getting on his quizzes: 95 percent, 87 percent, 89 percent, 86 percent. He makes some careless mistakes at times because he wants to finish fast.

Ese muchacho… No es una buena idea que se apresure. Es un poco impaciente.

I know. I wanted to ask you if you received the letter I sent at the beginning of the school year—the one that explains my homework policy.

Ay, señora. La verdad es que no recuerdo. Sé que hay días que tiene tarea y otros que no.

That's right. He has spelling assignments on Mondays, readings on Tuesday and Wednesday and math homework on Thursdays. Students don't have homework on weekends.

Sí. Recuerdo haberlo visto con una lista de palabras los lunes. También me ha dicho que tiene que leer el libro que se trae de la biblioteca.

Correct. He takes home a library book to read on Tuesdays and Wednesdays. He's supposed to read for thirty minutes.

Hay veces que le pregunto si tiene tarea y me dice que no.

He's supposed to read the book at home and in class. If he wants to read on weekends that is fine, but that is not a requirement. All students will be writing book reports about their chosen books.

¿Y esos informes lo va a tener que hacer en la casa o en clase? No sé si le pueda ayudar con eso. No sé leer en inglés.

Don't worry. We will be writing the reports in class. I want to make sure students understand the stories. I also want them to reflect on the meaning of what they have read. Javier has chosen some very interesting books.

Sí. La verdad es que hay días que lee por más de media hora. Parece que con tanta lectura va a estar mejor preparado. Y, dígame por favor, ¿Cómo se ha portado ultimamente?

He's behaving better now. His best friend, Paco, used to sit in back of him. Javier would turn around a lot. They'd talk and sometimes he'd get distracted.

Conozco a ese muchacho. Vive cerquita de nuestra casa. Hay veces que viene a comer, especialmente cuando sus papás regresan tarde del trabajo.

That's great. I'm glad they can see each other after class. I've had to move Javier to the corner of the room, next to the whiteboard. Now I can keep a better eye on him. I think the move has worked well for both boys.

Muchísimas gracias, maestra. Y si por cualquier razón se quiere comunicar conmigo me llama a mi celular.

Of course. Thank you very much for coming, and please take the coloring book with you.

Está bien. Muchas gracias, maestra. Vente chamaca. Nos vamos a la casa.

#1 Consecutive interpretation role play: Parent-teacher conference (grades 4–6), English-English

Hello. I'm Miss Young, Javier's teacher. You must be his mom. Please come in. You can sit right here.

Thank you for taking care of me. Javier helped me find his (your) class. And excuse me for bringing my little girl. I just had no one to leave her with.

That's fine. I am glad you were able to make it. What's her name?

Her name is Rubisol. That is also my dear aunt's name.

It's a beautiful name. Here. Let me give her a coloring book and some crayons. She can sit right here, not far from us. Javier can sit in the chair next to you. Here is Miss García, she will be your interpreter.

Nice to meet you. Thank you very much. I see that you have everything prepared for my visit. Sit there, honey. You are going to color that little book.

Javier told me that today was your day off. I am so glad you were able to come. First of all, I'd like to share his report card with you. Let's start with math.

Very well. I think he really likes math.

You're right. He's doing an excellent job in math. Here are the grades he's been getting on his quizzes: 95 percent, 87 percent, 89 percent, 86 percent. He makes some careless mistakes at times because he wants to finish fast.

That boy... It's not a good idea for him to rush. He is a little impatient.

I know. I wanted to ask you if you received the letter I sent at the beginning of the school year—the one that explains my homework policy.

Oh, ma'am. The truth is that I don't remember. I know that there are days he has homework and other days that he doesn't.

That's right. He has spelling assignments on Mondays, readings on Tuesday and Wednesday and math homework on Thursdays. Students don't have homework on weekends.

Yes. I remember seeing him with a list of words on Mondays. He has also told me that he has to read the book that he brings from the library.

Correct. He takes home a library book to read on Tuesdays and Wednesdays. He's supposed to read for thirty minutes.

There are times when I ask him if he has homework, and he says no.

He's supposed to read the book at home and in class. If he wants to read on weekends that is fine, but that is not a requirement. All students will be writing book reports about their chosen books.

And is he going to have to do those reports at home or in class? I don't know if I can help him with that. I can't read English.

Don't worry. We will be writing the reports in class. I want to make sure students understand the stories. I also want them to reflect on the meaning of what they have read. Javier has chosen some very interesting books.

Yes. The truth is that there are days he reads for more than half an hour. It seems that with so much reading he will be better prepared. And please tell me, how has he behaved lately?

He's behaving better now. His best friend, Paco, used to sit in back of him. Javier would turn around a lot. They'd talk and sometimes he'd get distracted.

I know that boy. He lives close to our house. There are times when he comes to eat, especially when his parents come home late from work.

That's great. I'm glad they can see each other after class. I've had to move Javier to the corner of the room, next to the whiteboard. Now I can keep a better eye on him. I think the move has worked well for both boys.

Thank you very much, teacher. And if for any reason you would like to communicate with me, you call me on my cell phone.

Of course. Thank you very much for coming, and please take the coloring book with you.

Ok. Thank you very much, teacher. Come, honey. We are going home.

👉 #2 Consecutive interpretation role play: Parent–teacher conference (grades 5–6)

Hello. I am Lucy Travis, Juan's teacher. Please take a seat right here.

Marta Rodriquez, para servirle.

We're going to talk about Juan's grades. Here are the ones for the second quarter: a B in spelling, a D in reading and a W in Writing. He does well in spelling.

¿Por qué le va tan mal con la lectura?

He is working below grade level in reading. He is trying hard but is still having difficulties with reading comprehension. The main reason I gave him a D was because he only completed five out of ten book reports that were assigned. Here is a sample book report form.

¿Cree Ud. que no ha leído los libros o que se le olvida entregar los informes?

He doesn't always finish reading the books he checks out of the library. At times he gets books that may be too difficult and has a hard time finishing them. Do you see him reading at home?

No creo que lea todos los días. Yo no me encuentro siempre en la casa, pero sé que prefiere jugar a los videojuegos.

He is supposed to read twenty minutes each night, from Monday to Thursday.

Hay veces que regreso tarde del trabajo. Cuando le pregunto si tiene tarea, me dice que ya la terminó. Hay veces que regreso temprano, pero esos días no lo veo leer. Pero sí me dice que acabó de hacer su tarea.

Next time, ask him specifically if he did his twenty minutes of reading. Have him show you the bookmark that lists the date and to what page he should have read at home. He'll be able to tell you how far he's supposed to have read. I write due dates on the marker.

Muy bien, maestra. Ahora que sé que es lo que tiene que hacer en la casa. Me tendré que fijar hasta dónde leyó. Y dígame usted, ¿cómo se porta?

Juan's behavior is good. What does concern me is that he doesn't always complete all his work. That's why sometimes I keep him in class during recess.

Bueno, maestra. Le quiero dar las gracias por todo lo que hace por él. Yo sólo quiero que se supere para que no tenga que piscar moras cuando sea mayor.

Yes. We'll help him here in whatever way we can. You can be sure of that. Meanwhile, I thank you for your support and for making it to this meeting.

A Ud. también. Muchísimas gracias.

☛ #2 Consecutive interpretation role play: Parent–teacher conference (grades 5–6), English-English

Hello. I am Lucy Travis, Juan's teacher. Please take a seat right here.

Marta Rodriquez, at your service.

We're going to talk about Juan's grades. Here are the ones for the second quarter: a B in spelling, a D in reading and a W in Writing. He does well in spelling.

Why is he doing so badly with reading?

He is working below grade level in reading. He is trying hard but is still having difficulties with reading comprehension. The main reason I gave him a D was because he only completed five out of ten book reports that were assigned. Here is a sample book report form.

Do you think he hasn't read the books or that he forgets to turn in the reports?

He doesn't always finish reading the books he checks out of the library. At times he gets books that may be too difficult and has a hard time finishing them. Do you see him reading at home?

I don't think he reads every day. I'm not always in the house, but I know he prefers to play video games.

He is supposed to read twenty minutes each night, from Monday to Thursday.

There are times when I come back late from work. When I ask him if he has homework, he tells me he's finished it. There are times when I return early, but those days I don't see him read. But he does tell me that he finished doing his homework.

Next time, ask him specifically if he did his twenty minutes of reading. Have him show you the bookmark that lists the date and to what page he should have read at home. He'll be able to tell you how far he's supposed to have read. I write due dates on the marker.

Very well, teacher. Now that I know what he has to do in the house. I'll have to look at how far he read. And tell me, how does he behave?

Juan's behavior is good. What does concern me is that he doesn't always complete all his work. That's why sometimes I keep him in class during recess.

Well, teacher. I want to thank you for everything you do for him. I just want him to better himself so that he doesn't have to harvest berries when he's older.

Yes. We'll help him here in whatever way we can. You can be sure of that. Meanwhile, I thank you for your support and for making it to this meeting.

You too. Thank you very much.

☛ #3 Consecutive interpretation role play: Parent-teacher conference (grades 6–8)

Good afternoon. Please come in. We were expecting you. I am Roger Garfield, Silvia's math teacher. Thank you for making it on time. We'll be assisted by our school interpreter, Ms. Sara Pascuara.

Mucho gusto. Traje a Silvia para que escuche lo que Ud. tiene que decirme. También pensé que Silvia me ayudaría a traducir. No hablo mucho inglés.

No. That won't be necessary. Silvia can sit next to you. You can sit here facing me, and Ms. Pascuara will sit right here between us.

Está bien. Quisiera saber cómo le va a mi hija con las matemáticas. Me parece que es algo bastante difícil para ella. Traté de ayudarla anoche, pero se puso a llorar.

Well…You're right. Let's take a look at the latest CAASPP test scores. This particular test measures her understanding of math. It is taken on a computer and students' scores fall into one of four levels. She scored in level two.

¿Y eso qué quiere decir?

Here is what the levels mean. Level one means the standard is not met. When the standard is nearly met it corresponds to a level two. When the standard is met, a level three. And when the standard is exceeded, a level four. Very few students make it to a level four.

Parece que va a necesitar mucha ayuda con este tipo de examen.

I have taken the liberty of making you a copy of the *Parent Road in Supporting Your Child in*

Eighth-Grade Math. It comes in Spanish and is only six pages long. You and your daughter can go over this booklet starting with page three.

Muchísimas gracias. Así que esto le va a servir para que comience a entender mejor las matemáticas. Puede que esté mejor preparada cuando tome los próximos exámenes.

That would be terrific. The booklet is a very useful tool. You might want to use some of the suggestions that appear on page five. These have to do with ways you can make math fun at home. For example, you can choose different objects you have around the house. You can pick up a soup can or a cereal box and ask her to take measurements to determine the volume of the containers. We are now working with spheres, cones and cylinders.

Me parece muy bien. ¿Hay algo más que pueda hacer con ella?

There are additional resources here. You or your daughter can access a list of math games. I have highlighted the link so that you and your daughter can easily find it.

Excelente. Sarita me lo va a tener que encontrar porque soy muy burro para las cosas de la computadora. Lo bueno es que tenemos una en la casa y mi hija la usa a diario.

Excellent. I am glad you are willing to work with her. Should you ever have any questions, or if she needs helps understanding anything, please call me or send me a note.

Se lo agradezco mucho. Sé que Ud. la aprecia mucho y eso me da mucho gusto.

That's good to hear. We have a very good relationship. I know she is willing to learn.

☞ #3 Consecutive interpretation role play: Parent-teacher conference (grades 6–8), English-English

Good afternoon. Please come in. We were expecting you. I am Roger Garfield, Silvia's math teacher. Thank you for making it on time. We'll be assisted by our school interpreter, Ms. Sara Pascuara.

Nice to meet you. I brought Silvia to listen to what you have to tell me. I also thought Silvia would help me translate. I don't speak much English.

That won't be necessary. Silvia can sit next to you. You can sit here facing me, and Ms. Pascuara will sit right here between us.

I would like to know how my daughter is doing with math. I think it's quite difficult for her. I tried to help her last night, but she started crying.

Well... You're right. Let's take a look at the latest CAASPP test scores. This particular test measures her understanding of math. It is taken on a computer and students' scores fall into one of four levels. She scored in level two.

And what does that mean?

Here is what the levels mean. Level one means the standard is not met. When the standard is nearly met it corresponds to a level two. When the standard is met, a level three. And when the standard is exceeded, a level four. Very few students make it to a level four.

It looks like she is going to need a lot of help with this type of exam.

I have taken the liberty of making you a copy of the *Parent Road in Supporting Your Child in Eighth-Grade Math.* It comes in Spanish and is only six pages long. You and your daughter can go over this booklet starting with page three.

Thank you so much. So, is this going to help her start to understand mathematics better. She may be better prepared when she takes the next tests.

That would be terrific. The booklet is a very useful tool. You might want to use some of the suggestions that appear on page five. These have to do with ways you can make math fun at home. For example, you can choose different objects you have around the house. You can pick up a soup can or a cereal box and ask her to take measurements to determine the volume of the containers. We are now working with spheres, cones and cylinders.

Looks good to me. Is there anything else I can do with her?

There are additional resources here. You or your daughter can access a list of math games. I have highlighted the link so that you and your daughter can easily find it.

Excellent. Sarita is going to have to find it for me because I am stupid for computer stuff. The good thing is that we have one in the house and my daughter uses it daily.

Excellent. I am glad you are willing to work with her. Should you ever have any questions, or if she needs helps understanding anything, please call me or send me a note.

Thank you very much. I know you appreciate her very much and that gives me great pleasure.

That's good to hear. We have a very good relationship. I know she is willing to learn.

#4 Consecutive interpretation role play: Parent-teacher conference (grade 8 history)

Hello, Mrs. Almejo. I am Mr. Murphy, Antonio's history teacher. I hope this will be a productive and informative conference. Please at any time feel free to ask any questions.

Muy bien. María Luisa Almejo, para servirle.

Antonio is in my third-period U.S. history class. During the course of the year, we cover events that occurred between the late 1770s and the beginning of the twentieth century.

Qué bien. Sé muy poco acerca de la historia de los Estados Unidos. Dejé de ir a la escuela después del tercer grado. Pero a Antonio le interesa la historia.

Antonio will be learning a lot of information. He is cooperative, polite and usually on task. He has been issued a textbook, *America's Voice*. Students are given assignments and homework. Usually students answer questions that appear at the end of a chapter.

¿Qué días tiene tarea? ¿Me puede enseñar el libro?

Of course. It's right here. Homework is turned in about once a week, usually on Thursday or Friday. I seldom give them homework during the weekends.

¿Qué más tiene que hacer en la casa?

Each quarter, I assign a complex project. You will receive detailed information about it. Luz María, our interpreter, will be translating the information about the project.

Y… ¿En qué consiste el proyecto?

The upcoming event will be the Supreme Court nomination. All students, including Antonio, will choose a role: senator, president, member of the press, nominee. Students research pertinent information regarding the confirmation process.

Me parece muy bien. Espero que a Antonio le interese el tema.

Yes. Of course. Students get very involved. When the project is completed, they will perform a reenactment. I invite parents to attend.

Supongo que se llevará a cabo durante la hora de clase, durante el tercer período, ¿verdad?

That's right. We will also record the reenactment so that the parents who cannot attend can view it on our website.

¡Qué buena idea! ¿Algo más?

Antonio is required to take notes of our class lectures. Many notes can be copied straight from the whiteboard. Please check his notebook regularly.

Muchísimas gracias, maestro. Estaré al tanto de lo que tiene que hacer.

One more thing. You can view my syllabus on the school website. It's been translated into Spanish. Feel free to contact me if you have any questions. Thank you very much for coming. It's been a pleasure meeting you.

👉 #4 Consecutive interpretation role play: Parent-teacher conference (grade 8 history), English-English

Hello, Mrs. Almejo. I am Mr. Murphy, Antonio's history teacher. I hope this will be a productive and informative conference. Please at any time feel free to ask any questions.

Very well. María Luisa Almejo, at your service.

Antonio is in my third-period U.S. history class. During the course of the year, we cover events that occurred between the late 1770s and the beginning of the twentieth century.

Very nice. I know very little about the history of the United States. I stopped going to school after third grade. But Antonio is interested in history.

Antonio will be learning a lot of information. He is cooperative, polite and usually on task. He has been issued a textbook, *America's Voice.* Students are given assignments and homework. Usually students answer questions that appear at the end of a chapter.

What days does he have homework? Can you show me the book?

Of course. It's right here. Homework is turned in about once a week, usually on Thursday or Friday. I seldom give them homework during the weekends.

What else does he have to do at home?

Each quarter, I assign a complex project. You will receive detailed information about it. Luz María, our interpreter, will be translating the information about the project.

And... What does the project consist of?

The upcoming event will be the Supreme Court nomination. All students, including Antonio, will choose a role: senator, president, member of the press, nominee. Students research pertinent information regarding the confirmation process.

Looks good to me. I hope Antonio is interested in the subject.

Yes. Of course. Students get very involved. When the project is completed, they will perform a reenactment. I invite parents to attend.

I guess it will take place during class time, during the third period, right?

That's right. We will also record the reenactment so that the parents who cannot attend can view it on our website.

What a good idea! Anything else?

Antonio is required to take notes of our class lectures. Many notes can be copied straight from the whiteboard. Please check his notebook regularly.

Thank you very much, teacher. I will be aware of what he has to do.

One more thing. You can view my syllabus on the school website. It's been translated into Spanish. Feel free to contact me if you have any questions. Thank you very much for coming. It's been a pleasure meeting you.

Chapter 12 — Introduction to Educational Interpreting and Translation

☛ #5 Consecutive interpretation role play: SST meeting

Mrs. Bynoe: Please, come in. Have a seat. You must be Mrs. Soria.

Sí, señora. Soy la mamá de Berta. Me vine directamente del trabajo.

Mrs. Bynoe: I'm Linda Bynoe, Berta's teacher. Mr. Robbins, the psychologist; Miss Denise Black, our speech and language specialist; Mrs. Meg Tobias, our resource specialist; Miss Sonia Lee, our bilingual specialist and Mr. Carl Ferguson, our assistant principal.

Mucho gusto. Se trata de una reunión muy formal, ¿verdad?

Mr. Ferguson: That's right. We're all here to make sure that Berta's needs are met. As a Chapter One school, we must ensure that all children have a fair and equal opportunity to obtain a high quality education.

¿Cuáles son los problemas de mi hija? ¿No se ha portado bien?

Mrs. Bynoe: She is a very well-behaved student, although rather shy. We're here to make sure she receives the type of education and interventions she needs in order to succeed.

Es cierto. Es algo tímida, pero muy obediente. En casa me hace caso y me ayuda.

Mrs. Bynoe: I am concerned about her reading. She is now in a two-dash-seven level reading group. Her reading ability should be at least a three-dash-seven. I believe she can improve her reading with additional help. In order to provide her with this help, we will need to assess her skills.

Entiendo. Me parece muy bien.

Mrs. Bynoe: Miss Black, would you like to explain what tests she will be administering?

Miss Black: It will be the PPVT and the CELF.

Uds. Me van a tener que explicar eso. ¿Cuándo piensan examinarla?

Miss Black: Of course. We hope to start in a week. The PPVT is the Peabody Picture Vocabulary Test, which measures her vocabulary comprehension. With the CELF, the Clinical Evaluation of Language Fundamentals, she responds to commands and also gives oral responses to a variety of stimuli. Once we complete the testing, we will schedule a meeting to go over the results with you.

Berta habla dos idiomas, inglés y español. ¿Eso le va a perjudicar?

Ms. Lee: Not at all. She scored a five on the WIDA ACCESS when she enrolled in school. This means that her English is well developed. She also knows Spanish and should continue to use it at home.

Muy bien. ¿Qué sugieren que yo haga con ella? Es muy callada. Habla poco.

Mrs. Tobias: Please encourage her to read books she enjoys. Rather than watching TV, give her a children's book to read. She can read it to you or read it silently. She checks out books from our library every week. Have her show you the books she brings home.

Me parece una buena idea. Muchas gracias. Espero que le puedan ayudar.

👉 #5 Consecutive interpretation role play: SST meeting, English-English

Mrs. Bynoe: Please, come in. Have a seat. You must be Mrs. Soria.

Yes, ma'am. I'm Berta's mom. I came straight from work.

Mrs. Bynoe: I'm Linda Bynoe, Berta's teacher. Mr. Robbins, the psychologist; Miss Denise Black, our speech and language specialist; Mrs. Meg Tobias, our resource specialist; Ms. Sonia Lee, our bilingual specialist and Mr. Carl Ferguson, our assistant principal.

Nice to meet you. This is about a very formal meeting, right?

Mr. Ferguson: That's right. We're all here to make sure that Berta's needs are met. As a Chapter One school, we must ensure that all children have a fair and equal opportunity to obtain a high quality education.

What are the issues with my daughter? Has she misbehaved?

Mrs. Bynoe: She is a very well-behaved student, although rather shy. We're here to make sure she receives the type of education and interventions she needs in order to succeed.

It's true. She is somewhat shy, but very obedient. At home she listens to me and helps me.

Mrs. Bynoe: I am concerned about her reading. She is now in a two-dash-seven level reading group. Her reading ability should be at least a three-dash-seven. I believe she can improve her reading with additional help. In order to provide her with this help, we will need to assess her skills.

I understand. Sounds good to me.

Mrs. Bynoe: Miss Black, would you like to explain what tests she will be administering?

Miss Black: It will be the PPVT and the CELF.

You are going to have to explain that to me. When do you think you will evaluate her?

Miss Black: Of course. We hope to start in a week. The PPVT is the Peabody Picture Vocabulary Test, which measures her vocabulary comprehension. With the CELF, the Clinical Evaluation of Language Fundamentals, she responds to commands and also gives oral responses to a variety of stimuli. Once we complete the testing, we will schedule a meeting to go over the results with you.

Berta speaks two languages, English and Spanish. Is that going to be detrimental?

Ms. Lee: Not at all. She scored a five on the WIDA ACCESS when she enrolled in school. This means that her English is well developed. She also knows Spanish and should continue to use it at home.

Very well. What do you suggest I do with her? She is very quiet. She speaks a little.

Mrs. Tobias: Please encourage her to read books she enjoys. Rather than watching TV, give her a children's book to read. She can read it to you or read it silently. She checks out books from our library every week. Have her show you the books she brings home.

I think that's a good idea. Thank you so much. I hope they are able to help her.

#6 Consecutive interpretation role play: Annual IEP meeting

Good morning, Mr. García. So good that you could join us so early this morning.

I am Vanessa Chapman, your student's special education specialist. We have already spoken a few times. Here are the members of our team. Jody Beckman, our speech pathologist; Mr. Robert Eastman, our psychologist; Ms. Mary Winning, your son's teacher and May Stanton, our principal.

Mucho gusto. Sé que estamos aquí para hablar de mi hijo y de unos exámenes.

Miss Chapman: That's right. As you recall, we met before to inform you that we would be assessing your son, Ivan, in all educational areas. I have administered two tests: the Kaufman Test of Educational Achievement and the informal Basic Reading Inventory.

¿Cuándo le administraron los exámenes? Supongo que me van a explicar los resultados.

Miss Chapman: Certainly. He completed the KTEA-3 on October 14. You agreed to the testing a month ago. Unfortunately, he scored below grade level in some areas. His scores were below average in letter-word recognition and in reading comprehension.

Así que tiene problemas con la lectura. Ya lo había notado cuando trataba de leerles un cuento a sus hermanos.

Miss Chapman: Right. And the other exams show deficiencies in his phonological abilities—the relationship between graphemes and phonemes.

¿Me podría explicar todo eso?

Miss Chapman: Certainly. This means that when Ivan hears a word, such as grow, hit, glad or pony, he misspells these words when he writes them. He does not process what he hears well enough to find a match to the sounds he hears, sounds that represent words and sentences. As a result, he is reading and writing below grade level.

Ay. ¿Qué se puede hacer?

Ms. Winning: We are proposing that he take part in a reading and language intervention program twice weekly, if you agree.

Claro que sí. ¿Cuánto tiempo va a estar participando en ese programa?

Miss Chapman: We can start next week. I can see him for forty minutes every Tuesday and Thursday afternoon. I will focus first on his receptive auditory skills. We can start with high frequency words and move into low frequency words. We will use the Read 180 program. We will also choose interesting stories for him to read. I will be sending some of these home. At the end of this school year, we will take a look at his progress.

Me parece muy bien.

Mr. Eastman: He will be receiving eighty minutes of pull-out services weekly. You will be signing a consent form indicating that you agree with this individualized education program.

Estoy de acuerdo. Sé que Uds. le van a poder ayudar.

☛ #6 Consecutive interpretation role play: Annual IEP meeting, English-English

Good morning, Mr. Garcia. So good that you could join us so early this morning.

I am Vanessa Chapman, your student's special education specialist. We have already spoken a few times. Here are the members of our team. Jody Beckman, our speech pathologist; Mr. Robert Eastman, our psychologist; Ms. Mary Winning, your son's teacher and May Stanton, our principal.

Nice to meet you. I know we're here to talk about my son and some exams.

Miss Chapman: That's right. As you recall, we met before to inform you that we would be assessing your son, Ivan, in all educational areas. I have administered two tests: the Kaufman Test of Educational Achievement and the informal Basic Reading Inventory.

When was he given the tests? I am guessing they will explain the results to me.

Miss Chapman: Certainly. He completed the KTEA-3 on October 14. You agreed to the testing a month ago. Unfortunately, he scored below grade level in some areas. His scores were below average in letter-word recognition and in reading comprehension.

So he has trouble reading. I had already noticed it when he tried to read a story to his siblings.

Miss Chapman: Right. And the other exams show deficiencies in his phonological abilities—the relationship between graphemes and phonemes.

Could you explain all that to me?

Miss Chapman: Certainly. This means that when Ivan hears a word, such as grow, hit, glad or pony, he misspells these words when he writes them. He does not process what he hears well enough to find a match to the sounds he hears, sounds that represent words and sentences. As a result, he is reading and writing below grade level.

Jeez. What can be done?

Ms. Winning: We are proposing that he take part in a reading and language intervention program twice weekly, if you agree.

Of course. How long will he be participating in that program?

Miss Chapman: We can start next week. I can see him for forty minutes every Tuesday and Thursday afternoon. I will focus first on his receptive auditory skills. We can start with high frequency words and move into low frequency words. We will use the Read 180 program. We will also choose interesting stories for him to read. I will be sending some of these home. At the end of this school year, we will take a look at his progress.

I think it's great.

Mr. Eastman: He will be receiving eighty minutes of pull-out services weekly. You will be signing a consent form indicating that you agree with this individualized education program.

I agree. I know you will be able to help him.

#7 Consecutive role play: Transitioning from middle school to high school

Participants: case manager, principal, parent (Mrs. Ortega), student (Robert), general education teacher, high school case manager

Case Manager: Welcome to the meeting. We are here to determine the steps that we will take in transitioning Robert into high school.

Case Manager: Good morning, Mrs. Ortega. First of all, let us go over the procedural safeguards that we have in place for your son, Robert. As you know, you have the right to participate in all meetings and to examine all education records concerning your son. You also have the right to obtain an independent educational evaluation of your son.

Mrs. Ortega: *Es cierto. Ud. me había explicado esto en otra ocasión.*

Case Manager: I would like to share with you his current reading and math levels. He is now reading at a high fifth-grade level, instead of the eighth-grade level. His reading comprehension is at 70 percent.

Mrs. Ortega: *Me he dado cuenta de que todavía lee muy despacio.*

Case Manager: Right. In the area of math, he is still working on the multiplication tables and doing math computations in the thousands. He is, however, struggling in solving equations with one unknown.

Mrs. Ortega: *¿Se va a poder graduar teniendo estas dificultades?*

Principal: This is an issue that we have to address. He can either receive a diploma or a certificate of completion. Based on his skills, it seems appropriate to recommend the certificate of completion rather than a graduation certificate.

Mrs. Ortega: *Está bien. Uds. son los expertos. Con tal que pueda continuar con su programa especializado en la "high school."*

Case Manager: I believe that he would benefit if he is placed in special education courses in math and reading, because these are the areas where he struggles the most.

Mrs. Ortega: *También se juntará con los muchachos de las clases regulares, ¿verdad?*

General Education Teacher: He can certainly participate with the general population in certain courses. He could take general education U.S. history and science and also PE.

Mrs. Ortega: *Me parece muy bien que se junte con más muchachos de su edad.*

Case Manager: Robert is a very hard-working student and asks for help when he needs it.

High School Case Manager: I look forward to helping Robert next year and making sure he receives the support he needs in the classroom.

Mrs. Ortega: *Muchas gracias a todos.*

Case Manager: Mrs. Ortega, once again you will need to sign your consent in order to proceed with this plan.

#7 Consecutive role play: Transitioning from middle school to high school, English-English

Participants: case manager, principal, parent (Mrs. Ortega), student (Robert), general education teacher, high school case manager

Case Manager: Welcome to the meeting. We are here to determine the steps that we will take in transitioning Robert into high school.

Case Manager: Good morning, Mrs. Ortega. First of all, let us go over the procedural safeguards that we have in place for your son, Robert. As you know, you have the right to participate in all meetings and to examine all education records concerning your son. You also have the right to obtain an independent educational evaluation of your son.

Mrs. Ortega: *That's right. You had explained this to me on another occasion.*

Case Manager: I would like to share with you his current reading and math levels. He is now reading at a high fifth-grade level, instead of the eighth-grade level. His reading comprehension is at 70 percent.

Mrs. Ortega: *I have noticed that he still reads very slowly.*

Case Manager: Right. In the area of math, he is still working on the multiplication tables and doing math computations in the thousands. He is, however, struggling in solving equations with one unknown.

Mrs. Ortega: *Will he be able to graduate having these difficulties?*

Principal: This is an issue that we have to address. He can either receive a diploma or a certificate of completion. Based on his skills, it seems appropriate to recommend the certificate of completion rather than a graduation certificate.

Mrs. Ortega: *Okay. You are the experts. As long as he can continue with his specialized program in high school.*

Case Manager: I believe that he would benefit if he is placed in special education courses in math and reading, because these are the areas where he struggles the most.

Mrs. Ortega: *He will also join the kids from the regular classes, right?*

General Education Teacher: He can certainly participate with the general population in certain courses. He could take general education U.S. history and science and also PE.

Mrs. Ortega: *I think it's great that he's getting together with more kids his age.*

Case Manager: Robert is a very hard-working student and asks for help when he needs it.

High School Case Manager: I look forward to helping Robert next year and making sure he receives the support he needs in the classroom.

Mrs. Ortega: *Thank you all very much.*

Case Manager: Mrs. Ortega, once again you will need to sign your consent in order to proceed with this plan.

#8 Consecutive role play: Parent-teacher conference based on #1 Sight translation role play: Report card

This is your opportunity to create your own dialogue between a teacher and a parent.

Using #1 Sight translation role play: Report card (see page 206), write out the verbal exchange in two languages that could potentially take place between the two people.

Teacher:

Parent:

Teacher:

Parent:

Scenarios similar to these present themselves with great frequency at public schools in all states where there are children with parents who don't yet understand or speak the English language. It is the duty of the school to provide these interpreting and translation services. As a result, English learner parents will be better able to understand classroom expectations and school procedures. Furthermore, when parents know that there are interpreters and translators available to assist with language needs, they will be more willing to participate in school matters.

Some of the more common expressions that appear on report cards are also utilized during parent-teacher conferences. Some also appear in drop-down menus on a website for the teacher to select as needed.

Commonly Used Phrases in English and Spanish:

The student is learning.	Está aprendiendo.
The student is responsible.	Es responsable.
The student completes his/her work.	Completa su trabajo.
The student is not a problem.	No causa ningún problema.
The student finishes his/her work on time.	Completa su trabajo a tiempo.
The student does his/her work well.	Hace bien su trabajo.
The student works independently.	Trabaja independientemente.
The student needs (a lot of) help.	Necesita (mucha) ayuda.
The student gets along well with others.	Se lleva bien con los demás.
The student fights with other children.	Se pelea con otros niños.
The student needs to play with other children.	Necesita jugar con otros niños.
The student prefers to play alone.	Prefiere jugar solo/a.
The student needs attention to work well.	Necesita atención para trabajar bien.
The student needs supervision.	Necesita que lo vigilen.
The student pays attention in class.	Presta atención en clase.
The student is careless.	Es descuidado/a.
The student has problems with…	Tiene problemas con…
The student behaves very well.	Se porta muy bien.

The student follows directions.	Sigue las instrucciones.
The student has difficulties with directions.	Las instrucciones le resultan difíciles.
The student is quiet.	Es callado/a.
The student needs to improve.	Necesita mejorar.
The student is cooperative.	Coopera.
The student has good work habits.	Tiene buenos hábitos de trabajo.
The student is well organized.	Está bien organizado.
The student asks for help.	Pide ayuda.
The student reads below (at, above) grade level.	Lee por debajo (a la par, por encima) del nivel del grado.
The student is highly motivated.	Muestra mucha motivación.
The student uses time well.	Emplea bien el tiempo.
He//she is obedient.	Es obediente.
The student tries hard to learn.	Se empeña mucho en aprender.
The student works well.	Trabaja bien.
The student needs to study more.	Necesita estudiar más.
The student has trouble concentrating.	Le cuesta concentrarse.
The student likes to help in class.	Le gusta ayudar en clase.
The student is interested in math (art).	Le interesan las matemáticas, el arte.
The student takes part in class activities.	Participa en las actividades de clase.
The student helps other children.	Ayuda a otros niños.
The student listens when others speak.	Escucha cuando otros hablan.
The student is showing improvement.	Está mejorando.
The student comes to class on time.	Llega a tiempo a clase.
The student sometimes arrives late.	A veces llega tarde.
The student has good attendance.	Su asistencia es buena.
The student needs to bring a note to school after being absent.	Necesita traer una nota a la escuela después de ausentarse.
The student needs to learn the multiplication tables.	Necesita aprender las tablas de multiplicar.
The student can add and subtract.	Sabe sumar y multiplicar.
The student is learning to divide.	Está aprendiendo a divider.
The student is learning to read.	Está aprendiendo a leer.
The student shows an interest in reading.	Demuestra interés en leer.
The student has difficulties with comprehension.	Tiene problemas con la comprensión.
The student reads with ease.	Lee fácilmente.
The student tries to finish on time.	Se esfuerza en terminar a tiempo.

Practice: Sight translation

For each sight translation exercise, first preview the material while paying close attention to any problematic terminology. The first time you sight translate the texts, start by skimming over the material and then deliver your sight translation without looking up any words. The second time you practice, note on a separate sheet of paper the problematic expressions or words. Look up two or three of these, but no more. You'll want to begin your rendition of the text without spending an unrealistic amount of time preparing for this task.

☛ #1 Sight translation role play: Report card

School: The Sky Is the Limit

Principal:_____

Location: 1000 Skyheaven Place, Merryland

Teacher:_____

Grade 4: Report Card

Date of Report:_____

Performance Levels for Habits of Mind

> C: Consistently U: Usually S: Sometimes R: Rarely
>
> X: Not covered this trimester

Performance Levels for Academic Standards

> Advanced (4): Students at this level demonstrate a comprehensive, in-depth understanding of rigorous subject matter and provide sophisticated solutions to complex problems.
>
> Proficient (3): Students at this level demonstrate a solid understanding of challenging subject.
>
> Progressing but Needs Improvement (2): Students at this level demonstrate a partial understanding of subject matter and solve some simple problems.
>
> Warning (1): Students at this level demonstrate a minimal understanding of subject matter and are unable to solve simple problems.

T1: Trimester 1; T2: Trimester 2; T3: Trimester 3

	T1	T2	T3
Absences			
Tardies			

Habits of Mind: Social Skills	T1	T2	T3
Shows self-control and makes responsible choices.	U		
Follows instructions; listens attentively.	U		
Respects self, others and community.	C		
Puts forth best effort.	C		
Turns in assignments on time.	U		
Engages in class discussions and activities.	U		

English / Language Arts	T1	T2	T3
Reads at grade level.	3		
Comprehends text at his/her level.	3		
Writes with focus and organization.	3		
Uses standard English conventions.	3		
Determines important aspects of text.	4		

Mathematics	T1	T2	T3
Uses the four operations with whole numbers to solve problems.	3		
Gains familiarity with factors and multiples.	3		
Uses place values and properties of operations to perform arithmetic.	3		
Understands decimal notation for fractions.	2		
Builds fractions by using understanding of operations in whole numbers.	2		
Solves problems involving measurement and conversion.	3		
Geometric measurement: Understands concepts of angle and angle measurement.	4		
Draws and identifies lines and angles; classifies shapes by their lines and angles.	3		

Social Studies	T1	T2	T3
Demonstrates mapping skills.	3		
Identifies the states within the United States.	3		
Describes the geography, climate, economy and immigrant influences in the United States.	3		
Identifies rights and responsibilities of U.S. citizens.	2		

Science	T1	T2	T3
Uses the skills of inquiry effectively.	3		
Understands the properties of earth materials.	3	X	X
Solves problems using simple and complex machines.	X		X
Recognizes the properties of electricity and magnetism.	X	X	
Identifies various types of circuits.	X	X	

Visual Arts	T1	T2	T3
Demonstrates an understanding of art concepts.	4		
Demonstrates skillful use of art materials.	4		

Physical Education			
Participates in individual and group activities.	3		
Meets physical fitness benchmarks.	2		

☞ #2 Sight translation role play: Consent form

Dear Parent or Guardian,

Your child will be asked to take a survey in class. This survey is anonymous.

It includes questions about drugs, alcohol and tobacco issues. Your child's participation in the survey is strictly voluntary. We are asking that you give permission for your child to participate in the survey so that his or their opinion and knowledge can be used to make improvements in our school environment. You also have the option of denying our request.

Neither the name of your child nor any other identifying information about your child will be disclosed, except for the name of the school.

If you have questions, please contact our district's testing coordinator, Elisa Magallanes at Vista Esperanza School District, phone number 877-100-0000. (emagallanes@vistaesperanza.com).

Should you want to read the survey, you may do so at our school office or on our district's website under the testing tab.

Sincerely,

Mr. Will Summerville

School Principal

____I hereby give permission for my child to take the aforementioned survey.

____I do not give permission for my child to take the aforementioned survey.

_____   _____

Your name   Date

_____

Signature

#3 Sight translation role play: Birth certificate

Estado de Guanajuato
Dirección General del Registro Civil
Nacimiento

En nombre del Estado Libre y Soberano de Guanajuato, certifico ser cierto que en el

Libro 4 de nacimientos que existe en el archivo de la oficialía del registro civil No 01

San Felipe del Municipio de San Felipe se encuentra asentada el acta No. 00896 fechada el 6 de febrero de 2015 del Tenor siguiente:

Fecha Registro: 6 de febrero de 2015

Lugar de Registro: San Felipe

Datos del registrado

Nombre: Rodrigo Manuel Larrañaga Martinez
Fecha de nacimiento: 25 de octubre de 2014
Lugar de Nacimiento: Guanajuato, Guanajuato, México
Nacionalidad: Mexicana   Registrado: vivo Sexo: masculino Compareció: ambos

Datos de los padres

Nombre padre: Pedro Mario Larrañaga Salazar
Nacionalidad: Mexicana   Edad padre: 28
Nombre madre: Sandra Mirta Martinez   Edad madre: 25
Nacionalidad: Mexicana

Datos de los abuelos

Nombre abuelo paterno: Rodrigo Manuel Larrañaga Pérez
Nacionalidad: Mexicana
Nombre abuela paterna: María Josefina Salazar Montes
Nacionalidad: Mexicana
Nombre abuelo materno: Francisco José Martínez Sánchez
Nacionalidad: Mexicana

Se extiene la presente conforme a lo dispuesto por el decreto gubernativo número 9 de fecha 4 de junio de 1998 y el artículo 1 fracción V del reglamento interior del registro civil vigente en el estado. Guanajuato, Guanajuato. 10 de marzo de 2014.

[Sello de la oficina]

#4 Sight translation role play: Classroom rules

For elementary schools

1. Be on time at the beginning of the day and after lunch or recess.
2. Come prepared with supplies and completed homework.
3. Be kind, polite and courteous to others.
4. Keep your hands and feet to yourself.
5. Treat your classmates, teachers and property with respect.
6. Listen to the teacher and classmates, and follow the teacher's instructions.
7. Work hard, and always do your best.
8. Be safe.
9. Raise your hand when you would like to speak in class or if you need to leave the classroom for any reason (e.g., going to the restroom, visiting the nurse, etc.).
10. Obey all school rules.

For high schools

1. Arrive on time.
2. Raise your hand before speaking.
3. Listen to others and participate in class discussions.
4. Do not distract your classmates.
5. Stay on task.
6. Do your assignments without getting sidetracked.
7. Bring classroom materials and have them ready.
8. Listen carefully to your teacher's instructions.

#5 Sight translation role play: Special education

Slingerland Screening Report Form A

Student _____Camilo Vargas_____

Parent _____Ignacio Vargas and María Elena Vargas_____

Date of screening _____5/12/21_____

Date of birth _____11/12/2013_____ C.A. _____7 years 6 months_____

Current grade _____1st_____

Handedness _____Right handed_____

Examiner _____Ralph Stacey_____

Chapter 12 — Introduction to Educational Interpreting and Translation

Test I Score ____29/30____ SC ____1____

Student is required to copy a paragraph from a chart. Tests ability to copy from a distance. This subset involves visual perception associated with kinesthetic motor response.

A. Reading

Camilo read the paragraph fluently and with no difficulties.

B. Copying

Camilo copied in print. Letter size discrimination, letter formation and spacing were good. He omitted one period in one sentence. Shorter words (had, two, big, fat, to, and) were copied as wholes, otherwise Camilo copied in two letter sequences.

Test II Score ____10/10____ SC ____---____

Student is required to copy a list of 10 words. Tests near-point copying and tracking abilities.

Camilo had problems in correctly spacing words in phrases but made no errors otherwise.

Score = # correct/total # possible   SC = self-corrections

Test III Score ____10/10____ SC____

Student is shown words or letter or number sequences on cards for 10 seconds each. After a brief pause, student attempts to find what was seen on the stimulus card among several similar possibilities. Tests short-term memory for words, letters and numbers.

Camilo had no difficulties on this subtest.

Test IV Score ____8/8____ SC____

Student is required to match a stimulus word with one of four visually confusing alternatives. Tests visual discrimination.

Camilo had no difficulties with this subtest.

Test V Score ____9/12____ SC____

Testing procedures are similar to Test III except this time the student is required to draw or write what was seen on the stimulus card. Tests short-term visual memory for letters, words, numbers and geometric designs associated with kinesthetic-motor response.

Camilo copied lowercase "crj" instead of the capital "CRJ." He inserted an "a" in the letter sequence "hgd" copying "hagd." In copying geometric designs, Camilo copied a right triangle instead of an isosceles triangle.

Test VI Score ____14/16____ SC ____3____

Student is required to write dictated letter sequences, words, numbers and word sequences following a brief pause. Tests short-term auditory memory and kinesthetic-motor response.

Camilo self-corrected a "p" for the "q" confusion and a poor formation of a "d." He substituted "ecg" for "bcg" (auditory discrimination). In the numeral sequences, Camilo inserted a "0" in the "326," writing "3206." Camilo made no errors in the dictated phrases. He did use a capital "G" in the phrase "to go," which was against instruction.

Test VII Score____13/16____ SC____

Student is required to write what makes beginning and ending sound in individually dictated one-syllable words. Tests student's ability to associate sounds with symbols.

Camilo had no difficulty isolating initial sounds of one syllable words for a written response. He did use capitals ("D") against instruction. He continued to isolate the initial sound of the stimulus word instead of the final sound on the final eight items of the subtest.

Test VIII Score____11/12____ SC____

Student is required to circle dictated words, letter sequences and numbers after a brief pause. Tests auditory memory associated with visual patterns.

Camilo chose the transposed letters "gril" for "girl."

Camilo was diligent and cooperative during the testing. He did require several repeats of oral instructions.

Screening Conclusions

Camilo demonstrates relative auditory processing strength and minimal visual perceptual deficits.

Screening Discussion Date:

Present:

Recommendations

    1. Summer school: manuscript level utilizing an integrated simultaneous, multisensory approach within a structured phonics program. Such a summer program would strengthen existing skills and give Camilo sequential strategies for encoding and decoding.

    2. Re-evaluation after summer school to determine proper fall program placement and tutoring assistance.

Names and Signatures

Date

Classroom teacher _____   _____

Speech and language specialist_____   _____

Resource specialist teacher _____   _____

Parent _____   _____

☞ #6 Sight translation role play: Exam instructions

May I please have your attention. I will be reading you some important information.

- No cell phones, electronic devices of any kind or personal items are permitted in the testing room. Anyone caught with these items will be asked to immediately place them on the test proctor's desk for the duration of the exam.
- Write your first and last name on the top portion of your form. Fill the bubbles on your Quick Score Answer Form to correspond with your first name and last name. Please make sure that your name is spelled correctly on the top of your Quick Score Answer Form.
- Make only 75 marks on your Quick Score Answer Form, not including the bubbles that correspond to your first and last names.
- Mark your Quick Score Answer Form for items 1 through 75 by marking either A, B, C or D.
- Make sure your marks are clear and dark and stay within the bubble.
- Use a number two pencil.
- Double-check that the test version number printed on the top of your Quick Score Answer Form matches the Written Test version number printed on your Written Test booklet.
- Raise your hand and tell your Written Test proctor if these version numbers do not match.
- Do not make any marks in your Written Test booklet. If you need to write anything down, please use the scratch paper that has been provided.
- If you need a calculator, quietly approach the test proctor and one will be provided for you.
- You will have a maximum of ninety minutes to complete the Written Test.
- You will be informed when there are fifteen minutes remaining. When you are finished with the Written Test, double-check the marks you have made on your Quick Score Answer Form and then quietly bring your test booklet, scratch paper, calculator and Quick Score Answer Form to the proctor.

Do you have any questions?

Good luck.

☞ #7 Sight translation role play: Planning and placement cover sheet for IEP

Planning and Placement Team Cover Page

Student: _____ DOB: _____ District: _____ Meeting Date: _____
Last Name, First Name _____ MM/DD/YYYY _____

Current Enrolled School:_____ Age:_____ Current Grade:_____

H.S. Credits:_____ Grade Next Yr:_____ Gender: Female___ Male___

Current Home School:_____ Next Year:_____ Home School Next Year:_____ SASID
#:_____ Case Manager:_____ Yes___ No___ NA___

Student Address: _____ Student Instructional Lang.: English _____

Other: _____ (specify) _____ Parent/Guardian (Name): _____ Home Dominant

Lang.: English _____ Other: (specify) _____ Parent/Guardian (Address): _____

Student Mobile Phone: _____

Parent Home Phone: _____ Surrogate Name: _____

Parent Mobile Phone: _____ Surrogate Address: _____

Most Recent Evaluation Date: _____

Next Re-evaluation Date: _____

Most Recent Annual Review Date: _____ Next Annual Review Date: _____

Reason for Meeting: _____ Review Referral _____ Plan Eval/Reeval _____ Review Eval/Reeval _____ Determine Eligibility _____ Determine Continuing Eligibility _____ Develop IEP _____ Review or Revise IEP _____ Conduct Annual Review _____ Transition Planning _____ Determination _____ Other (specify)

Primary Disability: ___ Autism ___ Emotional Disturbance ___ Multiple Disabilities ___ Orthopedic Impairment ___ Speech or Language Impaired ___ Other Health Impairment ___ Deaf ___ Blindness ___ Hearing Impairment (Deaf or Hard of Hearing) ___ Specific Learning Disabilities ___ Traumatic Brain Injury ___ OHI ___ ADHD ___ Developmental Delay (ages 3–5 only) ___ Intellectual Disability ___ Specific Learning Disabilities/Dyslexia ___ Visual Impairment ___ To be determined

The next projected PPT meeting date is: _____

- Eligible as a student in need of special education. (The child is evaluated as having a disability, and needs special education and related services.) ___ Yes ___ No
- Is this an amendment to a current IEP? ___ Yes ___ No

If Yes, what is the date of the IEP being amended? _____

Team members present (required): _____

☛ #8 Sight translation role play: Guardianship

TEMPORARY GUARDIANSHIP AGREEMENT

I, _____, the biological parent of the following minor children,

(Provide full names and dates of birth) _____

do hereby appoint and give temporary custody to (name and relationship to the children)

_____

This custody agreement shall take effect on _____

and will remain in full force and effect for one year or until such time that I wish to amend or revoke this affidavit. At that time I will provide a copy of the amended affidavit to the parties signing this agreement.

I currently reside at _____

The aforementioned guardians currently reside at

_____. Their telephone number is_____

I further give permission for _____to care for my

children in their home and to apply for, consent to, or otherwise obtain any medical

treatment, economical, educational, social or other services that the children may require.

_____   _____
Parent's signature   Date

_____   _____
Guardian's signature   Date

The parties signing the agreement appeared before me and provided satisfactory evidence of identification, and swore under penalty of perjury that the foregoing statements are true. Subscribed and sworn before the undersigned authority on_____

                                                                                                    Date

My commission expires _____

                                                                                                     [Seal]

Notary Public

Practice: Simultaneous interpretation

The following simultaneous role play texts are to be used for practice. These can be utilized in two ways. First, you can work with a partner who reads the material while you interpret. If that is not possible, you or someone else can record these texts. Afterward, you can listen to the recording as you interpret from the source language into the target language. Using another device, record your rendition into the target language. If you are not satisfied with your first rendition, repeat the exercise.

Keep in mind the speed of your recording. You may need to keep it at about 100 to 120 words per minute at first. Gradually increase your speed and rerecord the material until it reaches about 200 words per minute. If listening to a recording, you may want to wear a headset in order to maximize your concentration and to drown out distracting noises.

☛ #1 Simultaneous interpretation role play: Student success team meeting

Good afternoon, everyone. We're here to go over the results of the testing and the interventions that have taken place with Rafuelo Segura. But first we need to introduce ourselves. I am Minarita Buenaventura, the school vice principal.

My name is J.T., a special education coordinator and notetaker.

You know me. I am T.S., Rafuelo's classroom teacher.

I am the school psychologist, C.R.

I am the math interventionist. My name is R.D.

I am P.H., the Spanish interpreter.

Parent: Soy la mamá de Rafuelo, Margarita Lopez Segura.

P.H.: I am Rafuelo's mom, Margarita Lopez Segura

R.D.: I'd like to start out by summarizing the conversation that we had at our referral meeting last year. At that meeting, there was a concern raised regarding a disability. That meeting's summary is in your packet. So at the referral meeting we did talk about Rafuelo's areas of challenges and at that point his mom and the classroom teacher were concerned about how he was performing in fourth grade. He was having challenges in the winter and the spring in math and he began receiving some interventions. Now that he is in the fifth grade, we are seeing some of the same challenges, but to a lesser degree. At the meeting, we talked about the scores and looked at the assessments, and we looked at the intervention data. We felt that he was receiving comprehensive classroom instruction and that he had also been receiving at least two periods of sufficient intensive intervention in math. Despite this, the gap between his peers was not closing fast enough in the area of math. We felt that there might be a disability that was impacting his ability to succeed. We determined that a comprehensive evaluation would give us the information that we needed and we have asked members of this team to share and provide additional information about Rafuelo's math skills. We also needed to look at his achievement scores, particularly in math.

C.R.: Back in the winter of last year, in the fourth grade, I was informed that he was beginning to struggle in the area of math and wasn't quite where his peers were. That is when we started the interventions and he began receiving extra work. In the winter.

T.S.: He received extra math work on the classroom computer when he returned to school in the fifth grade. I was pleased to see that he was continuing to work with our math specialist, and I noticed that there was improvement in some areas of math.

R.D.: We started seeing him again in the fall and realized that he had lost a lot of ground during the summer. We started him on a daily program focusing on number problems. His progress was slow but steady. His memory skills have improved, and he has now memorized the times tables. We have looked at his growth during the interventions and have seen a little gain in each area, though he is still slightly below the rest of the fifth graders.

M.B.: His math progress is based on his general education math instruction, plus the interventions. The resources we use are aligned with the common core standards. His scores show that he is below proficient with scores of 50 percent, 60 percent and 53 percent. These correspond to math facts, calculation skills and applied problems.

J.T.: It seem to me that continued interventions would be beneficial.

M.B.: I agree. We now need to schedule our next meeting in order to continue monitoring his progress. Mrs. Segura, do you have any questions for us?

#2 Simultaneous interpretation role play: District board meeting

OK. It looks like everyone is here. Let's get started.

One, two, three. I pledge allegiance to the flag of the United States of America, and to the republic for which it stands, one nation under God, indivisible, with liberty and justice for all.

Do we hear a motion to approve the agenda? So moved. Moved by Guido de la Selva and seconded by Jovanna Hladik.

Any discussion? No. Anyone opposed? Motion is passed.

We will now move to the agenda. We have a lengthy presentation tonight and we have a special meeting with the board later to go over the results of the attendance data in depth. I will have Dr. Cuevas introduce what the data consists of and then have our director of research and assessment, Dr. Benitez, go through the slides that demonstrate the comparative data for attendance from September of this year to September of the year before, as well as semester one grades for comparison. And then we will allow principals who are here to ask questions about those two points of data. Later, I will ask the board to have a consensus vote to go over the data at an agreed on day and time.

At this time I will turn the meeting over to Dr. Cuevas.

Mr. Chair, thank you. I would like to remind everyone that although we are not going to see all the data tonight, the data that we will be seeing consists only of numbers on the screen. This quantitative data represents only one dimension of the complete picture of the students' experience. These numbers provide some insight about the 16,000-plus students in our district as well as staff who have been working very hard despite the life-altering experience that took place last March. Many have suffered loss, the loss of a loved one, the loss of their homes, their income security, and many of our students have also had added responsibilities, such as taking care of their younger siblings. And in so doing they have neglected their own studies, taking on jobs to support their families. While we continue to look at data and monitor student learning we have also been focusing on the well-being of these students. So tonight, as Dr. Marcus Benitez presents the data, please know that teachers continue to teach with rigor, and they continue to have high expectations of their students. They are also being patient and flexible. Our students are doing their very best under their new circumstances and their individual situations. So when we start looking at the numbers, think of the faces of our students. Thank you. And right now I would like to introduce to you Dr. Marcus Benitez. who will be focusing on these two data points: attendance and grades. Dr. Benitez, are you ready?

Good evening. I'd like to share my screen. Bear with me. I am looking forward to reviewing the data in greater depth with the board. Just a reminder as to where we are at this time. The staff has been focusing on teaching the standards, and this Friday we will be releasing the figures on our dashboard.

☛ #3 Simultaneous interpretation role play: District board meeting

Let us stand. One, two, three. I pledge allegiance to the United States of America and to the republic for which it stands, one nation under God, with liberty and justice for all.

Do we need a motion to approve the agenda?

So moved by Justin Campos and seconded by Mirtha Royce Any discussion? All approve? Say aye. Aye.

Anyone opposed? Motion is carried.

The board will now recognize our speaker, Rosina Lordaz Piñedo.

Buenos días, miembros de la mesa directiva del distrito escolar de Paz, presidente y superintendente Elogio Shukla. Mi nombre es Rosina Lordaz Piñedo. Soy madre de dos niños que asisten a la escuela A y a la escuela D. También soy miembro del Comité de Padres Unidos y del DELAC. Nosotros nos hemos visto en otras ocasiones. Quiero agradecerles por estar recibiendo comentarios públicos a través del correo electrónico ya que esto nos ayuda a poder expresarnos y seguir participando cívicamente en estos espacios. Otros miembros del comité de padres les han enviado mensajes a favor de su reciente propuesta. Gracias por escuchar nuestras necesidades. Nos complace poder formar parte de este distrito, el cual nos ha tratado y nos sigue tratando con mucho respeto. Al escuchar nuestras voces Uds. escuchan las voces de los padres hispanos de su distrito.

También agradezco su apoyo hacia las prioridades del distrito y también por su apoyo a los jóvenes del grupo "Unidos" quienes han estado trabajando desde comienzos del año para mejorar las condiciones de los ancianos hispanos de esta ciudad. Agradezco la iniciativa del profesor de historia, el señor Bruno Contreras, quien inició esta asociación entre los dos grupos. Como Uds. sabrán, diez de sus estudiantes han formado lazos estrechos con un grupo de viejitos que necesitan de esta ayuda. Han demostrado ser excelentes voluntarios al acompañar y ayudar a los ancianos del hogar "El Refugio." Les han llevado libros de la biblioteca para que los que quieren leer, los lean.

En muchos casos les han estado leyendo historias de gente famosa de la historia de los Estados Unidos. Con esto, este grupo de estudiantes se beneficia ya que ellos mismos aprenden acerca de la historia de este país. No es un esfuerzo fácil de llevar a cabo ya que requiere mucha dedicación, tiempo y paciencia. Felicito a estos muchachos y al profesor de historia.

Por otra parte les agradezco que podamos participar de una manera auténtica en el desarrollo de los planes para el distrito y la implementación de éstos para así lograr los resultados que nuestros jóvenes necesitan para tener éxito y ser académicamente competentes. Gracias por su atención y espero que Uds. tomen en cuenta mis sugerencias, las que les envié por correo electrónico para que éstas se puedan llevar a cabo. También les doy las gracias por su colaboración, y por ser colaboradores y compañeros en la vida de nuestros jóvenes estudiantes. Y con estas palabras me retiro.

☛ #4 Simultaneous interpretation role play: Special day class open house

Good afternoon, everyone. It's a pleasure to be here with you. This is your child's classroom and my classroom. We have an interpreter at the rear of the room who will be interpreting what I say, should you need her services. I will have her introduce herself.

Please take a seat by one of the desks that has your child's name on it. I have placed a folder on the desk where your child usually sits. You will be able to take it home with you. It contains information that is relevant to the education of your child.

Let me now describe some of the subjects and topics that we will be covering in class.

Your child is reading at an instructional level. We use the Read 180 program that includes reading comprehension, academic vocabulary and writing skills. I use it with small groups and also for independent student work. It comes with a workbook that is used for various writing activities. If you haven't seen it yet, I have placed a copy on the desk in front of you. It also comes with software and takes students through five learning zones: reading, words, spelling, success and writing. It's a wonderful program and my students like it and are making progress using it.

Now we are all reading a Harry Potter book that was selected by the class. It is a book that was approved by our district. It corresponds to the state standards. Once we finish reading it, the students will watch the movie. Afterward, they will be able to compare and contrast the written version with the movie version.

When it comes to mathematics, we use Math 180. Each lesson starts with a "Do now." We watch an introductory lesson with a video that shows what we will be working on. We do one of the problems together and then the students work on the rest of the problems. They get an "exit ticket" to show they understood the problem.

For U.S. history, the students keep a notebook. We watch documentaries and YouTube historical videos. We start from the very beginning of U.S. history, with the Indigenous settlers and continue with the history of the colonies, the Lewis and Clark expedition, the Civil War until the present, including the struggles for civil rights represented by Martin Luther King and Rosa Parks.

For science, I have them participate in various experiments. We just dissected owl pellets. They are also studying a body part. Each student chooses a body part, such as the heart, the lungs, an arm, the eye, the kidneys, etc. They research it in depth, write about it and then give a presentation to the entire class using visuals. One of our students just completed his project on the spinal cord. He was able to recreate the spine using toilet paper rounds to represent vertebrae. Students get very creative with this assignment.

Now I would like to answer any of your questions. I see one hand up already.

☛ #5 Simultaneous interpretation role play: Eighth-grade valedictorian speech

Hello friends, teachers, students and parents. We are so pleased that you were all able to come and celebrate with us on this special day. All of us seated here today, especially other students, may think that we have now reached the end of many chapters. In a sense, that is true. We have come a long way. This day signifies that we have reached chapter nine of our journey, a journey that started in kindergarten and has now taken us to the end of the eighth grade. We truly have so much to look forward to, but let us now do a mental review of what has happened to us in the last nine years.

We started kindergarten by entering a brand new environment. We made new friends. A teacher introduced us to many stories and poems while teaching us how to read. We had fun while playing games, and we began to learn how to behave with other kids. The days went by fast, but then we entered first grade and things changed. The pressure was on to read, to add and to subtract. We spent more time in school.

In first, second and third grades, tests became more important. We got good at filling bubbles. We were on our way to becoming critical thinkers. It wasn't always easy. I remember, though, some extraordinary field trips. Who could forget going to science camp in the woods in fifth grade? It was fun. We collected insects and leaves, we sang songs by the campfire at night and participated in science experiments. But after a week of nature adventures, back to the classrooms we went. Then it was time to leave our safe fifth-grade classroom and we entered middle school.

And what a change that was. We were issued lockers; our backpacks got heavier. We had to change classes throughout the day. We were the youngest ones there, and what a challenge that was, but many of us were able to participate in extracurricular activities. Some of us joined track and field, others joined the band, some joined softball teams.

Then it was time to move into seventh grade. We were no longer the youngest ones in school. With the help of the PTA, we were able to take part in some exciting activities. We took a field trip to the beach, to the aquarium and even a ballet performance in winter where we all saw the Nutcracker!

We were so fortunate to be able to take part in these activities. Now that we have reached the end of the eighth grade, we realize that we will be facing new challenges. We went on another field trip, and that time it was to our new high school. What a big place! We will once again be the youngest group of students in this new environment, but we're ready for this challenge. We have faced challenges before, and we have made it.

At this time, I would like to thank all the people who have helped us on our journey and who have helped us become who we are today, especially the teachers at ABC Middle School who have worked hard to instill in us values of respect and responsibility. We cannot forget our friends, those who have supported us and particularly our parents who have always been there to lend a helping hand.

And let me now close with a quote: "You never fail until you stop trying." Thank you.

☞ #6 Simultaneous role play: School-sponsored lecture about students and reading

Hello, everyone. My name is Leti Hadi. Thank you for inviting me to your school. I am so pleased that I can share some thoughts on how to help your child with reading at home. This is a topic that is very important to me and should also be important to you as parents. When teachers send homework assignments with your child, these often involve reading. In the lower grades, this will involve you much more than in the higher grades. As you can see by the displays, we have brought a number of books for you to view and purchase at a minimal cost.

Can you, as parents, model a love for reading in young children? Absolutely. Modeling can do wonders. A parent can certainly start reading to a child long before the child learns to read. As a parent, you can choose books that interest your child. If you haven't learned to read though, these could even be made-up stories without the use of a book. You may want to use a book with only pictures and no words. If you have a children's book at home, you or a family member can get into the habit of reading to a child before bedtime. Here are a few of my favorites on the display to my left. They are in English and other languages. We will have you look at these in a few minutes.

How do you find the right book for your child? It might be a good idea to include your child, if possible, when choosing a book. I see that some of you have brought your children. As a parent, you probably have a good idea as to what types of books your child enjoys. Younger students don't want too many words per page. They will prefer pictures that match a story line. Beginning readers may be able to handle just one word or one sentence per page. Some books follow a repetitive pattern.

You may want to go to a library near your home. In that case, a librarian can assist you in selecting a book that will match the interests and comfort level of your child. Encourage your relatives to gift appropriate books for your child. Teachers and students can also select books from the school library together. I can certainly assist you in selecting the right book from the ones I have brought to this school. Let us talk about your child's age, interests and reading level before you select a book.

How do you read with your child? Once you have chosen a book and taken it home, sit down next to your child. If you are too busy to do so, have a brother, sister, grandparent or neighbor take your place. That person can start by talking about the cover and the title to encourage a dialogue about the book's topic. You and your child can try to guess the story line as you flip the pages.

If the child can read the book, listen attentively and ask questions about its content as you listen to the narration. You can ask questions such as "What would have happened if… ?" or "Why do you think…?" rather than questions that require a yes-or-no answer. If a word is too difficult to read, you can wait a few seconds before telling your child the word. If the book is too advanced, you can take turns with your child and read parts of the book. To keep the flow of the reading, you might suggest reading one page, and your child can read the next one. Another idea would be to read one sentence or to read an entire paragraph as you take turns.

Right now, I invite you all to take a good look at our displays. I will be happy to answer any of your questions.

#7 Simultaneous interpretation role play: FAFSA explanation

We are here today to provide you with instructions for completing the FAFSA form. FAFSA stands for Free Application for Federal Student Aid. It is for students who want to enroll in college and graduate school. Students needing federal assistance with costs are encouraged to apply. The money received will pay for college-related expenses.

In order to get started students will first go to www.fafsa.gov to access the application form. I will now guide you with this PowerPoint, so that you can follow along visually. On the website, students will create an FSA ID by choosing a user name or an email address and a password. Parents will also need an FSA ID because they will also be sending information required for the completion of the application.

If a student is a non-US citizen without a Social Security number or had a number issued by the federal Deferred Action for Childhood Arrivals (DACA) program, filling out the California Dream Act Application will be necessary. This can be found at dream.csac.ca.gov.

When completing the FAFSA form, students must pay close attention to the box at the bottom of the page that reads "Next" or "Previous."

Both high school students, like those present, and the parents, like those who are attending this meeting, will be completing the FAFSA. Parents will need to submit information about their marital status and also their income tax filing information.

While completing the application, don't forget to use the SAVE key to save what you have been entering on the electronic form.

Students will also need to create a SAVE KEY, an eight-digit code that students can share with their parents so that these parents can complete the information required of them.

The first part requires the student to complete some basic information, such as a first name, last name and Social Security number. Students must also answer the question that asks about being registered with the Selective Service System. Students answer this part with a "yes" or a "no." Don't forget that the email address the student provides will become the main form of communication regarding the status of the application.

The student then completes the remaining sections: school of attendance and location; this is based on a dropdown menu. The school selection section asks what colleges the student wants to attend.

Up to ten can be selected. The dependency status section asks for information about the student's birth or adoptive parents. Under the heading of parent demographics, an FSA ID will be needed for the parents.

Financial information must be completed for the parents and for the student. Tax data can be transferred from the IRS to the application by clicking on the "Transfer My Tax Information into the FAFSA Form" and selecting the "Transfer Now" button. There are additional questions regarding taxed and untaxed income.

The FAFSA summary provides a quick check that allows the student to verify all the information that has been submitted. Students must make sure that all the information is correct and that the email address provided is the right one because that is the way communication will take place. The last section is the Sign and Submit section. This is where the student and one of the parents sign the form after agreeing to the terms and then clicking on "Sign This FAFSA." The last click is the "Submit My FAFSA Now."

Finally, students print, sign and mail the signature page.

☛ #8 Simultaneous interpretation role play: Kindergarten orientation

I welcome all of you to this kindergarten orientation experience. Thank you very much for being here. I am Mr. Tomas Jairo, the principal at this school. I would like to introduce you to our three kindergarten teachers: Miss Lueta Joshi, Mr. Luis Petulka, and Mrs. Paula Singh.

If you haven't signed in yet, please do so at the front table. We will be needing your full name, your child's name, your address, your phone number and your email address.

This is a very exciting time for your child. You are enrolling them in an outstanding school, with dedicated teachers, supportive staff and a very caring environment. This is the beginning of a long adventure for your child, one that will have positive outcomes and should lead to a love of learning. Before introducing you to our kindergarten program and watching the orientation video, I need to remind you of the requirements to enroll your child in school.

- You will need to complete a registration packet that includes important information about your child, emergency contacts and a Home Language Survey.
- You also need to provide us with a birth certificate, a passport or some type of hospital birth record.
- Please bring a record of your child's vaccinations against hepatitis B, polio, mumps, measles, diphtheria, tetanus and pertussis.
- You need to show us two proofs of residency by bringing a utility bill, an income tax statement, a rental agreement or proof of home ownership.

Our district offers a full-day kindergarten for children who have turned five years old by September fifth. Our teachers are here to instill behaviors that lead to respect toward others and cooperation. Our kindergarten program includes language arts, math, science, social studies, art, music and physical education. During reading time, engaging books are used to strengthen their literacy skills. Workstations during language arts may include a listening center, a phonics center or a fun vocabulary center. We also recognize the importance of technology. Each child is issued a Chromebook laptop to use in class.

In math, children are introduced to numbers and shapes using manipulatives. The science program goes hand in hand with the reading that is done in language arts. Children learn important social skills all day, especially during lunchtime and recess time. There is a music teacher at this school who will introduce the children to a variety of sounds, instruments and popular children's songs. Our very talented art teacher instructs them in the use of crayons, pens, watercolors and even clay.

I want you to see for yourselves what a typical day in the life of a kindergartener looks like. For this purpose, we have created a video showing our current kindergarteners from the time they arrive at school in the morning to the time they leave. Let's take a look.

Practice: Translations

Translate the following notices and announcements into the target language. Feel free to use any of the suggested apps or dictionaries.

☛ #1 Translation role play: Field trip permission slip

FIELD TRIP PERMISSION SLIP

ABC High School

Trip date:___May 12__Grade/class:_____11th_____

Please note the following regarding the field trip:

Where:_____Aquarium_____Activity:_____Observe and report on marine life found at the Aquarium.

Departure from School (Time): __8:10 A.M.__

Return to School (Time): __2:45 P.M.__

> 1. I have been informed of the details of this educational field experience. 2. My child has my permission to participate in this supervised field experience. 3. I agree to instruct my child to obey all rules, regulations and instructions given by teachers and/or authorized school personnel. 4. I further agree that no teacher or authorized personnel shall be held

responsible for injuries or other mishaps caused by my child's deliberate disobedience of rules, regulations or instructions. 5. This field experience is considered as school work and will be conducted as a regular class.

I GIVE PERMISSION TO TAKE THE FIELD TRIP TO: _____Aquarium_____

Name of student _____

Your signature indicates that you have read and agreed to the above and that we have your permission to take your child on this field trip experience.

Parent's name _____

Parent's signature _____

☞ #2 Translation role play: Invitation to a school concert

Dear Parents/Guardian:

On Saturday, May 21, from 3:00 P.M. to 5:00 P.M., our school will host the first annual Concert in the Auditorium. The purpose of this concert is to create and provide a community-oriented forum in which to highlight a wide range of students' musical talents from the elementary school level to high school.

We are partnering with our neighboring high school, CBA. You will hear solo performances on the violin and piano. You will also hear the CBA chorus sing songs from well-known American musicals. This year you will be hearing selections from *West Side Story* and *Hamilton*.

This concert will provide community members the opportunity to enrich their lives through the understanding, appreciation and performance of music. Proceeds from this program will support the music program at both schools.

Tickets are $15 per person and may be purchased at the school office. The last day to purchase tickets will be Wednesday, May 18. Pianísimo Coffee Shop is generously providing refreshments and pastries for your enjoyment. These will be available following the concert in the foyer of the auditorium.

Parents of performers can receive two free tickets. Please stop by the school office to pick these up.

If you want additional information about the concert, please telephone me at 999-999-9999.

Sincerely,

A.T.

Principal

#3: Sample translation for IEP explanation

Who needs a school IEP?

The student who has difficulties learning and functioning in a regular classroom may be a candidate for an IEP. Appropriate testing is required in order to diagnose the type of extra services that may be required. Students who struggle in school may qualify for support services as a result of various reasons such as:

- Learning disability
- Physical disability
- Development delay
- Attention-deficit / hyperactivity disorder (ADHD)
- Emotional disorders
- Cognitive challenges
- Speech and language impairment
- Hearing impairment
- Autism
- Visual impairment

How is the IEP implemented?

In most cases, the services and goals outlined in an IEP can be provided in a regular school environment. This can be done in a standard classroom (for example, a reading teacher assists a small group of students who need extra help while other students in the classroom read and write with the regular teacher) or in a special resource room with a special education resource teacher. A group of students with similar needs may be brought together to receive this extra support.

Some students who need additional and more specialized interventions may be taught in a special school environment. These classes have fewer students per teacher, allowing for more individualized attention.

Special education teachers usually have specific training and certification to help students with special educational needs. The children spend most of their day in a special classroom and join the regular classes for nonacademic activities (like music and physical education) or in academic activities in which they don't need extra assistance.

Because the goal of Individuals with Disabilities Education Act (IDEA) is to ensure that each child is educated in the least restrictive environment possible, effort is made to help students stay in a regular classroom.

☛ #4 Translation role play: Request for special education services

Dear _____   Date_____

I am the parent of _____ who is in the __ grade (enter grade) at _____ (enter school name) or ___not attending school. I am requesting a comprehensive assessment in all areas related to a suspected disability to determine whether_____ is eligible for special education and/or related services either under the Individuals with Disabilities Education Act (including the Other Health Impairment category) or Section 504 of the Rehabilitation Act of 1973.

I am requesting this assessment because:

_____

The following interventions and accommodations have already been tried:

_____

However, my child continues to struggle in school with_____

_____

It is my understanding that I will receive a response from you in writing within 15 days of this request. I look forward to finding solutions for my child's problems by bringing this matter to your attention.

☛ #5 Translation role play: Sixth grade daily schedule

8:00 to 8:15	School arrival. Check board work.
8:15 to 8:25	Attendance, flag salute, announcements, homework checks
8:25 to 8:30	Change classrooms
8:30 to 9:55	First period—language arts or math and science
9:55 to 10:15	Recess
10:15 to 10:20	Change classrooms
10:20 to 12:20	Second period—language arts or math and science
12:20 to 1:00	Lunch and recess
1:00 to 1:05	Change classrooms
1:05 to 1:55	Social studies
1:55 to 2:00	Change classrooms

2:00 to 2:30   Physical education (Monday, Wednesday, Friday)

   Art (Tuesday, Thursday)

2:30 to 2:35   Dismissal

The doors to the classrooms open for all students at 8:00 A.M. each morning. We would like to see all students arrive at that time so that the day starts without problems. When students arrive late, they have a harder time organizing themselves for the school day.

Let us teach our students good habits.

☛ #6 Translation role play: School site council's role

We are looking for school site council members for this school year.

What is the role of the school site council?

A school site council (SSC) is a decision-making body that represents all stakeholders of our school community. The school principal, teachers, other school personnel, parents and students (secondary level) make up this group. Its primary responsibility is to identify common goals and assist the leadership team in establishing a plan to achieve these goals.

The key to a successful SSC depends on a good working relationship among all members of the council. Each member of the council shares their unique perspective and knowledge of the school's needs, as they affect all students. The principal and teachers contribute background knowledge in instructional practices; parents provide the insights on how effective the school is working and how well their children understand their assignments; and students offer insight on the range and effectiveness of learning opportunities available. Other personnel at the school, such as counselors, instructional aides and clerical staff can share insights on how the school can function to support student learning.

School site councils operate under the policy, direction and approval of the local board of education. As the school leadership team and SSC develop, monitor and revise the single plan for student achievement, the SSC allocates resources to support the plan. The members determine the allocation of funds.

There should be continual communication between the SSC, grade levels and departments to ensure that each group supports the other. Communication usually takes place through the school newsletter, website, minutes of meetings being posted in prominent places and reports made during grade level and department meetings. By working cooperatively, all elements of the school population ensure that each school site plan focuses resources on improvement strategies, which guarantees that all students meet high standards.

School site council meetings should be open to the public with the date, time and location of meetings posted at the school site or other appropriate place accessible to the public, at least 72 hours before the time set for a meeting.

If interested in being a part of the SSC, please sign up in the school's office.

☞ #7 Translation role play: Eligibility for high school graduation ceremony

Eligibility to Participate in Our High School's Graduation Ceremony

Students who want to participate in the high school graduation ceremony must meet all requirements for graduation, satisfy district standards and pass any required assessments.

The governing board believes that these students deserve the privilege of a public celebration that recognizes the significance of their achievement. Students who will complete graduation requirements during the summer may participate in graduation exercises without receiving a diploma. High school students who have passed the California High School Proficiency Examination or the General Education Development Test must also meet district graduation requirements in order to participate in graduation ceremonies.

If a student successfully completes the district's graduation requirements while attending a juvenile court school or nonsectarian school or agency, the district will issue the student a diploma from the school the student last attended. This student will be able to participate in the graduation ceremony. Students suspended during the last 15 days of school preceding the commencement may not participate in the commencement exercises.

To honor superior academic achievement, graduation ceremonies shall include recognition of valedictorian and salutatorian, students selected based on establish criteria and procedures that use multiple measures of academic performance.

Any student participating in a graduation ceremony shall comply with district policies and regulations pertaining to student conduct.

In order to encourage high standards of student conduct, a principal may deny a student the privilege of participating in a graduation ceremony in accordance with school rules. Prior to the denial of this privilege, the student's parent or guardian shall receive written notice of this denial and the means whereby it can be appealed.

☞ #8 Translation role play: Discipline policy

Discipline Policy

Each school in the district will develop standards of conduct and discipline that are consistent with district policies and administrative regulations. Students and their parents/guardians shall be notified of district and school rules related to students' conduct. The following list of infractions could result in disciplinary action as stated in Education Code 48900-48925 and 48260.

Academic dishonesty

Alcohol /represented to be alcohol

Arson

Assault

Battery

Bullying

Causing physical injury to another, except in self-defense

Defiance of school personnel

Destruction, damage or defacement of school property

Disorderly conduct including profanity and obscene behavior

Disruptive bus conduct

Explosive devices

Extortion/robbery

Firearm possession, selling, furnishing

Forgery

Habitual disregard for school rules

Hate crimes

Hostile or intimidating school environment

Knife possession or brandishing

Plagiarism

Possession of controlled substances

Receiving stolen property

Tardiness and truancy

Terrorist threat

Theft

Threatening staff with intent to do harm

Tobacco possession

Weapons or objects represented to be weapons

Witness harassment, threatening, intimidating or retaliation

Violations could result in suspension, expulsion or transfer to alternative programs in accordance with board policy and administrative regulations.

Appendix

Appendix

- Resources for educational interpreters and translators
- Education sites and bilingual programs
- Dictionaries
- Translation apps
- Computer software tool
- Books and articles for interpreters and translators
- Training sites and links for practice
- Non-language specific role plays (in English only)
- Word games

RESOURCES FOR EDUCATIONAL INTERPRETERS AND TRANSLATORS

SPANISH/ENGLISH TERMINOLOGY BOOKS

Thuro, B. (2009). *A Bilingual Dictionary of School Terminology*. English-Spanish.

Valentán, R. (2018). *Glossary of Educational Terminology English to Spanish*. Valentán.

EDUCATION GLOSSARIES

For bilingual glossaries of Department of Education terminology in several languages (Arabic, Bengali, Chinese, Haitian Creole, Korean, Russian, Spanish and Urdu), go to the website of New York City Schools.

https://docs.steinhardt.nyu.edu/pdfs/metrocenter/atn293/ela/ela_spanish.pdf?_ga=2.198792748.2095639372.1695350436-1914873130.1695350436

https://steinhardt.nyu.edu/metrocenter/language-rbern/resources/bilingual-glossaries-and-cognates

Glossary of education terms (Virginia)

https://www.doe.virginia.gov/about-vdoe/search?q=glossary

Internet users' Spanish glossary.

http://www.ati.es/novatica/glosario/glosario_internet.html

Los Angeles Unified School District glossary

https://www.lausd.org/cms/lib/CA01000043/Centricity/Domain/1220/LAUSD%20Translation%20Unit%20EnglishSpanish%20Glossary%20of%20LAUSD%20Terminology.pdf

Education terminology

https://sedl.org/connections/engagement_webinars/webinar-2/glossary-of-ed-terms.pdf

LD glossary online

http://www.ldonline.org/glossary

Mental health terms

http://smhp.psych.ucla.edu/conted/gloss.htm#glossary

Helpful for special education terminology in English

Special education

https://texasprojectfirst.org/en/glossary

Autism

http://www.autism-resources.com/autismfaq-glos.html

Center for Parent Information & Resources
https://www.parentcenterhub.org/?s=glossary

Spanish language resources for education
https://www.trelliscompany.org/english-spanish-glossary/

English definitions of the most common terminology related to ELL
https://www.colorincolorado.org/ell-basics/ell-glossary

IDEA-Related Acronyms, Abbreviations, and Terms
https://sites.ed.gov/idea/acronyms/#A

Reading glossary
https://www.arlington.k12.ma.us/apps/pages/index.jsp?uREC_ID=2867829&type=d&pREC_ID=2329271#

English/Spanish glossary for educational settings from the California Department of Education
https://www.cde.ca.gov/sp/el/er/engspanglossary.asp

Definitions of words in English
www.yourdictionary.com

Online dictionary search engine: currently has links to over 7,500 bilingual and multilingual dictionaries and glossaries.
http://www.lexicool.com/

Translations in 14 language combinations such as Swahili, Russian, Serbian, Tagalog and others
http://www.thefreedictionary.com/

Ukrainian glossary of basic education terms
https://www.ukrainianlessons.com/ph-education/

English-Spanish speech pathology terms
https://bilinguistics.com/how-to-describe-speech-disorders-in-spanish/

Special Education terms in Mandarin Chinese and English
https://www.pps.net/cms/lib/OR01913224/Centricity/Domain/181/Parent/Chinese_SPED_terminology.pdf

Terms specific to SPED and IDEA developed by the Office of Special Education Programs (OSEP)
https://www.parentcenterhub.org/wp-content/uploads/repo_items/osep-english-spanish-glossary.pdf

Glossary in English and Spanish from Albuquerque Public Schools
https://www.aps.edu/language-and-cultural-equity/translation-and-interpretation-services/resources

EDUCATION SITES AND BILINGUAL PROGRAMS

CADRE. The National Center on Dispute Resolution in Special Education

http://www.directionservice.org/cadre/

ECLKC. Head start.

http://eclkc.ohs.acf.hhs.gov/hslc

http://eclkc.ohs.acf.hhs.gov/hslc/espanol

Bright Futures

http://www.brightfutures.org/georgetown.html

http://www.brightfutures.org/spanish/index.html

National Parent Teacher Association

http://pta.org/

http://www.pta.org/spanish/index.asp

Two-Way Immersion. Center for Applied Linguistics.

http://www.cal.org/twi/

Rubrics (Arlingotn, Virginia)

http://www.cal.org/twi/Rubrics/index.html

CAL Center for Applied Linguistics

http://www.cal.org/

Child welfare

http://www.childwelfare.gov/glossary/terms_english_spanish_t-z.cfm#W

Parent involvement

https://www2.ed.gov/about/offices/list/oela/newcomers-toolkit/chap5.pdf

Although the following publication targets educational interpreters for the Deaf, it may also interest spoken interpreters in education:

https://rid.org/

Educational Interpreting: A Collection of Articles from Views. RID Publications, 2000.
For interpreters, parents, school administrators and teachers. Includes 30 articles covering a wide range of educational interpreting topics. Also includes RID's Standard Practice Paper on Educational Interpreting and the Code of Ethics.

Individuals with Disabilities Education Act

http://idea.ed.gov/explore/home

Council for Exceptional Children

www.cec.sped.org

IDEA practices, law and regulations

The 2004 reauthorization of Individuals with Disabilities Education Improvement Act
http://www.p12.nysed.gov/specialed/idea/

http://idea.ed.gov/explore/home

Family and Advocates for Partnership in Education, 2004 reauthorization
https://www2.ed.gov/about/offices/list/ocr/docs/edlite-FAPE504.html

DICTIONARIES

There are a number of well-known dictionaries that can aid you in finding the right wording in English and Spanish:

- *Merriam-Webster's Spanish-English Visual Dictionary,* with over 22,500 technical and everyday terms.
- *Larousse Unabridged Dictionary: Spanish English,* with 250,000 words and phrases.
- *Collins English-Spanish Dictionary*, with over 100,000 Spanish translations of English words and phrases.
- *Oxford Spanish Dictionary,* with more than 300,000 words.
- *Simon & Schuster's International Spanish Dictionary,* with over 200,000 entries.

If you are looking for an excellent Spanish-only dictionary, you have a choice of these top two:

- *Diccionario de la Lengua Española* (Real Academia Española)
- María Moliner, *Diccionario de Uso del Español*

For an illustrated dictionary refer to:

- *Duden Español: Diccionario por la Imagen,* dictionary with illustrations

On-line dictionaries for Spanish

- *Pan-Hispanic Dictionary of Doubts*
- *Fundéu a dictionary focused on proper word usage*
- *An Etymological Dictionary of the Spanish language by Ricardo Soca*
- *El País—dictionary of Spanish synonyms and antonyms*
- *Spanish Collocations Dictionary*—DiCE—word usage and proper expressions in Spanish

TRANSLATION APPS

Google Translate is a popular app that can be used for a large number of language pairs.

Linguee offers two-way translation of words across a range of languages.

Microsoft Translator (what used to be Babel Fish and Bing Translator) has quick access.

WordReference offers two-way translations for 15 languages, most European languages, plus Korean, Japanese, Turkish and Arabic. It includes a large repository of advice and questions about language usage and allows you to ask questions about specific expressions.

Hola: Hola is a Spanish translator

SayHi is another option for quick references.

COMPUTER SOFTWARE TOOLS

Computer Aided (or Assisted) Interpretation (CAI) is a computer software tool that can benefit you in preparing for a job. Some examples of software support for managing terminology are: InterpretBank, Interpreters' Help, LookUp, Intragloss and The Interpreter's Wizard.

A very popular computer assisted translation software tool is Trados.

☞ Books and Articles for Interpreters and Translators

Aguirre, B., Barthelemy, R., David, B., Fequiere, A. and Fitzpatrick, J. (1997). Translating/ Interpreting for the Schools: A Burgeoning Field. In *Proceedings of the 38th Annual Conference of the American Translators Association,* Jerome-O'Keefe (ed.). American Translators Association.

Allen, E. and Bernofsky, S. (eds.). (2013). *In Translation: Translators on Their Work and What It Means.* Columbia University Press. A collection of essays dealing with translation studies.

Allen, K., Bancroft, M.A., González-Cestari, T., Meder, D., Remer, C., Runge, D. and Stockler-Rex, S. (2023). *The Remote Interpreter: An International Textbook for Remote Interpreting, Volume 1, Foundations in Remote Interpreting.* Culture & Language Press.

Allen, K., Sosa, V., Isidro, A. and Bancroft, M.A. (2018). *The Indigenous Interpreter®: A Training Manual for Indigenous Language Interpreting.* Natividad Medical Foundation.

Angelelli, C.V. (2004). *Revisiting the Interpreter's Role.* John Benjamins Publishing Company. Focuses on the interpreter's role in various settings.

Angelelli, C.V. (2016). Looking Back: A Study of (Ad-Hoc) Family Interpreters. *European Journal of Applied Linguistics 4, 1*, pp. 5-31.

Baddeley, A.D., Thomson, N. and Buchanan, M. (1975). Word Length and the Structure of Short-Term Memory. *Journal of Verbal Learning and Verbal Behavior 14,* pp. 575-589.

Biagini, M., Boyd, M.S. (2021). *The Changing Role of the Interpreter.* Routledge.

Chafin Seal, B. (2003). *Best Practices in Educational Interpreting.* Pearson. For those who work with hearing loss students.

Child, J. (2009). *Introduction to Spanish Translation,* 2nd edition. UPA. A manual intended for a third or fourth year university course; 24 lessons include translation exercises.

Durand, T.M. and Perez, N.A. (2013). Continuity and Variability in the Parental Involvement and Advocacy Beliefs of Latino Families of Young Children: Finding the Potential for a Collective Voice. *School Community Journal 23,* pp. 49-79.

Ferreira, A., Schwieter, J., (eds.). (2022*). Introduction to Translation and Interpreting Studies.* Wiley-Blackwell. This book covers the essential aspects of translation and interpreting studies.

Fulcher, G. and Davidson, F. (2007). *Language Testing and Assessment: An Advanced Resource Book.* Routledge.

García-Beyaert, S. (2015). The Role of the Community Interpreter. In *The Community Interpreter®: An International Textbook.* Culture & Language Press.

Gillies, A. (2005). *Note-Taking for Consecutive Interpreting: A Short Course.* Routledge.

Gillies, A. (2019). Consecutive Interpreting: A Short Course. Routledge.

González, E. (2005). *Exercise Manual for the Training of Translators and Interpreters.* XanEdu Publishing. This book contains more skills-building exercises than role plays.

Jakobsen, A.L. and Jensen, K.T. (2008). Eye Movement Behaviour Across Four Different Types of Reading Tasks. *Copenhagen Studies in Language 36*, pp. 103-124.

Joos, M. (1962). *The Five Clocks: A Linguistic Excursion into the Five Styles of English Usage.* Harcourt.

Klimova, B., Pikhart, M., Delorme Benites, A., Lehr, C. and Sanchez-Stockhammer, C. (2023). Neural Machine Translation in Foreign Language Teaching and Learning: A Systematic Review. *Education and Information Technologies 28,* pp. 663-682.

Lambert, S. and Moser-Mercer, B. (1994). *Bridging the Gap—Empirical Research in Simultaneous Interpretation*. John Benjamins Publishing Company.

Langdon, H.W. and Saenz, T. (2016). *Working with Interpreters and Translators: A Guide for Speech-Language Pathologists and Audiologists.* Plural Publishing Inc. Interpreting and translating in speech pathology and audiology with important steps.

Lee, T.K. and Wang, D. (eds.). (2022). *Translation and Social Media Communication in the Age of the Pandemic.* Taylor and Francis.

Mazzei, C.A., Aibo, I. and Jay-Rayon, L. (2022). *The Routledge Guide to Teaching Translation and Interpreting Online.* Routledge.

McKay, C. (2015). *How to Succeed as a Freelance Translator,* 3rd edition. Two Rat Press.

Miller, G. (1956). The Magical Number Seven, Plus or Minus Two: Some Limits on Our Capacity for Processing Information. *Psychological Review 63,* pp. 81-97.

Monacelli, C. (2009). *Self-Preservation in Simultaneous Interpreting: Surviving the Role.* John Benjamins Publishing Company.

Munday, J. (2016). *Introducing Translation Studies: Theories and Applications,* 4th edition. Routledge.

Nolan, J. (2012). *Interpretation: Techniques and Exercises (Professional Interpreting in the Real World),* 2nd edition. Multilingual Matters.

Payne, R. (2005). *A Framework for Understanding Poverty: A Cognitive Approach,* 6th edition. aha! Process.

Pochhacker, F. and Minhua, L. (2014). *Aptitude for Interpreting.* John Benjamins Publishing Company. Analyses aptitude for interpreting based on tests and looks at psychological traits such as learning style, motivation and cognitive flexibility.

Rozan, J-F. (1956). *Note-Taking in Consecutive Interpreting.* Tertium.

Shreve, G.M., Lacruz, I. and Angelone, E. (2010). Cognitive Effort, Syntactic Disruption, and Visual Interference in a Sight Translation Task. *Translation and Cognition,* pp. 63-84.

Sofer, M. (2009). *The Translator's Handbook,* 7th edition. Schreiber Publishing.

Weisskirch, R.S. (2010). Child Language Brokers in Immigrant Families: An Overview of Family Dynamics. *mediAzion 10.*

Winston, E. (ed.). (2005). *Educational Interpreting: How It Can Succeed.* Gallaudet University Press. Aimed at Deaf students and interpreters.

Youdelman, M. (2019). *Summary of State Law Requirements Addressing Language Needs in Health Care.* National Health Law Program.

TRAINING SITES AND LINKS FOR PRACTICE

Provides training and practical advice for all modes of interpreting:

http://www.orcit.eu/resources-shelf-en/story.html

Interpreter training for all levels:

https://interpretertrainingresources.eu

Presentation by Natalia Abarca, of the Orange County Department of Education, on the role of the school interpreter:

https://www.youtube.com/watch?v=yvT9rnB6OiY

Graciela Zozaya speaks about "Interpreting for Special ed and Other School Settings:"

https://www.youtube.com/watch?v=6CdKh4ayAzM

Mock ARD meeting without an interpreter:

https://www.youtube.com/watch?v=0CmXhw95a_0

Interpreting in Educational Settings: on line course from the Academy of Interpretation:

https://www.academyofinterpretation.com/courses/interpreting-in-educational-settings#course-materials

Interpreting Spoken Languages in Educational Settings: advanced online course from the NAETISL:

https://naetisl.mylearnworlds.com/home

University of Georgia online Professional Interpreter in Education Certificate 30 hr course for professional interpreters:

https://www.georgiacenter.uga.edu/courses/teaching-and-education/languages/professional-interpreters-edu

NON-LANGUAGE SPECIFIC ROLE PLAYS (IN ENGLISH ONLY)

MEDICAL: Cross Cultural Communication Systems, Inc. (CCCS). (2009). *The Art of Medical Interpretation*, 3rd edition. CCCS.

GENERAL/TELEPHONIC: Kelly, Nataly, (2008). *Telephone Interpreting: A Comprehensive Guide to the Profession*, Trafford Publishing.

Materials at www.interpretrain.com

WORD GAMES

Merriam-Webster provides a free online dictionary, thesaurus, audio pronunciations, Word of the Day, word games and other English language resources.

http://www.m-w.com/game/

University participants learn English vocabulary in context (grades 5-12) with free word puzzles. Thematic word games and creative activities.

www.vocabulary.com/

Learn about word origins and etymology. Tough and educational word games.

www.etymologic.com/

Free online interactive word games, boggle, anagrams, puzzles, crosswords, cryptograms, crypoquotes and jumbles. Play and solve word games.

www.wordplays.com/

Additional word games.

https://www.arkadium.com/free-online-games/word/

Vocabulary University® recommended word-related websites.

https://myvocabulary.com/word-games-puzzles/

www.vocabulary.com/VUogoodlinks.html

Bibliography

ACTFL. (2012). *ACTFL Proficiency Guidelines.* ACTFL.

Allen, K., Bancroft, M.A., González-Cestari, T., Meder, D., Remer, C., Runge, D. and Stockler-Rex, S. (2023). *The Remote Interpreter: An International Textbook for Remote Interpreting, Volume 1, Foundations in Remote Interpreting.* Culture & Language Press.

Allen, K. et al. (forthcoming 2024). *The Remote Interpreter: An International Textbook, Volume 2: Specializations and Advanced Skills in Remote Interpreting.* Culture & Language Press.

Allen, K., Sosa, V., Isidro, A. and Bancroft, M.A. (2018). *The Indigenous Interpreter®: A Training Manual for Indigenous Language Interpreting.* Natividad Medical Foundation.

Baddeley, A.D., Thomson, N. and Buchanan, M. (1975). Word Length and the Structure of Short-Term Memory. *Journal of Verbal Learning and Verbal Behavior 14,* pp. 575-589.

Ballentine, J.A. (1969). *Ballentine's Law Dictionary.* Lawyers Co-operative Pub. Co., p. 422.

Durand, T.M. and Perez, N.A. (2013). Continuity and Variability in the Parental Involvement and Advocacy Beliefs of Latino Families of Young Children: Finding the Potential for a Collective Voice. *School Community Journal 23,* pp. 49-79.

García-Beyaert, S. (2015). The Role of the Community Interpreter. In *The Community Interpreter®: An International Textbook.* Culture & Language Press.

Gillies, A. (2019). Consecutive Interpreting: A Short Course. Routledge.

Gillies, A. (2005). *Note-Taking for Consecutive Interpreting: A Short Course*. Routledge.

Jakobsen, A.L. and Jensen, K.T. (2008). Eye Movement Behaviour Across Four Different Types of Reading Task. *Copenhagen Studies in Language 36*, pp. 103-124.

Joos, M. (1962). *The Five Clocks: A Linguistic Excursion into the Five Styles of English Usage.* Harcourt.

Lambert, S. and Moser-Mercer, B. (1994). *Bridging the Gap—Empirical Research in Simultaneous Interpretation*. John Benjamins Publishing Company.

McKay, C. (2015). *How to Succeed as a Freelance Translator,* 3rd edition. Two Rat Press.

Miller, G. (1956). The Magical Number Seven, Plus or Minus Two: Some Limits on Our Capacity for Processing Information. *Psychological Review 63,* pp. 81-97.

Munday, J. (2016). *Introducing Translation Studies: Theories and Applications,* 4th edition. Routledge.

NAETISL. (2022). *Code of Ethics and Standards of Practice for Educational Translators and Interpreters of Spoken Languages.* National Association of Educational Translators and Interpreters of Spoken Languages.

NAIE. (2021). *Educational Interpreter Code of Ethics.* National Association of Interpreters in Education.

NCIHC. (2004). *A National Code of Ethics for Interpreters in Health Care*. The National Council on Interpreting in Health Care.

NCLB. (2004). *Parental Involvement, Title I, Part A, Non-Regulatory Guidance.* A-5, p. 4.

Payne, R. (2005). *A Framework for Understanding Poverty: A Cognitive Approach,* 6th edition. aha! Process.

Rozan, J-F. (1956). *Note-taking in Consecutive Interpreting.* Tertium.

Shreve, G.M., Lacruz, I. and Angelone, E. (2010). Cognitive Effort, Syntactic Disruption, and Visual Interference in a Sight Translation Task. *Translation and Cognition,* pp. 63-84.

Weisskirch, R.S. (2010). Child Language Brokers in Immigrant Families: An Overview of Family Dynamics, *mediAzion 10.*

Youdelman, M. (2019). *Summary of State Law Requirements Addressing Language Needs in Health Care.* National Health Law Program.

Bilingual Glossary for Educational Interpreters

* Words modeled by their English counterpart and accepted as Spanish words in the United States.

A

English	Español
ability	habilidad; capacidad; destreza
abnormality	anormalidad
above average	superior al (por encima del) nivel promedio
absence	ausencia; falta
abused	maltratado; abusado
academic achievement	rendimiento académico; logro académico
academic achievement goals	metas de rendimientos (logros) académicos
academic calendar	calendario académico
academic standards	normas académicas; estándares académicos
accelerated courses	cursos acelerados
accessibility resources	recursos de accesibilidad
accommodate, to	adaptar; tomar en cuenta; modificar
accommodation	adaptación; acomadación; modificación
accomplish, to	lograr; conseguir; cumplir
accountability, interventions and support	rendición de cuentas, intervenciones y apoyo
accountability model	modelo de rendición de cuentas
accurate	exacto; preciso
achieve, to	lograr; progresar
achievement	logro; rendimiento; progreso
achievement gap	brecha del rendimiento académico
achievement level	nivel de rendimiento; nivel de desempeño
achievement test	prueba de rendimiento académico
acquisition	adquisición
acronym	sigla
act	decreto; ley

action plan	plan de acción
activities	actividades
acute	agudo
adaptive behavior	conducta adaptiva
adaptive skills	habilidades de adaptación; destrezas adaptables
address, to	dirigirse, referirse
adequate yearly progress (AYP)	progreso anual adecuado (AYP, por sus siglas en inglés)
ADHD, attention-deficit / hyperactivity disorder	TDAH trastorno por déficit de atención por hiperactividad
adjustment	ajuste
administer, to	administrar (una prueba); dirigir
administration	administración
administrator	administrador/a
adolescent	adolescente
adopt, to	adoptar
adopted materials	materiales adoptados
adoption	adopción
adult education	educación de adultos
advanced performance level	nivel avanzado
advanced students	estudiantes avanzados
advantage	ventaja
advice	consejo; recomendación
advisory committee	comité consultivo; comité asesor
advocacy	abogacía; defensoría
advocate, to	abogar por; proponer
affidavit	declaración jurada; afidávit
aforementioned	ya mencionado; arriba mencionado
African American	afroamericano/a
after-school program	programa para después de clases regulares
age	edad
age equivalent	edad equivalente
agree, to	ponerse de acuerdo

aide	ayudante; asistente
all English program of instruction	programa de instrucción totalmente en inglés
allocate, to	distribuir; repartir; asignar
alternative assessments	pruebas alternativas; examenes alternativos
amend, to	enmendar
amendment	enmienda
American Sign Language (ASL)	Lenguaje de señas americano (ASL, por sus siglas en inglés)
Americans with Disabilities Act (ADA), U.S.	ley para americanos con discapacidades (ADA, por sus siglas en inglés)
annual assessment	evaluación anual; prueba anual
annual goals	metas anuales
anxiety	ansiedad; inquietud
application	solicitud; aplicación*
apply, to	solicitar; aplicar*
appointment	cita
approve, to	aprovar
art show	exposición de arte
Asperger syndrome (AS)	síndrome de Asperger (AS por sus siglas en inglés)
assault, to	atacar; agredir
assembly bill (AB)	proyecto de ley de la asamblea legislativa
assess, to	evaluar; analizar; determinar
assessment	evaluación; prueba; examen; análisis
assessment requirements	requisitos de evaluación
assistance	ayuda; apoyo
assistant principal	subdirector/a; vicedirector
assistant teacher	auxiliar del maestro/a; asistente o ayudante al maestro/a
assistive technology device	aparato tecnológico de asistencia
associate of arts (AA) degree	título de asociado en artes
at-risk students	estudiantes con riesgo de fracaso
attack	ataque; agresión

attend, to	asistir
attendance	asistencia
attendance rate	tasa de asistencia (escolar)
attention deficit disorder (ADD) *Note: term considered outdated*	trastorno por déficit de atención (ADD, por sus siglas en inglés)
attention-deficit/ hyperactivity disorder (ADHD)	trastorno por déficit de atención con hiperactividad (ADHD, por sus siglas en inglés)
audiology	audiología
audit	auditoria
auditory	auditivo
autism spectrum disorder (ASD)	trastorno del espectro del autism (ASD, por sus siglas en inglés)
average daily attendance (ADA)	promedio de asistencia diaria (ADA por sus siglas en inglés)
avoid, to	evitar; eludir
award	premio

B

English	Español
bachelor of arts (BA) degree	licenciatura o título en humanidades
bachelor of science (BS) degree	licenciatura o título en ciencias
background	antecedente; historial; contexto
back-to-school night	noche de regreso a clases o a la escuela
balance	equilibrio; saldo
ballpoint pen	pluma; bolígrafo; birome
baseline data	datos iniciales; datos de base
bashful	tímido; vergonzoso
basic interpersonal communicative skills (BICS)	habilidades básicas de comunicación interpersonal (BICS, por sus siglas en inglés)
basic performance level	nivel básico de rendimiento
basic sight words	palabras básicas reconocibles de vista
basic skills test	prueba para la evaluación de destrezas básicas
battery	agresión grave; agresión física

BDAC, bilingual parent advisory committee	comité consejero bilingüe del distrito (BDAC, por sus siglas en inglés)
bear with me	ten(ga) paciencia
beginner	principiante
beginning performance level	nivel de rendimiento inicial
beginning readers	lectores principiantes
behave, to	comportarse; portarse; conducirse
behavior	conducta; comportamiento
behavior disorder	trastorno del comportamiento
behavior rating scale	escala del índice de la conducta
behavioral objective	objetivo del comportamiento
below average	por debajo del promedio
below basic performance level	por debajo del nivel básico
below expectations	por debajo de las expectativas
below grade level	por debajo del nivel del grado
below standard	por debajo de las normas
benchmark	indicadores; punto de referencia
benefit, to	beneficiar
bias	preferencia; inclinación
bilingual advisory committee (BAC)	comité consultivo bilingüe
bilingual cross-cultural language and academic development (BCLAD)	desarrollo académico del lenguaje intercultural y bilingüe (BCLAD, por sus siglas en inglés)
bilingual education	educación bilingüe
bilingual educational aide	auxiliar educativo/a bilingüe
bilingual evaluation	evalución bilingüe
bilingual immersion program	programa de inmersión bilingüe
bilingual individual learning plan	programa de aprendizaje bilingüe individual
bilingual resource teacher	maestro de recursos bilingües
biliteracy	lectoescritura en dos idiomas
biliterate	que domina la lectoescritura en dos idiomas
bill	proyecto de ley
binder	carpeta
bipartisan	bipartidista

birth certificate	acta de nacimiento; partida de nacimiento
birth date	fecha de nacimiento
blackboard	pizarra; pizarrón
Blindness	ceguera
board meeting	junta del consejo directivo
board of directors	consejo directivo; junta directiva
board of education	consejo de educación; junta de educación
board of trustees	junta directiva
bodily harm	daño corporal
bomb threat	amenaza de bomba
bookkeeping	contabilidad
booklet (as in test booklet)	cuadernillo o libreta (de prueba)
bracket [square mark]	corchete; paréntesis
Braille	Braille
brainstorm	lluvia de ideas; tormenta de ideas
break	descanso; recreo; pausa
bubble, to	rellenar el círculo
budget shortfall	insuficiencia del presupuesto
bulletin	boletín
bulletin board	tablero de anuncios; tablero informativo
bullying	"bullying"*; intimidación; acoso escolar

C

English	Español
cafeteria	cafetería
California Association of Bilingual Education (CABE)	Asociación de Educación Bilingüe para California (CABE, por sus siglas en inglés)
California High School Proficiency Examination (CHSPE)	prueba de aptitud de la escuela preparatoria de California (CHSPE, por sus siglas en inglés)
campfire	fogata; fuego de campamento
campus	campus; plantel escolar
cap and gown	toga y birrete

capable	capaz
care	cuidado; supervisión
career counseling	asesoriamiento sobre carreras
career pathway	trayectoria de una carrera
career training	capacitación para una carrera universitaria o profesión
caring	comprensivo; bondadoso; amable; cariñoso
carryover funds	fondos remanentes
case manager	administrador del caso; coordinador del caso
categorical funds	fondos categóricos
categorical programs	programas categóricos
categorically funded programs	programas con financiamiento categórico
categorize, to	categorizar
cerebral palsy (CP)	parálisis cerebral (CP, por sus siglas en inglés)
certificate of proficiency	certificado de aptitud académica
challenge, to	desafiar: retar
chart	gráfica
charter school	escuela de convenio; escuela especial financiada por el estado
check out (item from library)	tomar prestado; prestar
chickenpox	varicela
child	niño; menor de edad
child abuse prevention program	programa para la prevención del maltrato de menores
child advocate	defensor de menores
child and family services	servicios para menores de edad y familias
child development program	programa de desarrollo infantil
child development training consortium (CDTC)	programa para la capacitación del desarrollo infantil (CDTC, por sus siglas en inglés)
child protective services (CPS)	servicios de protección a los menores de edad
child study team	equipo de estudio del niño
child welfare	bienestar de menores
childcare	guardería infantil; supervisión de niños

childhood development	desarrollo infantil; desarrollo del niño
children with disabilities	niños con discapacidades
children's health insurance program	programa de seguro médico para niños
chronological age	edad cronológica
citizenship	ciudadanía
civil registry	registro civil
claim, to	reclamar; asegurar
class size reduction	reducción de la proporción de estudiantes por maestro
classified personnel or staff	personal clasificado o sin certificado educativo de maestro
classroom	salón; aula; sala de clase
coach	entrenador
coach, to	entrenar
code of student behavior	código de conducta o comportamiento estudiantil
college	universidad
college preparation program	programa de preparación para ingresar a la universidad
command	orden
commencement	ceremonia de graduación
commend, to	elogiar
commission on teacher credentialing	comisión de acreditación para maestros
common core standards	normas estatales académicas de base común
community advisory committee (CAC)	comité asesor comunitario (CAC por sus siglas en inglés)
community college	universidad pública de dos años; instituto comunitario; colegio comunitario*
compensatory education	educación compensatoria
competency	capacidad; aptitud
competency-based curriculum	programa de estudios basado en las aptitudes del alumno
complainant	querellante
compliance	cumplimiento; conformidad
compliance review	evaluación del cumplimiento con los reglamentos

comply, to	cumplir
compose, to	redactar; escribir
composition	redacción; composición; ensayo
computer adaptive test/testing (CAT)	prueba adaptada administrada a través de una computadora (CAT, por sus siglas en inglés)
computer literacy	habilidades y conocimientos fundamentales informáticos
computer-based test/testing	prueba administrada a través de una computadora
conduct	comportamiento; conducta
confidence	confianza
confidential	confidencial
confidentiality	confidencialidad
congenital infections	infecciones congénitas
congratulate, to	felicitar
connectivity	conectividad
consent	consentimiento
consolidated application (ConApp)	solicitud consolidada (ConApp, por sus siglas en inglés)
consortium	consorcio
content knowledge	conocimiento académico
content standards	normas de contenido académico; estándares de contenido
continuing education units (CEU)	unidades de educación continuas (CEU, por sus siglas en inglés)
continuity of instruction	continuidad de instrucción
conventions of standard English grammar and usage	convenciones de la gramática y el uso estándar del inglés
cooperative learning	aprendizaje cooperativo
coordinator	coordinador
core academic classes	clases académicas principales; clases académicas básicas
core content connectors	conectores de contenido principal
core curriculum	currículo fundamental
core literature	obras literarias fundamentales
core program	programa de materias fundamentales

core subjects	materias fundamentales
correct, to	corregir
corrective action	acción correctiva; medidas correctivas
counseling	asesoramiento; orientación
counselor	consejero
country of origin	país de origen; país de procedencia
county office of education (COE)	oficina de educación del condado (COE, por sus siglas in inglés)
courtyard	patio
crayon	crayón; crayola
credential	credencial
criterion-referenced test	prueba basada en objetivos específicos
critical thinking	razonamiento crítico, razonamiento analítico
cross-cultural, language and academic development (CLAD)	desarrollo lingüístico, académico y transcultural (CLAD, por sus siglas en inglés)
cumulative file	expediente cumulativo
curriculum	currículo; plan de estudios
curriculum-based assessments	evaluaciones basadas en el currículo; pruebas basadas en el currículo
cursive	cursiva; letra pegada
custody	custodia

D

English	Español
damage	daño
dashboard	tablero de información
data	datos; información
data reporting office	Oficina de informes de datos
day care center	guardería infantil; cuidado para niños pequeños
day off	día libre
deadline	fecha límite; fecha de entrega
Deaf-Blind	sordoceguera

Deafness	sordera
decision-making	toma de decisiones
decline, to	rechazar
decode, to	decodificar; descrifrar
deficiency	deficiencia
deficit	déficit
delay	retrazo
demanding	exigente
deny, to	rechazar; negar
department of education (ED)	departmento de educación
department of justice (DOJ)	departamento de justiciar (DOJ, por sus siglas en Inglés)
depth of knowledge	profundidad o intensidad del conocimiento
descriptive essay	ensayo descriptivo
designated primary language test (DPLT)	prueba designada en la lengua natal (DPLT, por sus siglas en inglés)
designated supports	apoyos designados
development standards	normas de desarrollo
developmental bilingual program	programa formativo bilingüe
developmental delay	retraso del desarrollo
developmental disability	discapacidad de desarrollo(DD, por sus siglas en inglés)
devices	dispositivos; aparatos
diagnostic assessment	evaluación diagnóstica
dictation	dictado
differentiated instruction	instrucción diferenciada
digital library	biblioteca digital
diligent	diligente; cuidadoso
diphtheria	difteria
directions for test administration	instrucciones para la administración de pruebas
disabilities	discapacidades; incapacidades
disabled	discapacitado; incapacitado
disadvantage	desventaja; obstáculo

disciplinary core ideas (DCI)	ideas centrales disciplinarias
disclosure	revelación; divulgación
discourage	disuadir a
discrimination	discriminación
discuss	tratar, hablar sobre, dialogar
dishonest	deshonesto
disobedient	desobediente
disorder	trastorno; problema
display, to	exhibir; mostrar
disrespectful	irrespetuoso; grosero
disrupt, to	interrumpir; perturbar
dissect	diseccionar
distance learning	aprendizaje a distancia
distance learning professional development	capacitación docente a distancia
district English language advisory committee (DELAC)	comité asesor de padres de aprendices de inglés del distrito (DELAC, por sus siglas en inglés)
districtwide	de todo el distrito; por todo el distrito
disturb, to	interrumpir; molestar; inquietar
disturbance	alboroto; disturbio
domain	campo; dominio; ámbito
door to door	de puerta en puerta
double-check, to	volver a revisar; chequear de nuevo
Down syndrome	síndrome de Down
download	descargar; bajar
draft	borrador
dress code	código de vestir; reglamento de vestimenta
dropdown menu	menú desplegable
dropout	estudiante que abandona los estudios
dropout rate	tasa de abandono escolar
dual language development	desarrollo de dos idiomas
dual language immersion	inmersión dual; doble inmersión
dual language learner	aprendiz de dos idiomas

due process	proceso debido
durable medical equipment	equipo médico duradero
dyslexia	dislexia

E

English	Español
early advanced performance level	nivel de rendimiento avanzado inicial
early assessment program (EAP)	programa de evaluación temprana (EAP, por sus siglas en inglés)
early childhood	primeros años de la infancia; primera infancia
early childhood education	educación en la primera infancia
early intermediate performance level	nivel de rendimiento intermedio
early intervention	intervención temprana
early intervention program	programa de intervención temprana
early literacy	lectoescritura temprana; alfabetización temprana
early literacy assessment	prueba de lectoescritura temprana; prueba de alfabetización temprana
early literacy program	programa de lectoescritura temprana; programa de alfabetización temprana
early release day	día de salida temprana
earth and space science	ciencia de la tierra y el espacio
earthquake drill	simulacro de un terremoto
economic impact aid	ayuda de impacto económico
economically disadvantaged	de bajos recursos económicos
education center	centro educativo
education code (EC)	código de educación (EC, por sus siglas en inglés)
education data	datos escolares
Education for All Handicapped Children (EHA)	educación para todos los niños con discapacidad (EHA; por sus siglas en inglés)
education level	nivel de educación
education programs consultant	consultor de programas educativos
education reform	reforma educativa

educational performance	desempeño académico
effective communication skills	habilidad para la comunicación eficaz
effective date	a partir de la fecha; fecha de entrada en vigor
effective expression	expresión eficaz
effort	esfuerzo
elective classes	materias o clases opcionales
electronic device	dispositivo; accesorio electrónico
Elementary and Secondary Education Act (ESEA), U.S.	ley federal para la educación primaria y secundaria (ESEA, por sus siglas en inglés)
elementary education	educación primaria
eligibility	idoneidad; requisites; elegibilidad*
eligible	con derecho a; cumple con los requisites; elegible*
email	correo electrónico; mail*
embedded performance task	ejercicio de rendimiento integrado o de rendimiento incrustado
emerging level	nivel emergente
emotional disturbance	trastorno emocional (ED, por sus siglas en inglés)
emotionally disturbed	individuo emocionalmente trastornado
enact, to	promulgar; decretar
encode, to	codificar
encourage, to	animar; motivar
engage, to	propiciar la participación; lograr la participación; participar
engineering, technology, and application of science	ingeniería, tecnología, y aplicación de la ciencia
English as a second language (ESL)	inglés como segundo idioma (ESL, por sus siglas en inglés)
English language acquisition	proceso de aprendizaje del inglés como segundo idioma; adquisición del inglés como segundo idioma
English language arts (ELA)	artes del lenguaje inglés (ELA, por sus siglas en inglés)
English language arts standards	normas académicas de las artes del lenguaje inglés
English language arts/literacy	artes del lenguaje inglés y la lectoescritura

English language development (ELD)	desarrollo del inglés (ELD, por sus siglas en inglés)
English language development standards	normas para el desarrollo del inglés (ELL, por sus siglas en inlés)
English language learner (ELL)	estudiante del idioma inglés (ELL, por sus siglas en inglés)
English language proficiency	dominio del inglés
English learner (EL)	aprendiz del inglés; estudiante que está aprendiendo inglés (EL, por sus siglas en inglés)
English learner advisory committee (ELAC)	comité asesor de padres de aprendices de inglés (ELAC, por sus siglas en inglés)
English learners (ELs)	aprendices del inglés (ELs, por sus siglas en inglés)
English placement test (EPT)	examen de colocación en lengua y lectura en inglés (EPT, por sus siglas en inglés)
English proficient	competente o proficiente en inglés
enrichment	enriquecimiento
enroll	matricular; inscriber; registrar*
enrollment	inscripción; matrícula
entry level mathematics (ELM) test	examen de colocación en matemáticas (ELM, por sus siglas en inglés)
environment	medio ambiente; ambiente
equal opportunity	igualdad de oportunidades
equation	ecuación
equity	equidad
eraser	goma de borrar; borrador
essential understanding	comprensión esencial
establish, to	establecer
ethnic group	grupo étnico
ethnicity	etnicidad; origen étnico
evaluation	evaluación
Every Student Succeeds Act (ESSA), U.S.	la ley que cada estudiante triunfa (ESSA, por sus siglas en inglés)
evidence-based decisions	decisiones basadas en pruebas
examination	examen
examples	ejemplos

excited	emocionado; animado
exempt	exento (de)
exempt, to	eximir
exemption	exención
expanded learning time	tiempo de aprendizaje aumentado
expanding performance level	nivel de rendimiento en ampliación; nivel de rendimiento ampliado
expectation	expectativa
expected schoolwide learning results (ESLR)	resultados de aprendizaje previstos para todos los estudiantes de la escuela (ESLR, por sus siglas en inglés)
expel, to	expulsar
expenses	gastos
expiration	vencimiento; terminación
expire, to	expirar; vencer
extended school year	año escolar prolongado; año escolar extendido
extracurricular	extracurricular

F

English	Español
facilitator	coordinador
facilities	instalaciones
faculty	facultad; profesorado; cuerpo docente
fail, to	reprobar; no pasar; fracazar
family cost share	costo familiar compartido
family directed assessment	evaluación enfocada en la familia
Family Educational Rights and Privacy Act (FERPA), U.S.	ley de privacidad y derechos educativos de la familia (FERPA, por sus siglas en inglés)
family engagement	participación de la familia
federal disability category	categoría federal de discapacidad
fee	cuota; honorario; precio
feedback	retroalimentación; respuesta; sugerencia

field test	ensayo de campo; investigación preliminar
field trip	excursión; viaje de estudios; paseo escolar
figure	número; cifra
file folder	carpeta; fólder
file, to	archivar
financial literacy	el conocimiento financiero
fine motor skills	habilidades motrices finas
fire drill	simulacro de incendios
first aid kit	botiquín de primeros auxilios
flag salute	saludo a la bandera
flexibility	flexibilidad
fluency	fluidez; dominio
fluent English proficient (FEP)	con fluidez competente en inglés; con dominio del inglés ; con conocimiento avanzado de inglés (FEP, por sus siglas en inglés)
fluent reader	lector con fluidez
flyer	volante; panfleto
focus areas	áreas de enfoque
focus, to	enfocarse; concentrarse
folder	carpeta; archive; fólder
forgery	falsificación
form (for documents)	formulario; forma*
formative assessment	evaluación formativa
formative assessment practices	prácticas de la evaluación formativa
formative tools and processes	instrumentos y procesos formativos
forum	foro
foster care	cuidado temporal; hogar sustituto
foster home	hogar de acogida; hogar de crianza
foster parent	padres de jóvenes en hogar temporal; padre sustituto
foster youth	joven en hogar temporal; niño adoptivo
foundation	fundamento
foundational skills	habilidades fundamentales

fraction	fracción
framework	marco curricular
free and appropriate public education (FAPE)	educación pública gratuita y apropiada (FAPE, por sus siglas en inglés)
frequently asked questions (FAQs)	preguntas frecuentes (FAQs, por sus siglas en inglés)
full-time equivalent (FTE)	equivalente a un puesto de tiempo completo (FTE, por sus siglas en inglés)
fully mainstreamed	totalmente integrado al programa educativo regular
functional behavioral assessment (FBA)	evaluación de la conducta functional (FBA, por sus siglas en inglés
functional performance	desempeño funcional
fundraiser	recaudación de fondos; recaudador de fondos
funds	fondos
fussy	meticuloso; quisquilloso; exigente

G

English	Español
gain, to	obtener; conseguir; get; alcanzar
game	partido; juego
game plan	estrategia; proyecto; esquema; plan básico
gang prevention program	programa para la prevención de pandillas
gap	brecha
gather relevant information, to	recopilar información pertinente
general academic and domain-specific words and phrases	palabras y frases de uso académico general o específico de una disciplina
general education program	programa de educación general
general equivalency diploma (GED)	prueba del desarrollo educativo general (GED, por sus siglas en inglés)
gifted and talented education (GATE) program	educación para estudiantes talentosos y dotados (GATE, por sus siglas en inglés)
glue	pegamento
goal	meta; objetivo

good cause	motivo justificado
governing board	junta directiva
grade level	grado escolar; nivel de grado
grade point average (GPA)	promedio de calificaciones (GPA, por sus siglas en inglés)
grade, to	corregir; calificar
grade-level standards	normas al nivel del grado escolar
graduate, to	graduarse
graduation	graduación
graduation ceremony	ceremonia de graduación
graduation rates	índice de graduación
grant	subvención; beca; donación
grant writer	redactor de propuestas para solicitar subvenciones
gross motor skills	habilidades motrices gruesas
growth	crecimiento
guardian	tutor (legal); guardian*
guardianship	tutela legal; custodia; guarda y custodia
guide	guía
guidelines	directrices; reglas generales; pautas; normas
gym	gimnasio; gimnasia

H

English	Español
habit	costumbre; hábito
habits of mind	hábitos del pensamiento
habitual truant	estudiante que falta a la escuela de manera habitual, sin justificación
handbook	manual
handicap *Note: term considered outdated*	discapacidad; impedimemnto; desventaja; limitación
handwriting	letra manuscrita; caligrafía; escritura

harass, to	acosar; hostigar
harassment	acoso; hostigamiento
harmful	dañino
Head Start program, U.S.	"Head Start"*
health assessment	evaluación de la salud
health impairment	impedimento de salud; discapacidad médica
healthy fitness zone	zona de aptitud física saludable
hearing	audiencia; oído
hearing impairment	impedimento auditivo; hipoacusia
heritage language program	programa de idiomas de herencia
high academic level	alto nivel académico
high achievement	alto rendimiento
high expectations	expectativas altas
high frequency	alta frecuencia
high performance school	escuela de alto redimiento
high school	escuela secundaria; la preparatoria
high school equivalency tests	pruebas de equivalencia de secundaria
higher education	educación superior
highest obtainable scale score	el puntaje de escala más alto que se puede obtener
highlight, to	destacar; resaltar
highly qualified teacher	maestro altamente acreditado
high-quality assessment	evaluación de alta calidad
high-stakes assessment	evaluación con consecuencias mayores
high-stakes testing	pruebas con consecuencias mayores
history, social science	historia-ciencias sociales
hit, to	golpear; pegar
hole punch	perforadora; taladradora
holiday	día festivo
holistic	holístico; global
home instruction	instrucción en el hogar
home language	lengua materna o nativa; idioma del hogar

home language survey (HLS)	encuesta de la lengua materna; encuesta del idioma del hogar (HLS, por sus siglas en inglés)
home schooling	enseñanza en el hogar; educación en la casa
home study program	programa de cursos a distancia; programa de cursos en casa
home visit	visita al hogar
homeless	sin hogar; desalojado
household	hogar; casa
hybrid adaptive test	prueba de adaptación híbrida
hyperactivity	hiperactividad

I

English	Español
icebreaker	rompehielos; actividad para romper el hielo
illiteracy	analfabetismo
illiterate	analfabeto
immature	inmaduro
immigrant	inmigrante
immunization	vacuna; inmunización; vacunación
impairment	discapacidad; impedimento
implementation	implementación
improve, to	mejorar
improvement plan	plan de mejora
inappropriate	inapropiado
incapable	incapaz
inclusive education	educación inclusiva
independent study program	programa de estudios independientes; programa de estudios autónomos
individual family service plan (IFSP)	plan de servicio individualizado para la familia (IFSP, por sus siglas en inglés)
individualized education program (IEP)	programa individualizado de educación (IEP, por sus siglas en inglés)

individualized service plan (ISP)	plan de servicios individualizados (ISP, por sus siglas en inglés)
Individuals with Disabilities Education Act (IDEA), U.S.	ley de la educación para individuos con discapacidades (IDEA, por sus siglas en inglés)
indoor	adentro; bajo techo
information bulletin	boletín informativo
informed clinical opinion (ICO)	opinión clínica informada (ICO, por sus siglas en inglés)
initial assessment	evaluación inicial
initial identification	identificación inicial
initially fluent English proficient (I-FEP)	inicialmente designado como un estudiante con dominio del inglés (I-FEP, por sus siglas en inglés)
in-person instruction	instrucción presencial
in-service	entrenamiento; capacitación en el trabajo
insight	conocimiento
instructional aide	ayudante de maestro; asistente de maestro
instructional materials	materiales de enseñanza
instructional strategies	estrategias de enseñanza
integer	número entero
integrated English language development	desarrollo del inglés integrado
intellectual disability	discapacidad intelectual
intelligence quotient (IQ)	cociente intelectual; coeficiente intelectual (IQ, por sus siglas en inglés)
interdistrict transfer	transferencia interdistrital (a otra escuela de otro distrito)
interface	interfaz; interrelacción
interim alternative educational setting (IAES)	ambiente educativo provisional alternativo (IAES, por sus siglas en inglés)
interim alternative educational setting (IAES)	ambiente educativo provisional (IAES< por sus siglas en inglés)
interim assessments	evaluaciones interinas; evaluaciones provisionales
interim comprehensive assessment (ICA)	Evaluación integral provisional (ICA, por sus siglas en inglés)

intermediate performance level	nivel de rendimiento intermedio
intern	pasante; practicante; interno
internship	pasantía; práctica
intervention program	programa de intervención
intradistrict	intradistrital (dentro del distrito escolar)
introduce claims, to	presentar reclamaciones; reclamar
involvement	participación; involucramiento;
issue	asunto; cuestión; tema
issue, to	expedir; emitir

J

English	Español
join, to	formar parte
journey	viaje; trayecto
jump rope	cuerda de saltar
junior high school	escuela secundaria (grados 6 al 8); escuela de enseñanza media
juvenile court school	escuela del tribunal de menores
juvenile justice system	sistema de justicia juvenil

K

English	Español
keep up, to	mantenerse al día
keyboard	teclado
kind	amable; bondadoso
kindergarten	jardín de infancia; jardín infantil; kindergarten
kindergarten continuance form	formulario de permanencia en kindergarten
kinesthetic	cenestésico

L

English	Español
language	idioma; lengua; lenguaje
language acquisition program	programa de adquisición de idiomas
language arts	artes del lenguaje; gramática y literatura
language assessment results	resultados de la evaluación de idiomas
language assessment scales (LAS)	escalas de evaluación del lenguaje (LAS, por sus siglas en inglés)
language development	desarrollo de la lengua
language other than English	un idioma aparte del inglés
language policy and leadership office (LPLO)	oficina de liderazgo en la política del lenguaje (LPLO, por sus siglas en inglés)
language proficiency	dominio del idioma
language reclassification	reclasificación del lenguaje
large-scale assessment	evaluación a gran escala
last name	apellido
latest technology	tecnología más avanzada o reciente
lead agency	agencia principal
learner	aprendiz
learning continuity and attendance plan template	modelo del plan de continuidad de aprendizaje y asistencia
learning disability	discapacidad o limitación en el aprendizaje
learning loss	pérdida de aprendizaje
learning strategies	estrategias de aprendizaje
least restrictive environment (LRE)	ambiente lo menos restrictivo (LRE, por sus siglas en inglés)
letter grade	calificación con letra(s); nota con letra(s)
life science	ciencias naturales
limited English proficient (LEP)	limitado en su conocimiento del inglés (LEP por sus siglas en inglés)
link (as in internet or web link)	enlace
listening comprehension	comprensión auditiva
literacy	lectoescritura; alfabetización
literacy standards for history, social studies	normas literarias en historia y estudios sociales

literate	alfabetizado; que sabe leer y escribir
litter	basura
local control	control local
local control and accountability plan (LCAP)	plan de rendición de cuentas con control local (LCAP, por sus siglas en inglés)
local control funding formula (LCFF)	fórmula de financiamiento con control local (LCFF, por sus siglas en inglés)
local education agency (LEA)	agencia de educación local; agencia educativa local (LEA, por sus siglas en inglés)
locate	localizar; ubicar
locker	casillero
long-term English learner (LTEL)	aprendiz de inglés de largo plazo (LTEL, por sus siglas en inglés)
low achiever	de bajo rendimiento
low incidence	de incidencia baja
low income	bajos ingresos
lowercase letter	letra minúscula
lowest obtainable scale score	puntaje de escala más baja de la que se puede obtener
low-income families	familias de bajos ingresos
low-performing schools	escuelas de bajo rendimiento
lowest obtainable scale score	puntaje de escala más baja de la que se puede obtener

M

English	Español
magnet school	escuela especializada
mainstream English	inglés regular; inglés convencial
maintenance	mantenimiento
malicious mischief	agravio malicioso
mandatory	obligatorio
manipulatives	manipulativos
marital status	estado civil
marker	marcador

master schedule	horario general
mastery	dominio
Maternal and Child Health Bureau (MCHB), U.S.	Oficia Federal de la Salud materna e infantil (MCHB, por sus siglas en inglés)
math facts	datos matemáticos; operaciones matemáticas
mathematics	matemáticas
mathematics coach	entrenador de instrucción de matemáticas
maturity	madurez
mean	promedio
meaning making	construcción de significados
measles, mumps, rubella (MMR) vaccine	sarampión, paperas, rubeola (MMR, por sus siglas en inglés)
measurable objectives	objetivos medibles
Measures of Academic Progress (MAP), U.S.	medida del rendimiento y progreso académico (MAPP, por sus siglas en inglés)
meeting	reunión; junta
mental health	salud mental
mentally retarded[29]	retrasado mental; con retraso mental
mentor, to	servir como mentor
message	mensaje
method	método
middle school	escuela secundaria (grados 6 a 8); escuela intermedia
Migrant Education Program, U.S.	programa de educación para alumnos migrantes
minimum academic requirements	requisitos académicos mínimos
minimum skills	destrezas mínimas
minor	menor de edad
minorities	minorías
minority children	niños de grupos minoritarios
minutes	actas; minutas
misbehave, to	portarse mal
mischievous	travieso

---

[29] This term is normally no longer used, though as the interpreter you may hear it said in rare cases.

misdemeanor	delito menor
mishap	percance; accidente; contratiempo
modifications	modificaciones
modified educational assessment	prueba modificada de la evaluación educativa
molest, to	abusar sexualmente; acosar
monitor academic progress	monitorear el progreso académico
monitor, to	supervisar; monitorear
monolingual	monolingüe
most significant cognitive disabilities	discapacidades cognitivas más significantes
motion	petición; moción
motor skills	habilidades motoras
move (a proposal), to	proponer
multicultural education	educación multicultural
multidisciplinary evaluation	evaluación multidisciplinaria
multiple disabilities	discapacidades múltiples
multiple measures	medidas múltiples
multiple-choice questions	preguntas de opción múltiple
multiplication tables	tablas de multiplicar
multisensory	multisensorial
multitrack schools	escuelas multipistas
mumps	paperas

N

English	Español
National Assessment of Educational Progress (NAEP), U.S.	evaluación nacional del progreso educativo (NAEP, por sus siglas en inglés)
National Center and State Collaborative (NCSC), U.S.	colaboración nacional de centros y estados (NCSC, por sus siglas en inglés)
national origin	origen nacional
Native American	nativo americano
Native American Indian	indio nativo americano
native English speakers	angloparlantes; hablantes nativos del inglés

native language	lengua materna; idioma principal
near standard	cerca de la norma
neat	ordenado; aseado
need improvement, to	necesita mejorar
needs assessment	evaluación de necesidades
needy	necesitado
neglected	abandonado; descuidado
network	red; sistema; enlace
newcomer center	centro para recien llegados
newsletter	boletín informativo
No Child Left Behind (NCLB) Act, U.S.	ley de 2001 que ningún niño se quede atrás (NCLB, por sus siglas en inglés)
non-English speaking	que no habla inglés
nontechnical language	lenguaje que no sea técnico
norm-referenced results	resultados con referencia a las normas (de rendimiento académico)
not yet ready	aún no está preparado/a
notarized	notarizado
notice	notificación; aviso
notice of disclosure of student records	Aviso de divulgación de registros escolares
novice	principiante
nuances in word meanings	matices en el significado de las palabras
nurse	enfermero
nurse's office	enfermería
nursery school	guardería de niños; guardería infantil

O

English	Español
objection to disclosure of student information and records	objeción a la publicación de información y registros de los estudiantes
objective	objetivo
occupation	ocupación; puesto; oficio

occupational therapy	terapia ocupacional
offer, to	ofrecer
Office for Civil Rights (OCR), U.S. Department of Health and Human Services	oficina para derechos civiles (OCR, por sus siglas en inglés) del departamento de educación de los EEUU
Office of Special Education Programs (OSEP), U.S. Department of Education	oficina de los Programas de Educación especial (OSEP, por sus siglas en inglés)
Office of the Secretary, U.S. Department of Education	Oficina de la secretaría de educación
official records	expedientes oficiales
omit, to	omitir; olvidar
on task	enfocado; concentrado en su deber
online	en línea
online reporting system	sistema de reportes por línea
onsite	en el mismo lugar; in situ; allí mismo
on-task	enfocado; concentrado en su deber
open house	exposición escolar
opening	puesto disponible; vacante
opt out	optar por negar; no participar; rechazar
oral language	expresión oral
oral language skills	destrezas de expresión oral
oral vocabulary	vocabulario oral
orderly	ordenado; metódico
orthopedic impairment	impedimento ortopédico
outdoor	al aire libre; afuera
outline, to	hacer un esquema; resumir; señalar
outsource, to	subcotratar; terceriar
outstanding	sobresaliente; extraordinario; excelente
over-the-phone interpreting (OPI)	interpretación por teléfono (OPI, por sus siglas en inglés)
overall	total; global; en general
overall performance level	nivel de rendimiento total; nivel de rendimiento global
override	anular; invalidar

overview	resumen, descripción
owl pellets	egagrópilos; regurgitaciones de buhos o lechuzas

P

English	Español
pamphlet	folleto
paraprofessional	paraprofesional; ayudante de maestro
parent advisory council (PAC)	consejo asesor de padres de familia (PAC, por sus siglas en inglés)
Parent Teacher Association (PTA)	organización de padres y maestros (PTA, por sus siglas en inglés)
parent-teacher conference	reunión de padres y maestros; conferencia de padres y maestros
parent training and information center	centro de capacitación e información para padres
parental notification	notificación para padres de familia
parents and guardians	padres y tutores
parking lot	estacionamiento; parqueo
participation criteria	criterio para la participación
partner, to	colaborar; asociar
partnership for assessment of readiness	asociación para la evaluación de la preparación
party	parte
pass, to	aprobar; pasar
pattern	patrón
peer	compañero; colega
peer counseling	consejo por compañeros
peer pressure	presión de amigos
penalty of perjury	pena de perjurio
penmanship[30]	caligrafía
percentage	porcentaje
performance	rendimiento; desempeño; representación

---

[30] The more inclusive and preferred term is *handwriting*.

performance assessments	evaluaciones de rendimiento
performance level	nivel de rendimiento
performance report	informe de rendimiento
performance standards	normas de rendimiento
performance tasks	ejercicios de rendimiento
personally identifiable information (PII)	información personal identificable (PII, por sus siglas en inglés)
persuade, to	persuadir
phoneme	fonema
physical education	educación física
physical fitness test (PFT)	examen de aptitud física (PFT, por sus siglas en inglés)
physical science	ciencia física
physical therapy (PT)	terapia física; fisioterapia
pilot test	examen piloto
place value	lugar posicional
placement test	examen de colocación
plagiarism	plagio
playground	patio de recreo
pledge of allegiance	promesa de lealtad
poke, to	dar un toque; clavar; empujar
policy	reglamento; regla
population sampling	muestra de la población
positive behavioral interventions and support (PBIS)	apoyos e intervenciones para obtener una conducta positive (PBIS, por sus siglas en inglés)
post test	prueba posterior
post, to (on board, on web)	publicar; mostrar; compartir; enviar
postmark	sello postal
postsecondary	postsecundario
pout, to	poner mala cara; hacer pucheros
practice tests	exámenes de práctica
preliminary indicators	indicadores preliminares
preschool	escuela preescolar; parvulario; jardín de infancia;

preschool children	niños en edad preescolar
preschool learning foundations	fundamentos de aprendizaje preescolar
preschool teacher	maestro/a de preescolar o de guardería
present claims and findings, to	presentar resultados y postulaciones
pretesting	prueba preliminar
preview, to	ver previamente
primary language	lengua materna; idioma natal
principal	director
print, to	escribir con letra de molde; escribir de imprenta
printer	copiadora
prior written notice	notificación previa por escrit
problem-solving	resolución de problemas
procedure	procedimiento
proceeds	ganancias; ingresos
process server	oficial notificador; agente judicial
proctor	supervisor
proctor, to	supervisar
profanity	grosería, maldición
professional development or learning (PD)	capacitación; desarrollo profesional (PD) por sus siglas en inglés
proficiency	aptitud; dominio; competencia
proficiency level	nivel de competencia
proficient	proficiente
proficient performance level	nivel de rendimiento proficiente
program improvement (PI)	mejora de programa (PI, for sus siglas en inglés)
program of study	programa de estudios
progress report	informe de progreso; boleta de calificaciones
project	proyecto
proof	constancia; verificación; comprobante; prueba
proposal	propuesta
proposition	iniciativa de ley
protected	protegido

provide, to	suministrar; ofrecer; proporcionar
provision	disposición
psychiatrist	psiquiatra
psycholinguistic	psicolingüístico
psychologist	psicólogo
public reporting	informes públicos
public school	escuela pública
pull-out program	programa en otro salón; programa en un salón diferente
punch, to	golpear; dar un puñetazo
pupil learning loss	pérdida de aprendizaje del alumno
Pythagorean theory	teoría pitagórea

Q

English	Español
qualification	cualificación; título; certificación
qualitative information	información cualitativa
quality improvement	mejora de calidad
quantitative information	información cuantitativa
quarter	trimestre
questionnaire	cuestionario
quiz	prueba; examen

R

English	Español
range of reading and level of text complexity	rango de lectura y nivel de complejidad del texto
rate of transiency	tasa de movilidad estudiantil
ratio	proporción
raw score	puntuación bruta
readiness	disposición, preparación

reading	lectura
reading comprehension	comprensión de lectura
reading placement	colocación para la lectura
reading readiness skills	aptitudes para la lectura
ready	preparado; listo
reason	razón
reauthorization	reautorización
recently arrived English learner	aprendiz de inglés recién llegado
receptive language	idioma receptivo
recess	recreo; descanso
reclassification	reclasificación
reclassified fluent English proficient (R-FEP)	estudiante reclasificado competente en inglés; reclasificado con dominio del inglés (R-FEP, por sus siglas en inglés)
record	expediente (académico); datos; registro; récord
register, to	matricular; inscriber; registrar*
registration fees	cuota de matrícula; cuota de inscripción
registration form	formulario de matrícula; formulario de inscripción
regulations	reglamentos
reject, to	rechazar
related services	servicios relacionados
release days	días libres
reliability	fiabilidad; confiabilidad
reliable	fiable; confiable; responsable
remedial course	curso de nivelación; curso correctivo
removal from bus	sacar del autobús
report card	reporte de calificaciones; libreta de calificaciones
reporting cluster	conjunto que forma parte del reporte
required	obligatorio; necesario; requerido
requirement	requisito
research-based	basado en la investigación
resign, to	renunciar

resolution	acuerdo; resolución
resource room	salón de recursos (en educación especial)
resource specialist	especialiata en recursos
response to intervention	respuesta a la intervención
restructuring	reestructuración
retain, to	retener; quedarse con
retention	retención; quedarse en el mismo grado
revocation of consent	revocación del consentimiento
reward, to	recompensar; premiar
right	derecho
robbery	robo
roll call	pasar lista; tomar lista
row	fila; hilera
rubella	rubeola; sarampión alemán
rubric	rúbrica
rule	regla

S

English	Español
safe	seguro
salary	sueldo; salario; ingreso
salutatorian	estudiante que da la bienvenida
sample (as in sample report)	muestra; ejemplo
scaffolding	apoyo estructurado; enseñanza estructurada
scale score	puntuación escalada
schedule	horario
schedule, to	programar; citar
scholarship	beca
scholastic aptitude test	prueba de aptitud escolar
school accountability report card (SARC)	reporte escolar de rendición de cuentas (SARC, por sus siglas en inglés)

school advisory committee	comité consultivo de la escuela
school based	escolar
school board	mesa directiva escolar; junta directiva de la escuela
school calendar	calendario escolar
school choice	opción de escuela
school district	distrito escolar
school improvement plan	plan de mejoramiento escolar
school nutrition	nutrición escolar
school property	propiedad escolar
school records	registros escolares; expedientes escolares
school reform	reforma educativa; reforma escolar
school site administrator	administrador de la escuela
school site council (SSC)	consejo directivo escolar (SSC, por sus siglas en inglés)
school year	año escolar
schoolwide program	programa escolar; programa a nivel escolar
science and engineering practices (SEP)	prácticas de ciencia e ingeniería (SEP, por sus siglas en inglés)
science camp	campamento de ciencias
science framework	marco curricular para las ciencias
scientifically based methods	métodos científicos
score	puntaje; nota; calificación
scoring guide	guía de puntaje o de notas
scratch paper	papel borrador
screen	pantalla
screening	evaluación
script	guión
seal	sello
second language acquisition	adquisición del segundo idioma
secondary education	enseñanza secundaria; enseñanza media; educación secundaria
secretary of education	secretaría de educación

self-advocacy	auto-abogacía; auto-defensoría; auto-representación
self-concept	autoestima; amor propio
self-contained placement	colocación en un salón especial por tiempo completo
self-control	autocontrol; dominio propio
self-correction	autocorrección
self-esteem	autoestima; amor propio
Senate bill (SB), U.S.	proyecto de ley del senado (SB)
sensory impairments	impedimentos sensoriales
set forth, to	exponer; expresar
severely emotionally disturbed	con perturbaciones emocionales serias; con severo trastorno emocional
share the screen, to	compartir la pantalla
sheltered English instruction	instrucción estructurada en inglés; instrucción contextualizada en inglés
short-term objectives	objetivos a corto plazo
showcase, to	exhibir; mostrar
sibling	hermano o hermana
significant cognitive disabilities	discapacidades cognitivas significativas
single plan for student achievement (SPSA)	único plan escolar de rendimiento (SPSA, por sus siglas en inglés)
skills	destrezas; habilidades; capacidades
slogan	lema
slur	insulto; agravio
Smarter Balanced Assessment Consortium (Smarter Balanced)	consorcio de exámenes (conocido en inglés como Smarter Balanced)
social and emotional well-being	bienestar social y emocional
social skills	habilidades sociales
socioeconomically disadvantaged students	estudiantes desfavorecidos socioeconómicamente
somewhat developed	algo desarrollado
sound symbol association	asociación de sonidos y símbolos
Spanish language	idioma español; idioma castellano

Spanish language assessment procedures	procedimientos de evaluación en el idioma español
Spanish language development standards	normas del desarrollo de la lengua española
Spanish speaker	hispanohablante; de habla hispana
speaking	expresión oral; producción oral
speaking and listening	expresión oral y comprensión auditiva
special day class	clase especial de día
special day class (SDC)	clase para estudiantes con discapacidades; clase especial de día (SDC, por sus siglas en inglés)
special education	educación especial; educación inclusiva
special education local planning area (SELPA)	área de planificación local para la educación especial (SELPA, por sus siglas en inglés)
specific learning disability (SLD)	discapacidad especifica de aprendizaje (SLD, por sus siglas en inglés)
speech or language impairment	trastorno del habla o lenguaje
speech therapist	terapeuta del habla; fonoaudiólogo
speech therapy	terapia del habla; logopedia
spelling	ortografía; deletreo
spring recess	vacaciones de primavera
staff	personal docente; empleados
staff development	capacitación del personal; entrenamiento del personal
staffroom	salón o sala de profesores o maestros
stakeholder engagement	involucramiento de las partes interesadas
stakeholders	partes interesadas
stalk, to	seguir; acechar; acosar
standard exceeded	norma superada
standard met	norma lograda
standard nearly met	norma casi lograda
standard not met	norma no lograda
standardized testing	pruebas estandarizadas o normalizadas
standards	normas
standards-aligned instruction	enseñanza alineada con las normas
standards-based curriculum	currículo basado en las normas

staple	grapa; grampa
stapler	engrapadora; grapadora
state accountability report card	informe de rendición de cuentas estatal
state assigned student identifier (SASID)	identificación estatal asignada al estudiante (SASID, por sus siglas en inglés)
state board of education (SBE)	mesa directiva estatal de educación (SBE, por sus siglas en inglés)
state curriculum framework	marco curricular del estado
state department of education	departamento de Educación del Estado
state education agency (SEA)	agencia de Educación del Estado (SEA, por sus siglas en inglés)
state exams	exámenes estatales
state network of educators	red estatal de educadores
state performance plan (SPP)	plan de rendimiento del estado (SPP, por sus siglas en inglés)
state seal of biliteracy (SSB)	sello estatal de alfabetización bilingüe (de California) (SSB, por sus siglas en inglés)
state superintendent of public instruction (SSPI)	superintendente de instrucción pública del estado (SSPI, por sus siglas en inglés)
state-determined assessment calendar	calendario de pruebas determinado por el estado
state-mandated program	programa estatal obligatorio
status and change	estado y cambio
status level	nivel de aptitud
stepfather	padrastro
stepmother	madrastra
stimuli	estímulos
strengths	puntos fuertes
strike, to	golpear; pegar; cancelar
strive, to	esforzarse; tratar de
structured English immersion	inmersión estructurada en inglés
struggle, to	tener dificultades
student achievement	desempeño del estudiante
student achievement data	datos de rendimiento estudiantil
student body	alumnado; estudiantado

student oral language observation matrix (SOLOM)	matriz de observación del language oral (SOLOM por sus siglas en inglés)
student outcomes	resultados de los estudiantes
student score report information web page	página web de información sobre los informes de puntaje de los estudiantes
student scores	puntaje de los estudiantes
student study team (SST)	equipo de especialistas que estudian al estudiante; Comité de evaluación pedagógica (SST, por sus siglas en inglés)
students' strengths and weaknesses	puntos fuertes y débiles del alumno
subject	materia; tema; asignatura
substitute teacher	maestro suplente
succeed, to	tener éxito; lograr; triunfar
successful	exitoso
suggestion	sugerencia
summary	resumen; sumario
summative assessment	evaluación sumativa
summer break	vacaciones de verano
sunflower	girasol; mirasol
supervise, to	supervisar; vigilar
supplemental	suplementario
supplementary materials	materiales suplementarios
support services	servicios auxiliaries; servicios de apoyo
support staff	personal auxiliar; personal de apoyo
support, to	apoyar
surrogate parent	padre o madre suplente; padre sustituto
survey	encuesta
suspend, to	suspender
suspension	suspensión; exclusión
sustained silent reading	lectura en silencio continua
syllabus	plan de estudios; programa didáctico
systematic	sistemático
systemic	sistémico

T

English	Español
take effect	entrar en vigor; entrar en vigencia
tardy	tardanza; llegada tarde
targeted assistance schools	escuelas que reciben asistencia específica
task	ejercicio; tarea; deber
task force	grupo encargado de un proyecto; operativo
task, to be on	estar enfocado; concentrarse
teacher and leader evaluation and support systems including student learning and observations	evaluación de los maestros y directores y sistemas de apoyo que incluyen el aprendizaje estudiantil y observaciones
teacher qualifications	calificaciones del maestro
teacher quality	calidad del maestro
team teaching	enseñanza en equipo; instrucción en equipo
technical assistance	asistencia técnica
technical assistance and monitoring office (TAMO)	oficina de asistencia técnica y monitoreo (TAMO, por sus siglas en inglés)
technical school	escuela técnica
technical support	apoyo técnico
technology-enhanced tests	pruebas que incluyen tecnología
term	término
test	examen; prueba
test administration window	período de administración de las pruebas o exámenes
test administrator	examinador; administrador del examen
test assessing secondary completion (TASC)	prueba de evaluación de finalización secundaria (TASC, por sus siglas en inglés)
test blueprint	plan del contenido de la prueba
test results	resultados del exámen o prueba
test score guide web page	página web de la guía de los resultados de los exámenes
textbook	libro de texto
theater arts	arte dramático
theft	robo

third party	terceros
threat	amenaza
threaten, to	amenazar
three ring binder	carpeta de tres argollas; archivador de tres argollas
thumbtack	tachuela; chinche
ticket	boleto; billete
ticket stub	talón del boleto; resguardo; comprobante
timeline	cronología; plazo de tiempo
timetable	calendario de eventos; horario; itinerario
toddler	niño que empieza a caminar; niño de 1 a 3 años
topic	tema
track	grupo; itinerario; ruta
trade school	escuela de oficios; escuela vocacional
training	entrenamiento; adiestramiento; capacitación
transcript	certificado de estudios; constancia de estudios; expediente académico
transfer	transferencia; cambio (de escuela)
transition	transición
traumatic brain injury (TBI)	lesión cerebral traumática (TBI, por sus siglas en inglés)
truancy	ausentismo escolar; inasistencias; falta injustificada
truant	ausente sin permiso
tryout	prueba
turnout	asistencia; participación
tutor, to	dar clases (particulares); instruir
tutoring	tutoría; clases particulares
typing key	tecla

U

English	Español
unacceptable	inaceptable

unbiased	imparcial
underachiever	alumno de bajo rendimiento
undersigned	abajo firmante
unfit	inadecuado; no apto
unique	especial; único
unmanageable	incontrolable
unsafe	peligroso
unsupervised	sin supervisión; sin vigilancia
update, to	poner al día; actualizar
uppercase letter	letra mayúscula
upset	molesto
utilities	servicios públicos

V

English	Español
vaccination	vacunación
valedictorian	graduado con las mejores calificaciones
valid	legítimo; vigente
vandalism	vandalismo
verbal warning	advertencia verbal
verification	verificación; confirmación; comprobación
vice-principal	vicedirector
video remote interpreting (VRI)	interpretatción remota por video; (VRI, por sus siglas en inglés)
violate (the law)	infringer (la ley)
violation	transgresion; violación
visual impairment	impedimento visual
vocational education	educación vocacional
volunteer	voluntario

W

English	Español
wad of paper	bola de papel
wait list	lista de espera
waive, to	renunciar; desistir
warning	advertencia
warranted	explicable; justificado
website	sitio web; página web
welfare	asistencia pública
well-balanced	bien equilibrado
whiteboard	pizarra blanca; pizarra interactiva
whole number	número entero
willful	intencional; deliberado
winter break	vacaciones de invierno
work habits	costumbres de trabajo; hábitos de trabajo
work station	estación de trabajo; cubículo
wrestling	lucha libre
writing assessment	evaluación de la escritura
written accent	acento ortográfico
written consent	consentimiento por escrito
written prior notice	notificación escrita previamente
wrongdoing	fechoría; mala conducta; acto indebido
wrongful	injusto

Y

English	Español
year round	año redondo; año contínuo
youngster	jovencito; joven; chico